COMPOSITION-RHETORIC

BY

STRATTON D. BROOKS
Superintendent of Schools, Cleveland, Ohio

AND

MARIETTA HUBBARD
Formerly English Department, High School
La Salle, Illinois

NEW YORK ·:· CINCINNATI ·:· CHICAGO

AMERICAN BOOK COMPANY

To MARCIA STUART BROOKS
WHOSE TEACHING FIRST DEMONSTRATED
TO THE AUTHORS THAT COMPOSITION
COULD BECOME A DELIGHT AND PLEAS-
URE, THIS BOOK IS DEDICATED . . . .

PREFACE

THE aim of this book is not to produce critical readers of literature, nor to prepare the pupil to answer questions about rhetorical theory, but to enable every pupil to express in writing, freely, clearly, and forcibly, whatever he may find within him worthy of expression.

Three considerations of fundamental importance underlie the plan of the book:—

First, improvement in the performance of an act comes from the repetition of that act accompanied by a conscious effort to omit the imperfections of the former attempt. Therefore, the writing of a new theme in which the pupil attempts to avoid the error which occurred in his former theme is of much greater educational value than the copying of the old theme for the purpose of correcting the errors in it. To copy the old theme is to correct a result, to write a new theme correctly is to improve a process; and it is this improvement of process which is the real aim of composition teaching.

Second, the logical arrangement of material should be subordinated to the needs of the pupils. A theoretical discussion of the four forms of discourse would require that each be completely treated in one place. Such a treatment would ignore the fact that a high school pupil has daily need to use each of the four forms of discourse, and that some assistance in each should be given him as early in his course as possible. The book, therefore, gives in Part I the elements of description, narration, exposition, and argument, reserving for Part II a more complete treatment of each. In each part the effort has been made to adapt the material presented to the maturity and power of thought of the pupil.

Third, expression cannot be compelled, it must be coaxed. Only under favorable conditions can we expect that reaction of intellect and emotion which renders possible a full expression of self. A most important one of these favorable conditions is that the pupil shall write something he wishes to write, for an audience which wishes to hear it. With this in view, the suggested subjects are those in which it has been found that high school pupils are interested and about which they wish to write. It is hoped that the work will be so conducted by the teacher that every theme will be read aloud before the class. It is essential that the criticism of a theme so read shall, in the main, be complimentary, pointing out and emphasizing that which the pupil has done well; and that destructive criticism be largely impersonal and be directed toward a single definite point. Only thus may we avoid personal embarrassment to the pupil, give him confidence in himself, and assure him of a sympathetic audience — all of which are essential conditions of effective teaching of composition.

The plan of the book is as follows: —

1. Part I provides a series of themes covering description, narration, exposition, and argument. The purpose is to give the pupil that inspiration and confidence in himself which comes from the frequent repetition of an act.

2. Each theme differs from the preceding usually by a single point, and it will be found desirable to confine the teaching effort to that point. It is a false standard of accuracy which demands that every error be corrected every time it appears. Such a course loses sight of the main point in a multiplicity of details. It renders instruction ineffective by scattering effort, produces hopeless confusion in the mind of the pupil, and robs composition of that inspiration without which it cannot succeed. In composition, as in other things, it is better to do but one thing at a time.

3. Accompanying the written themes is a series of exercises, each designed to emphasize the point presented in the text, but

more especially intended to provide for frequent drills in oral composition.

4. The paragraph is the unit of composition throughout the first four chapters, but for the sake of added interest some themes of greater length have been included. Chapter V, on the Whole Composition, serves as a review and summary of the methods of paragraph development, shows how to make the transition from one paragraph to another, and discusses the more important rhetorical principles underlying the union of paragraphs into a coherent and unified whole.

5. The total result of the training furnished by Part I should be to give the pupil some fluency of expression, some confidence in his ability to make known to others that which he thinks and feels, and some power to determine that the theme he writes, however rough-hewn and unshapely it may be, yet in its major outlines follows closely the thought that is within his mind. If he has failed in this, it will be of little advantage to him to have mastered some of the minor matters of technique, or to have learned how to improve his phrasing, polish his sentences, and distribute his commas.

6. Part II provides a series of themes covering the same ground as Part I, but the treatment has been made more complete and the material has been adapted to the increased maturity and thought power of the pupils. By means of references the pupil is directed to all former treatments of the topic he is studying.

7. Part II discusses some topics usually treated in college courses in rhetoric. These have been included for three reasons : first, because comparatively few high school pupils go to college; second, because the increased amount of time now given to composition enables the high school to cover a wider field than formerly ; and third, because the topics included can with profit be handled by pupils in the upper years of the high school course.

8. It is not intended that the text shall be recited. Its pur-

pose is to furnish a basis for discussion between teacher and pupil before the pupil attempts to write. The real test of the pupil's acquisition of a principle discussed in the text will be his ability to put it into practice in his theme writing.

Any judgment of the success or failure of the book should be based upon the quality of the themes which the pupils write. Criticisms and suggestions will be welcomed from those who use the book.

The authors wish to express their obligation for advice and assistance to Professor Edward Fulton, Department of Rhetoric, University of Illinois; Mr. Gilbert I. Blakely, Instructor in English, Morris High School, New York; Miss Elizabeth Richardson, Girls' High School, Boston; Miss Katherine H. Shute, Boston Normal School; Miss E. Marguerite Strauchon, Kansas City High School.

The selections from Hawthorne, Longfellow, Lowell, Holmes, Whittier, Warner, Burroughs, Howells, and Trowbridge are used by permission and by special arrangement with Houghton, Mifflin, and Company, publishers of their works.

Grateful acknowledgment is made to Harper and Brothers; The Century Company; Doubleday, Page, and Company; and Charles Scribner's Sons for permission to use the selections to which their names are attached; to the publishers of the *Forum, Century, Atlantic Monthly, McClure's, Harper's, Scribner's,* and the *Outlook* for permission to use extracts; and to Scott, Foresman, and Company; D. Appleton and Company; Henry Holt and Company; G. P. Putnam's Sons; Thomas Y. Crowell and Company; and Benjamin H. Sanborn and Company for permission to use copyrighted material.

CONTENTS

PART I

PART II

PART I

I. EXPRESSION OF IDEAS ARISING FROM EXPERIENCE

1. Pleasure in Expressing Ideas. — Though we all enjoy talking, we cannot write as we talk, nor do we find the same pleasure in it. We seldom talk about topics in which we are not interested and concerning which we know little or nothing, but we often have such topics assigned to us as subjects for compositions. Under such conditions it is no wonder that there is little pleasure in writing. The ideas that we express orally are those with which we are familiar and in which we are interested, and we tell them because we wish to tell them to some one who is likewise interested and who desires to hear what we have to say. Such expression of ideas is enjoyed by all. If we but choose to express the same kinds of ideas and for the same reason, there is an equal or even greater pleasure to be derived from the expression of ideas in writing. It is the purpose of this book to show you how to express ideas *clearly* and *effectively* and at the same time *to enjoy doing it.*

2. Sources of Ideas. — We must have ideas before we can express them. There are three sources from which they arise. We may gain them from experience; we may recombine them into new forms by the imagination; and we may receive them from others through the medium of language, either by conversation or reading.

Every day we add to our knowledge through our senses. We see and hear and do, and so acquire ideas about things. These are the ones that we gain through experience, and by far the greater part of expression has to do with such ideas. The first chapter is concerned with the expression of ideas that come to us because of our experience.

We may, however, think about things that have not actually occurred. We may allow our minds to picture a football game that we have not seen or to plan a story about a boy who never existed. Nearly every one takes pleasure in such an exercise of the imagination. The second chapter will have to do with the expression of ideas of this kind.

We also add to our knowledge through the medium of language. Through conversation and reading we learn what others think, and it is often of value to restate these ideas. The expression of ideas so acquired is treated in the third chapter.

3. Advantages of Expressing Ideas Gained from Experience. — Young people sometimes find difficulty in writing because they "have nothing to say." Such a reason will not hold in regard to ideas gained from experience. Every one has a multitude of experiences every day, at least one of which is of sufficient interest to cause him to wish to tell it. Much of that which happens to you or to your friends, especially that which occurs outside of the regular routine of school work, is interesting and worth telling. Experience furnishes an abundance of material suitable for composition purposes, but a greater advantage comes from the fact that the ideas are *sure to be* *your own.* This is the first requisite of successful composition. To express ideas that are not your own is mere copy work, and seldom worth doing.

In the third place, the ideas are not only your own, but they are likely to be *clear* and *definite.* You know what you do and what you see; or, if you do not, the effort to express it so that it will be clear to others will make you observe closely for yourself.

Still another advantage comes from the fact that your experiences are not presented to you through the medium of language. The experience furnishes the ideas, but you are left free to choose for yourself the words that best set forth what you wish to tell. Because the things of your experience are the ones with which you are most familiar, the words that best apply to them are the ones that you most often use and whose meanings are best known to you.

Because experience supplies an abundance of interesting, clear, and definite ideas, which are your own and which may be expressed in familiar language, it furnishes better material for training in expression than does either imagination or reading.

4. Essentials of Expression. — There are two essentials of the proper expression of ideas : first, to say what you mean ; and second, to say it clearly. Without these, what you say may be not only valueless, but positively misleading. If you wish your hearer to understand what has occurred at a certain time and place, you must first of all know yourself exactly what did occur. You must then express it in language that shall make him understand clearly the situation as you understand it. You will learn much about clearness, later, but even now you can tell whether you know what is meant by a sentence which you hear. It is not so easy to tell whether what you say will convey clearly to another the meaning you intend to convey, but it will help in this if you ask yourself the questions : "Do I know exactly what happened?" "Have I said what I intended to say?" "Have I said it so that it will be clear to the listener?"

Oral Composition I. — *Report orally on one of the following : —*

1. Were you so interested in anything yesterday that you told it to your parents or friends? Tell the class about it.

2. Tell about something that you have done this week, so that the class may know exactly what you did.

3. Name some things in which you have been interested within the last two or three months. Tell the class about one of them.

4. Tell the class about something that happened during vacation. Have you told the event exactly as it occurred?

5. Interest. — In order to enjoy listening to a story we must take an interest in it, and the story should be so told as to arouse and maintain this interest. As you have listened to the reports of your classmates you have been more pleased with some than with others. Even though the meaning of each was clear, yet the interest aroused was in each case different. Since the purpose of a story is to entertain, it falls short of the purpose when it ceases to be interesting. We must at all times say what we mean and say it clearly ; but in story telling especially it is desirable to give some attention to saying it so that it may arouse and maintain interest.

6. The Introduction. — Clearness has an important bearing upon interest. The interest aroused by a story will depend upon the hearers' knowing enough of the circumstances to enable them to understand clearly what occurred; therefore, the introduction should include these circumstances. In order to render our account of an event clear it will be desirable to tell the hearers *when* and *where* it occurred and *who* were present. Their further understanding of it may be helped by telling some of the attendant circumstances. These usually answer the question, *Why?* If I begin my story by saying, "Last summer John Anderson and I were on a camping trip in the Adirondacks," I have told when, where, and who; and the addition of the words "on a camping trip" tells why we were in the Adirondacks, and may serve to explain some of the events that are to follow. Even the statement of the place indicates in some degree the trend of the story, for many things that might occur "in the Adirondacks" could not occur in a country where there were no mountains. Certainly the story that would follow such an introduction would be expected to differ from one beginning with the words, "Last summer John Anderson and I went to visit a friend in New York."

While it is not always necessary to include these four elements in the introduction, yet it is desirable to do so in most cases of oral story telling. Incidents taken from books may not have them stated because the reader is already familiar with them from the preceding portions of the book. The title of a printed or written story may serve as an introduction and give us all needed information. In relating personal incidents the time element is seldom omitted, though it may be indirectly stated or indefinitely designated by such expressions as 'once' or 'lately.' In many stories the interest depends upon the plot, and the time is not definitely stated:

EXERCISE

Notice what elements are included in each of the following introductions : —

1. Saturday last at Mount Holly, about eight miles from this place, nearly three hundred people were gathered together to see an experiment or two tried on some persons accused of witchcraft.

2. On the morning of the 10th instant at sunrise, they were discovered from Put-in-Bay, where I lay at anchor with the squadron under my command.

3. It was on Sunday when I awoke to the realization that I had quitted civilization and was afloat on an unfamiliar body of water in an open boat.

4. Up and down the long corn rows Pap Overholt guided the old mule and the small, rickety, inefficient plow, whose low handles bowed his tall, broad shoulders beneath the mild heat of a mountain June sun. As he went — ever with a furtive eye upon the cabin — he muttered to himself, shaking his head.

5. After breakfast, I went down to the Saponey Indian town, which is about a musket shot from the fort.

6. The lonely stretch of uphill road, upon whose yellow clay the midsummer sun beat vertically down, would have represented a toilsome climb to a grown and unencumbered man. To the boy staggering under the burden of a brimful carpet bag, it seemed fairly unscalable ; wherefore he stopped at its base and looked up in dismay to its far-off, red-hot summit.

7. One afternoon last summer, three or four people from New York, two from Boston, and a young man from the Middle West were lunching at one of the country clubs on the south shore of Long Island, and there came about a mild discussion of the American universities.

8. "But where is the station?" inquired the Judge.

"Ain't none, boss. Dis heah is jes a crossing. Train's about due now, sah ; you-all won't hab long fer to wait. Thanky, sah ; good-by ; sorry you-all didn't find no birds."

The Judge picked up his gun case and grip and walked toward his two companions waiting on the platform a few yards away. Silhouetted against the moonlight they made him think of the figure 10, for Mr. Appleton was tall and erect, and the little Doctor short and circular.

9. I sprang to the stirrup, and Joris and he;
   I galloped, Dirck galloped, we galloped all three;
   "Good speed!" cried the watch, as the gate bolts undrew,
   "Speed!" echoed the wall to us galloping through.
   Behind shut the postern, the lights sank to rest,
   And into the midnight we galloped abreast.
   — BROWNING.

Oral Composition II. — *Relate orally to the class some incident in which you were personally concerned.*

The following may suggest a subject: —

1. How I caught a woodchuck.
2. A trick of a tame crow.
3. Why I missed the train.
4. Why the teacher was angry.
5. Lost and found.
6. When I met a bear.

(When preparing to relate this incident ask yourself first whether you know exactly what happened. Consider then how to begin the story so that your hearer will know when and where it happened and who were there. Include in the beginning any statement that will assist the reader in understanding the events which follow.)

7. The Point of a Story. — It is not necessary that a story be concerned with a thrilling event in order to be interesting. Even a most commonplace occurrence may be so told that it is worth listening to. It is more important that a story have a point and be so told that this point will be readily appreciated than that it deal with important or thrilling events. The story should lead easily and rapidly to its point, and when this is reached the end of the story should not be far distant. The beginning of a story will contain statements that will assist us in appreciating the point when we come to it, but if the point is plainly stated near the beginning, or even if it is too strongly suggested, our story will drag.

At what point in the following selection is the interest greatest?

During the Civil War, I lived in that portion of Tennessee which was alternately held by the conflicting armies. My father and brothers were away, as were all the other men in the neighborhood, except a few very old ones and some half-grown boys. Mother and I were in constant fear of injury from stragglers from both armies. We had never been disturbed, for our farm was a mile or more back from the road along which such detachments usually moved. We had periods of comparative quiet in which we felt at ease, and then would come reports of depredation near at hand, or rumors of the presence of marauding bands in neighboring settlements.

One evening such a rumor came to us, and we were consequently anxious. Early next morning, before the fog had lifted, I caught sight of two men crossing the road at the far end of the orchard. They jumped over the fence into the orchard and disappeared among the trees. I had but a brief glimpse of them, but it was sufficient to show me that one had a gun over his shoulder, while the other carried a saber.

"Quick, Mother, quick!" I cried. "Come to the window. There are soldiers in the orchard."

Keeping out of sight, we watched the progress of the men through the orchard. Our brief glimpses of them through the trees showed that they were not coming directly to the house, but were headed for the barn and sheds, and in order to keep out of sight, were following a slight ravine which ran across the orchard and led to the back of the barns.

Mother and I were very much excited and hardly knew what to do. Finally it was determined to hide upstairs in hopes that the men were bent on stealing chickens or pigs, and might leave without disturbing the house. We locked the doors and went upstairs, taking with us the old musket and the butcher knife. We could hear the men about the barn, and after what seemed an interminable time we heard them coming towards the house.

Though shaking all over, I summoned courage enough to go to the window and look out of a hole in the shade. As the men came into sight around the corner, I screamed outright, but from relief rather than fear, for the men were not soldiers, but Grandpa Smith and his fourteen-year-old grandson. They stopped at the well to get a drink, and when we opened the window, the old man said, " We're just on our way to mow the back lot and stopped to grind the scythe on your stone. We broke ours yesterday."

Then he picked up the scythe which in the fog I had taken for a saber, while the grandson again shouldered his pitchfork musket.

What effect would it have on the interest aroused by the preceding story to begin it as follows ?

" One morning during the Civil War, I saw two of my neighbors, Grandpa Smith and his grandson, crossing our orchard, one carrying a scythe and the other a pitchfork."

Why is the expression, " before the fog had lifted," used near the beginning of the story?   Would a description of the appearance of the house, the barn, or the persons add to the interest aroused by the story?   Is it necessary to add anything to the story ?

EXERCISE

In each of the following selections decide where the interest reaches its climax.   Has anything been said in the beginning of any of them which suggests what the point will be, or which helps you to appreciate it when you come to it ?

1. The next evening our travelers encamped on a sand bar, or rather a great bank of sand, that ran for miles along one side of the river. They kept watch as usual, Leon taking the first turn. He seated himself on a pile of sand and did his best to keep awake ; but in about an hour after the rest were asleep, he felt very drowsy and fell into a nap that lasted nearly half an hour, and might have con-

tinued longer had he not slid down the sand hill and tumbled over on his side. This awoke him. Feeling vexed with himself, he rubbed his eyes and looked about to see if any creature had ventured near. He first looked towards the woods, for of course that was the direction from which the tigers would come; but he had scarcely turned himself when he perceived a pair of eyes glancing at him from the other side of the fire. Close to them another pair, then another and another, until, having looked on every side, he saw himself surrounded by a complete circle of glancing eyes. It is true they were small ones, and some of the heads which he could see by the blaze were small. They were not jaguars, but they had an ugly look. They looked like the heads of serpents. Was it possible that a hundred serpents could have surrounded the camp?

Brought suddenly to his feet, Leon stood for some moments uncertain what to do. He believed that the eyes belonged to snakes which had just crept out of the river; and he feared that any movement on his part would lead them to attack him. Having risen to his feet, his eyes were above the level of the blaze, and he was able in a little while to see more clearly.

He now saw that the snakelike heads belonged to creatures with large oval bodies, and that, besides the fifty or more which had come up to look at the fire, there were whole droves of them upon the sandy beach beyond. As far as he could see on all sides, the bank was covered with them. A strange sight it was, and most fearful. For his life he could not make out what it meant, or by what sort of wild animals he was surrounded.

He could see that their bodies were not larger than those of small sheep; and, from the way in which they glistened in the moonlight, he was sure they had come out of the river. He called to the Indian guide, who awoke and started to his feet in alarm. The movement frightened the creatures round the fire; they rushed to the shore, and were heard plunging by hundreds into the water.

The Indian's ear caught the sounds, and his eye took in the whole thing at a glance.

"Turtles," he said.

"Oh," said the lad; "turtles, are they?"

"Yes, master," answered the guide. "I suppose this is one of their great hatching places. They are going to lay their eggs in the sand."
— CAPTAIN MAYNE REID.

Would the preceding incident be interesting if we were told at the beginning that the boy and the Indian had encamped near a hatching place of turtles?

2. Not every story that reads like fiction is fact, but the *Brooklyn Eagle* assures its readers that the one here quoted is quite true. The man who told it was for many years an officer of the Chicago, Burlington & Quincy Railroad Company in Illinois, and had annual passes over all the important railroads in the country. His duties took him to Springfield, the state capital, and as he generally went by the Chicago, Alton & St. Louis road, the conductors on that line knew him so well that they never asked to see his pass.

"One day I received a telegram summoning me to meet one of the officers of my company at Aurora the next morning. I had only a short time to catch my train to Chicago, and in my haste left my pass-book behind. I did not find this out until I reached Chicago, and was about to take the last train for Aurora that night. Then I saw that the conductor, a man brought over from the Iowa division, was a stranger, and the fact that I would need my pass reminded me that I did not have it.

"I told the conductor the situation, but he said he could not carry me on my mere representation that I had a pass.

"'Why, man,' said I, 'I am an officer of the company, going to Aurora on company business, and this is the last train that will get me there in time. You must take me.'

"He was polite, but firm. He said he was a new man on this division, and could not afford to make any mistakes.

"When I saw that he was determined, I rushed off to the telegraph office; but it was too late to catch anybody authorized to issue passes, so I settled it in my mind that I must go by carriage, and the prospect of an all-night ride over bad roads through the dark was anything but inviting. Indeed, it was so forbidding that I resolved to make one more appeal to the conductor.

"'You simply must take me to Aurora!' I said, with intense earnestness.

"'I can't do it,' he answered. 'But I believe you are what you represent yourself to be, and I will lend you the money personally. It is only one dollar and twelve cents.'

"Well, sir, you could have knocked me down with the flat side of a palm-leaf fan. I had more than two thousand dollars in currency in my pocket, but it had never for an instant occurred to me that I could pay my fare and ride on that train. I showed the conductor a wad of money that made his eyes stick out.

"'I thought it was funny,' said he, 'that a man in your position couldn't raise one dollar and twelve cents. It was that that made me believe you were playing a trick to see if I would violate the rule.'

"The simple truth was, I had ridden everywhere on passes so many years, that it did not occur to me that I could ride in any other way."

Oral Composition III.[1] — *Relate to the class some personal incident suggested by one of the following subjects:* —

1. A day with my cousin.
2. Caught in the act.
3. A joke on me.
4. My peculiar mistake.
5. My experience on a farm.
6. My experience in a strange Sunday school.
7. What I saw when I was coming to school.

(In preparation for this exercise, consider the point of your story. What must you tell first in order to enable the hearers to understand the point? Can you say anything that will make them want to know what the point is without really telling them? Can you lead up to it without too long a delay? Can you stop when the point has been made?)

8. Theme Writing and Correcting. — Any written exercise, whether long or short, has been called a theme

---

[1] Oral compositions should be continued throughout the course. The exercises will furnish abundant opportunities for work of this kind. A few minutes may be profitably used once or twice each week in having each member of the class stand before the class and relate briefly some incident which he has witnessed since the last meeting of the class.

throughout this book. Just as one learns to skate by skating, so one learns to write by writing; therefore many themes have been required. Since the clear expression of thought is one of the essential characteristics of every theme, theme correction should be primarily directed to this end. The teacher will need to assist in this correction, but the really valuable part is that which you do for yourself. After you leave school you will need to decide for yourself what is right and what is best, and it is essential that you learn now how to make such decisions.

To aid you in acquiring a habit of self-correction, questions or suggestions follow the directions for writing each theme. In Theme I you are to express clearly to others that which is already clear to you.

Theme I. — *Write a short theme on one of the subjects that you have used for an oral composition.*

(After writing this theme, read it aloud to yourself. Does it read smoothly? Have you told what actually happened? Is it so expressed that the hearers will understand you? Have you said what you meant to say? Consider the introduction. Has the story a point?)

9. The Conclusion. — Since the point of a story marks the climax of interest, it is evident that the conclusion must not be long delayed after the point has been reached. If the story has been well told, the point marks the natural conclusion, and a sentence or two will serve to bring it to a satisfactory end. If a suitable ending does not suggest itself, it is better to omit the conclusion altogether than to construct a forced or flowery one. Notice the conclusion of the incident of the Civil War related on page 18.

Theme II. — *Write a short theme suggested by one of the following subjects:* —

1. A school picnic.
2. A race.
3. The largest fire I have seen.   .
4. An accident while skating.
5. A queer mistake.
6. An experience with a tramp.

(Correct with reference to meaning and clearness.   Consider the introduction ; the point ; the conclusion.)

10. Observation of Actions. — Many of our most interesting experiences arise from observing the actions of others. A written description of what we have observed will gain in interest to the reader, if, in addition to telling what was done, it gives some indication of the way in which it was done.   A list of tools a carpenter uses and the operations he performs during the half hour we watch him, may be dull and uninteresting; but our description may have an added value if it shows his manner of working so that the reader can determine whether the carpenter is an orderly, methodical, and rapid worker or a mere putterer who is careless, haphazard, and slow.   Two persons will perform similar actions in very different ways.   Our description should be so worded as to show what the differences are.

Theme III. — *Write a theme relating actions.*

Suggested subjects: —

1. A mason, blacksmith, painter, or other mechanic at work.
2. How my neighbor mows his lawn.
3. What a man does when his automobile breaks down.
4. Describe the actions of a cat, dog, rabbit, squirrel, or other animal.

5.   Watch the push-cart man a half-hour and report what
     he did.

(Have you told exactly what was done? Can you by
the choice of suitable words show more plainly the way
in which it was done? Does this theme need to have an
introduction? A point? A conclusion?)

11. Selection of Details. — You are at present concerned
with telling events that actually happen; but this does
not mean that you need to include everything that occurs.
If you wish to tell a friend about some interesting or
exciting incident at a picnic, he will not care to hear
everything that took place during the day. He may
listen politely to a statement of what train you took and
what you had in your lunch basket, but he will be little
interested in such details. In order to maintain interest,
the point of your story must not be too long delayed.
Brevity is desirable, and details that bear little relation
to the main point, and that do not prepare the listener to
understand and appreciate this point, are better omitted.

Theme IV. — *Write about something that you have
done. Use any of the following subjects, or one suggested
by them :* —

     1. My first hunt.
     2. Why I was tardy.
     3. My first fishing trip.
     4. My narrow escape.
     5. A runaway.
     6. What I did last Saturday.

(Read the theme aloud to yourself. Does it read
smoothly? Have you said what you meant to say? Is
it clearly expressed? Consider the introduction; the
point; the conclusion.   Reject unnecessary details.)

12. Order of Events. — The order in which events occur will assist in establishing the order in which to relate them. If you are telling about only one person, you can follow the time order of the events as they actually happened; but if you are telling about two or more persons who were doing different things at the same time, you will need to tell first what one did and then what another did. You must, however, make it clear to the reader that, though you have told one event after the other, they really happened at the same time.

In the selection below notice how the italicized portions indicate the relation in time that the different events bear to one another.

At the beach yesterday a fat woman and her three children caused quite a commotion. They had rigged themselves out in hired suits which might be described as an average fit, for that of the mother was as much too small as those of the children were too large. They trotted gingerly out into the surf, wholly unconscious that the crowd of beach loungers had, for the time, turned their attention from each other to the quartet in the water. By degrees the four worked out farther and farther until a wave larger than usual washed the smallest child entirely off his feet, and caused the mother to scream lustily for help. The people on the beach started up, and two or three men hastened to the rescue, but their progress was impeded by the crowd of frightened girls and women *who were scrambling and splashing towards the shore*. The mother's frantic efforts to reach the little boy were rendered ineffectual by the two girls, *who at the moment of the first alarm had been strangled* by the salt water and *were now clinging* desperately to her arms and *attempting* to climb up to her shoulders. *Meanwhile*, the lifeboat man was rowing rapidly towards the scene, but it seemed to the onlookers *who had rushed to the platform railing* that he would never arrive. *At the same time* a young man, *who had started from the diving raft some time before*, was swimming towards shore with powerful strokes. He *now* reached the spot, caught hold of the boy, and lifted him into the lifeboat, which had *at last* arrived.

Such expressions as *meanwhile, in the meantime, during, at last, while,* etc., are regularly used to denote the kind of time relations now under discussion. They should be used when they avoid confusion, but often a direct transition from one set of actions to another can be made without their use. Notice also the use of the relative clause to indicate time relations.

Theme V. — *Write a short theme, using some one of the subjects named under the preceding themes or one suggested by them. Select one which you have not already used.*

(Have you told enough to enable the reader to follow easily the thread of the story and to understand what you meant to tell? If your theme is concerned with more than one set of activities, have you made the transition from one to another in such a way as to be clear to the reader, and have you expressed them with the proper time relations? What other questions should you ask yourself while correcting this theme?)

SUMMARY

1. There is a pleasure to be derived from the expression of ideas.
2. There are three sources of ideas: experience, imagination, language.
3. Ideas gained from experience may be advantageously used for composition purposes because —
   a. They are interesting.
   b. They are your own.
   c. They are likely to be clear and definite.
   d. They offer free choice of language.
4. The two essentials of expression are—

    a. To say what you mean.

    b. To say it clearly.

5. A story should be told so as to arouse and maintain interest. Therefore, —

    a. The introduction usually tells when, where, who, and why.

    b. Every story worth telling has a point.

    c. Only such details are included as are essential to the development of the point.

    d. The conclusion is brief. The story comes to an end shortly after the point is told.

6. Care must be taken to indicate the time order, especially when two or more events occur at the same time.

7. The correction of one's own theme is the most valuable form of correction.

II. EXPRESSION OF IDEAS FURNISHED BY IMAGINATION

13. Relation of Imagination to Experience. — All ideas are based upon and spring from experience, and the imagination merely places them in new combinations. For the purpose of this book, however, it is convenient to distinguish those themes that relate real events as they actually occurred from those themes that relate events that did not happen. That body of writing which we call literature is largely composed of works of an imaginative character, and for this reason it has sometimes been carelessly assumed that in order to write one must be possessed of an excellent imagination. Such an assumption loses sight of the fact that imaginative writings cover but one small part of the whole field. The production of literature is the business of a few, while every one has occasion every day to express ideas. It is evident that by far the greater part of the ideas we are called upon to express do not require the use of the imagination, but exercises in writing themes of an imaginative character are given here because there is pleasure in writing such themes and because practice in writing them will aid us in stating clearly and effectively the many ideas arising from our daily experiences.

14. Advantages and Disadvantages of Imaginative Theme Writing. — Ideas furnished by the imagination are no less your own than are those furnished by experience, and the same freedom in the choice of language prevails. They are, however, not apt to be so clear and definite. At the time of their occurrence they do not make so deep and vital an impression upon you. If not recorded as they occur, they can seldom be recalled in the original form. Even though you attempt to write them down as you think them, you can and do change and modify them as you go along. This lack of clearness and permanent form, while it seems to give greater freedom, carries with it disadvantages. In the first place the ideas are less likely to be worth recording, and in the second place it is more difficult to give them a unity and directness of statement that will hold the attention and interest of the reader until the chief point is reached.

15. Probability. — Not everything that the imagination may furnish is equally worth expressing. If you choose to write about something for which imagination supplies the ideas, you may create for yourself such ideas as you wish. Their order of occurrence and their time and place are not determined by outward events, but solely by the mind itself. The events are no longer real and actual, but may be changed and rearranged without limit. An imaginative series of events may conform closely to the real and probable, or it may be manifestly improbable. Which will be of greatest interest will depend upon the reader, but it will be found that generally that story is most satisfactory which comes nearest to reality. In fairy tales we confessedly attempt to tell of events not possible in the real world, but tales of real life, however imaginary, should be so told that everything seems both possible and probable. An imaginative story, in which the persons seem to be real persons who do and say the things that real persons do and say, will be found much more satisfactory than a story that depends for its outcome on something manifestly impossible. From this it appears that he who really does the best in imaginative writing is the one who has most closely observed the real events of everyday life, and states his imaginary ones so that they seem real.

Theme VI. — *Write a short theme, using one of the subjects below. You need not tell something which actually happened, but it should be so told that your readers will think it might have happened.*

1. A trip in a sailboat.
2. The travels of a penny.
3. How I was lost.
4. A cat's account of a mouse hunt.
5. The mouse's account of the same hunt.
6. My experience with a burglar.
7. The burglar's story.

16. Euphony. — Besides clearness in a composition there are other desirable qualities. To one of these, various names have been applied, as "euphony," "ease," "elegance," "beauty," etc. Of two selections equally clear in meaning one may be more pleasing than the other. One may seem harsh and rough, while the other flows along with a satisfying ease and smoothness. If the thought that is in our mind fails to clothe itself in suitable language and appropriate figures, we can do little by conscious effort toward improving the beauty of the language. We can, however, do much to avoid choppy sentences and inharmonious combinations of words and phrases, and so remove from our compositions much that is harsh and rough. That quality which we call ease or euphony is better detected by the ear than by the eye, and it was for this purpose that it has been suggested that you read each theme aloud to yourself before presenting it to the class. Such a reading will assist you to determine whether you have made your meaning clear and to eliminate some of the more disagreeable combinations.

17. Variety. — Of the many elements which affect the euphony of a theme none is more essential than variety. The constant repetition of the same thing grows monotonous and distasteful, while a pleasing variety maintains interest and improves the story. For sake of it we avoid the continual use of the same words and phrases, substituting synonyms and equivalent expressions if we have need to repeat the same idea many times.

Most children begin every sentence of a story with "and," or perhaps it is better to say that they conclude many sentences with "and-uh," leaving the thought in suspense while they are trying to think of what to say next. High school pupils are not wholly free from this habit, and it is sometimes retained in their written work. This excessive use of *and* needs to be corrected. An examination of our language habits will show that nearly every one has one or more words which he uses to excess. A professor of rhetoric, after years of correcting others, discovered by underscoring the word *that* each time it occurred in his own writing that he was using it twice as often as necessary. *Got* is one of the words used too frequently, and often incorrectly.

EXERCISE

1. In the following selection notice how each sentence begins. Compare it with one of your own themes.

I was witness to events of a less peaceful character. One day when I went out to my woodpile, or rather my pile of stumps, I observed two large ants, the one red, and the other much larger, nearly half an inch long, and black, fiercely contending with each other. Having once got hold, they never let go, but struggled and wrestled and rolled on the chips incessantly. Looking farther, I was surprised to find that the chips were covered with such combatants; that it was not a *duellum*, but a *bellum*, — a war between two races of ants, the red always pitted against the black, and frequently two red ones to one black. The legions of these Myrmidons covered all the hills and vales in my woodyard, and the ground was already strewn with the dead and the dying, both red and black.

It was the only battle which I have ever witnessed — the only battlefield I ever trod while the battle was raging. . . . On every side they were engaged in deadly combat, yet without any noise that I could hear, and human soldiers never fought so resolutely. — THOREAU.

2. Examine one of your own themes. If some word occurs frequently, underscore it each time, and then substitute words or expressions for it in as many places as you can. If necessary, reconstruct the sentences so as to avoid using the word in some cases. Notice how these substitutions give a variety to your expression and improve the euphony of your composition.

Theme VII. — *Write a short story suggested by one of the following subjects:* —

1. The trout's revenge.
2. A sparrow's mistake.
3. A fortunate shot.
4. The freshman and the professor.
5. What the bookcase thought about it.

(Correct with reference to meaning and clearness. Cross out unnecessary *ands*. Consider the beginnings of the sentences. Can you improve the euphony by a different choice of words?)

18. Sentence Length. — Euphony is aided by securing a variety in the length of sentences. In endeavoring to avoid the excessive use of *and*, some pupils obtain results illustrated by the following example : —

Jean passed through the door of the church. He saw a child sitting on one of the stone steps. She was fast asleep in the midst of the snow. The child was thinly clad. Her feet, cold as it was, were bare.

A theme composed wholly of such a succession of short sentences is tedious. Especially when read aloud does its monotony become apparent. Though the thought in each sentence is complete, the effect is not satisfactory to the reader, because the thought of the whole does not come to him as fast as his mind can act. Such an arrangement of sentences might be satisfactory to young children, because it would agree with their habits of thought; but as one grows in ability to think more rapidly, he finds that longer and more complicated sentences best express his thoughts and are best understood by those for whom he writes. We introduce sentences of different length and different structure, because they more clearly express the thought of the whole and state it in a form more in accordance with the mental activity of the hearer. When we have done this, we at the same time secure a variety that avoids monotony.

In attempting to avoid a series of short sentences, care should be taken not to go to the other extreme. Sentences should not be overloaded. Too many adjectives or participles or subordinate clauses will render the meaning obscure. The number of phrases and clauses that may safely be introduced will be determined by the ability of the mind to grasp the meaning readily and accurately. It is sometimes quite as important to separate a long sentence into shorter ones as it is to combine short ones into those of greater length.

Notice in the following selection the different ways in which several ideas have been brought into the same sentence without rendering the meaning obscure: —

Loki made his way across a vast desert moorland, and came, after three days, into the barren hill country and among the rugged mountains of the South. There an earthquake had split the rocks asunder, and opened dark and bottomless gorges, and hollowed out many a low-walled cavern, where the light of day was never seen. Along deep, winding ways, Loki went, squeezing through narrow crevices, creeping under huge rocks, and gliding through crooked clefts, until he came at last into a great underground hall, where his eyes were dazzled by a light that was stronger and brighter than the day; for on every side were glowing fires, roaring in wonderful little gorges, and blown by wonderful little bellows.

Theme VIII. — *Write a story suggested by one of the following subjects:* —

1. School in the year 2000.
2. The lost door key.
3. Our big bonfire.
4. Kidnaped.
5. A bear hunt.
6. A mistake in the telegram.
7. How Fido rescued his master.

(Can you render the meaning more clear by uniting short sentences into longer ones, or by separating long sentences into shorter ones? Can you omit any *ands?* How many of the sentences begin with the same word? Can you change any of those words? Pick out the words which show the subordinate relation of some parts to others. Do all of the incidents in your story seem probable?)

19. Conversation. — It must not be inferred from the preceding section that short sentences are never to be used. They are quite as necessary as long ones, and in some cases, such as the portraying of strong emotion, are more effective. Even a succession of short sentences may be used with good results to describe rapid action. In conversation, also, sentences are generally short, and often grammatically incomplete, though they may be understood by the hearer. Sometimes this incompleteness is justified by the idiom of the language, but more often it is the result of carelessness on the part of the speaker. The hearer understands what is said either because he knows about what to expect, or because the expression is a familiar one. Such carelessness not only causes the omission of words grammatically necessary, but brings about the incorrect pronunciation of words and their faulty combination into sentences.

You speak much more often than you write. Your habits of speech are likely to become permanent and your errors of speech will creep into your written work. It is important therefore that you watch your spoken language. Occasions will arise when the slang expressions that you so freely use will seem inappropriate, and it will be unfortunate indeed if you find that you have used the slang so long that you have no other words to take their place. An abbreviated form of *gymnasium* or of *mathematics* may not attract attention among your schoolmates, but there are circles where such abbreviations are not used. By watching your own speech you will find that some incorrect forms are very common. Improvement can be made by giving your attention to one of them, such as the use of *guess*, or of *got*, or of *don't* and *doesn't*.

In making a written report of conversation you should remember that short sentences predominate. A conversation composed of long sentences would seem stilted and made to order. What each person says, however short, is put into a separate division and indented. Explanatory matter accompanying the conversation is placed with the spoken part to which it most closely relates. Notice the indentations and the use of quotation marks in several printed reports of conversation.

20. Ideas from Pictures. — If you look at a picture and then attempt to tell some one else what you see, you will be expressing ideas gained by experience. A picture may, however, cause a very different set of ideas to arise. Look at the picture on page 38. Can you imagine the circumstances that preceded the situation shown by the picture? Or again, can you not begin with that situation and imagine what would be done next? If you write out either of the series of events, the theme, though suggested by the picture, would be composed of ideas furnished by the imagination. In attempting to write a story suggested by a picture it will be best to make the situation given in the picture the point of greatest interest, and account for it by relating a series of events supposed to have preceded it.

Theme IX. — *Write a story that will account for the condition shown in the picture on page 38.*

(Correct with reference to clearness and meaning. Do you need to change the sentence length either for the sake of clearness or for the sake of variety? Cross out unnecessary *ands*. Underscore *got* and *then* each time you have used them. Can the reader follow the thread of your story to its chief point?)

21. Vocabulary. — A word is the symbol of an idea, and the addition of a word to one's vocabulary usually means that a new idea has been acquired. The more we see and hear and read, the greater our stock of ideas becomes. As our life experiences increase, so should our supply of words increase. We may have ideas without having the words with which to express them, and we may meet with words whose meanings we do not know. In either case there is chance for improvement. When you have a new idea, find out how best to express it, and when you meet with a new word, add it to your vocabulary.

It is necessary to distinguish between our reading vocabulary and our writing vocabulary. There are many words that belong only to the first. We know what they mean when we meet them in our reading, but we do not use them in our writing. Our speaking vocabulary also differs from that which we use in writing. We use words and phrases on paper that we seldom use in speech, and, on the other hand, many of the words that we speak we do not use in writing. There is, however, a constant shifting of words from one to another of these three groups. When we meet an unknown word, it usually becomes a part of our reading vocabulary. We learn its meaning, but we do not use it. Later it may appear in our written work, and finally we may use it in speaking. We add a word to our reading vocabulary when we determine its meaning, but *we must use it* in order to add it to our writing and speaking vocabulary. A conscious effort to aid in this acquisition of words is highly desirable.

A limited vocabulary indicates limited ideas. If one is limited to *awfully* in order to express a superlative; if his use of adjectives is restricted to *nice, jolly, lovely,* and *elegant;* if he must always *abominate* and never *abhor, detest*, *dislike*, or *loathe;* if he can only *adore* and not *admire*, *respect*, *revere*, or *venerate*, — then he has failed, indeed, to know the possibilities and beauties of English. Such a language habit shows a mind that has failed to distinguish between ideas. The best way to study the shades of meaning and the choice of words is in the actual production of a theme wherein there is need to bring out these differences in meaning by the use of words; but some help may be gained from a formal study of synonyms and antonyms and of the distinction in use and meaning between words which are commonly confused with each other. For this purpose such exercises are given in the Appendix.

22. Choice of Words. — Even though our words may express the proper meaning, the effect may not be a desirable one unless we use words suited to the occasion described and to the person writing. Pupils of high school age know the meaning of many words which are too " bookish " for daily use by them. Edward Everett Hale might use expressions which would not be suitable for a freshman's composition. Taste and good judgment will help you to avoid the unsuitable or grandiloquent.

The proper selection of words not only implies that we shall avoid the wrong one, but also that we shall choose the right one. A suitable adjective may express more than a whole sentence; a single verb may tell better how some one acted than could be told by a lengthy explanation. Since narration has to do with action, we need in story telling to be especially careful in our choice of verbs.

What can you say of the suitability of the words in the following selection, taken from a school reader of seventy-five years ago?

Mrs. Lismore. You are quite breathless, Charles; where have you been running so violently?

Charles. From the poultry yard, mamma, where I have been diverting myself with the bravado of the old gander. I did not observe him till he came toward me very fiercely, when, to induce him to pursue me, I ran from him. He followed, till, supposing he had beaten me, he returned to the geese, who appeared to receive him with acclamations of joy, cackling very loud, and seeming actually to laugh, and to enjoy the triumph of their gallant chief.

Emma. I wish I had been with you, Charles; I have often admired the gambols of these beautiful birds, and wondered how they came by the appellation of *silly*, which is generally bestowed on them. I remember Martha, our nursery maid, used often to call me a *silly goose*. How came they to deserve that term, mamma? they appear to me to have as much intelligence as any of the feathered tribe.

Mrs. Lismore. I have often thought with you, Emma, and supposed that term, like many others, misapplied, for want of examining into the justice of so degrading an epithet.

23. Improbability. — Up to this point we have been concerned with relating events that *could* exist, though we knew that they *did* not. We may, however, imagine a series of events that are manifestly impossible. There is a pleasure in inventing improbable stories, and if we know from the beginning that they are to be so, we enjoy listening to them. Such tales are more satisfactory to young persons than to older ones, as is shown by our declining interest in fairy stories as we grow older.

By limiting the improbability to a part of the story, it is possible to give an air of reality to the whole. Though the conditions described in a story about a trip to the moon might be wholly impossible, yet the reader for the time being might feel that the events were actually happening if the characters in the story were acting as real men would act under similar circumstances. In stories such as those of Thompson-Seton, where the animals are personified, the impossibilities·are forgotten, because the actions and situations are so real. In fairy stories and similar tales neither characters nor actions are in any way limited by probability.

Theme X. — *Write a short story suggested by one of the subjects below. Make either the characters or their surroundings seem real.*

1. A week in Mars.
2. Exploring the lake bottom.
3. The fight between the dog and the cat.
    (*a*) As told by the dog.
    (*b*) As told by the cat.
4. How the fox fooled the hound.
5. Diary of a donkey.
6. A biography of Jack Frost.

(Correct with reference to meaning and clearness and two other points to be assigned by the teacher.)

24. How to Increase One's Vocabulary. — In your daily work do what you can to add words to your reading vocabulary, and especially to increase your writing vocabulary. In the conversation of others and in reading you will meet with many new words, and you should attempt to make them your own. To do this, four things must be attended to : —

1. *Spelling*. Definite attention should be given to each new word until its form both as written and as printed is indelibly stamped upon the mind. In your general reading and in each of the subjects that you will study in the high school you will meet unfamiliar words. It is only by mastering the spelling of each new word *when you first meet it* that you can insure yourself against future

chagrin from bad spelling. A part of the time in each high school subject may well be devoted to the mastering of the words peculiar to that subject.

2. *Pronunciation.* The complete acquisition of a word includes its pronunciation. In reading aloud and in speaking, we have need to know it, and faulty pronunciation is considered an indication of lack of culture.

3. *Meaning.* This includes more than the ability to give the definition as found in the dictionary. It is possible to recite such definitions glibly without in reality knowing the meaning of the word defined. It is necessary to connect the word definitely and permanently in our mind with the idea for which it is the symbol and to be able to distinguish the idea clearly from others closely related to it.

4. *Use.* This is by far the most important of the four. If the word is to come into our speaking and writing vocabulary, we must use it. It is important that the spelling, pronunciation, and meaning be determined when you *first* meet the word, and it is equally important that the word be *used* soon and often.

Theme XI. — *Write a short story suggested by one of the following subjects. It may be wholly improbable, if you choose.*

1. The wicked fairy.
2. Mary's luck.
3. The man in the moon.
4. The golden apple.
5. A wonderful fountain pen.
6. The goobergoo and the kantan.

(Correct with reference to meaning and clearness and two other points to be assigned by the teacher.)

SUMMARY

1. The clear expression of the ideas connected with our daily experiences is of greater importance to most of us than is the production of literature.

2. Ideas furnished by imagination may be advantageously used for composition purposes, because —
     a. They are your own.
     b. They offer free choice of language.
   They are less desirable than those gained from experience, because —
     a. They are apt to lack clearness and permanency.
     b. They are less likely to be worth recording.
     c. It is more difficult to give them that unity and directness of statement that will keep the interest of the reader.

3. An imaginative series of events may seem probable or improbable. He who most closely observes real life and states his imaginary events so that they seem real will succeed best in imaginative writing.

4. Euphony is a desirable quality in a composition.

5. Variety aids euphony. It is gained by —
     a. Avoiding the repetition of the same words and phrases.
     b. Beginning our sentences in various ways.
     c. Using sentences of different lengths.

6. Conversation is usually composed of short sentences.

7. Pictures may suggest ideas suitable for use in compositions.

8. Our reading, writing, and speaking vocabularies differ. Each should be increased. With each new word attention should be given to —

a. Spelling.　*b.* Pronunciation.　*c.* Meaning.　*d.* Use.

III. EXPRESSION OF IDEAS ACQUIRED THROUGH LANGUAGE

25. Language as a Medium through Which Ideas are Acquired. — We have been considering language as a means of expression, an instrument by which we can convey to others the ideas which come to us from experience and imagination. We shall now consider it from a different point of view. Language is not only a means of expressing ideas, but it is in itself a medium through which ideas are acquired. It has a double use; the writer must put thought into language, the reader must get it out. A large share of your schooling has been devoted to this latter process, and ideas so acquired may be used for purposes of composition. *Since it is absolutely necessary to have ideas before you can express them,* it will be worth while to consider for a time how to get them from language.

26. Image Making. — Read the following selection from Hawthorne and form a clear mental image of each scene: —

At first, my fancy saw only the stern hills, lonely lakes, and venerable woods. Not a tree, since their seeds were first scattered over the infant soil, had felt the ax, but had grown up and flourished through its long generation, had fallen beneath the weight of years, been buried in green moss, and nourished the roots of others as gigantic. Hark! A light paddle dips into the lake, a birch canoe glides around the point, and an Indian chief has passed, painted and feather-crested, armed with a bow of hickory, a stone tomahawk, and flint-headed arrows. But the ripple had hardly vanished from the water, when a white flag caught the breeze, over a castle in the wilderness, with frowning ramparts and a hundred cannon. . . . A war party of French and Indians were issuing from the gate to lay waste some village of New England. Near the fortress there was a group of dancers. The merry soldiers footing it with the swart savage maids; deeper in the wood, some red men were growing frantic around a keg of the firewater; and elsewhere a Jesuit preached the faith of high cathedrals beneath a canopy of forest boughs, and distributed crucifixes to be worn beside English scalps.

Did you form clear mental images? Can you picture them all at one time, or must you turn your attention from one image to another? The formation of the proper mental images will be aided by making an effort to create them.

Many words do not cause us to form images; for example, *goodness*, *innocence*, *position*, *insurance;* but when the purpose of a word is to set forth an image, we should take care to get the correct one. In this the dictionary will not always help us. We must distinguish between the ability to repeat a definition and the power to form an accurate image of the thing defined. The difficulty of forming correct images by the use of dictionary definitions is so great that the definitions are frequently accompanied by pictures.

EXERCISES

Notice the different mental images that come to you as you read each of the following selections. Distinguish words that cause images to arise from those that do not.

1. Before these fields were shorn and tilled,
   Full to the brim our rivers flowed;
   The melody of waters filled
   The fresh and boundless wood;
   And torrents dashed, and rivulets played,
   And fountains spouted in the shade.
   —BRYANT: *An Indian at the Burial Place of his Fathers.*

2. At that moment the woods were filled with another burst of cries, and at the signal four savages sprang from the cover of the driftwood. Heyward felt a burning desire to rush forward to meet them, so intense was the delirious anxiety of the moment; but he was restrained by the deliberate examples of the scout and Uncas. When their foes, who leaped over the black rocks that divided them, with long bounds, uttering the wildest yells, were within a few rods, the rifle of Hawkeye slowly rose among the shrubs and poured out its fatal contents. The foremost Indian bounded like a stricken deer and fell headlong among the clefts of the island.

— COOPER: *Last of the Mohicans.*

3. The towering flames had now surmounted every obstruction, and rose to the evening skies, one huge and burning beacon, seen far and wide through the adjacent country. Tower after tower crashed down, with blazing roof and rafter; and the combatants were driven from the courtyard. The vanquished, of whom very few remained, scattered and escaped into the neighboring wood. The victors, assembling in large bands, gazed with wonder, not unmixed with fear, upon the flames, in which their own ranks and arms glanced dusky red. The maniac figure of the Saxon Ulrica was for a long time visible on the lofty stand she had chosen, tossing her arms abroad with wild exultation, as if she reigned empress of the conflagration which she had raised. At length, with a terrific crash, the whole turret gave way, and she perished in the flames which had consumed her tyrant.

— SCOTT: *Ivanhoe.*

4.　　　　　Under a spreading chestnut tree
　　　　　　　The village smithy stands;
　　　　　The smith, a mighty man is he,
　　　　　　　With large and sinewy hands;
　　　　　And the muscles of his brawny arms
　　　　　　　Are strong as iron bands.

— LONGFELLOW: *The Village Blacksmith.*

5. Once upon a midnight dreary, while I pondered weak and weary,
　Over many a quaint and curious volume of forgotten lore —
　While I nodded, nearly napping, suddenly there came a tapping,
　As of some one gently rapping, rapping at my chamber door;
　"'Tis some visitor," I muttered, "tapping at my chamber door —
　　　　Only this, and nothing more."

— EDGAR A. POE: *The Raven.*

6.
    Where with black cliffs the torrents toil,
    He watch'd the wheeling eddies boil,
    Till, from their foam, his dazzled eyes
    Beheld the River Demon rise;
    The mountain mist took form and limb
    Of noontide hag or goblin grim.
                —SCOTT: *Lady of the Lake.*

7. On nearer approach he was still more surprised at the singularity of the stranger's appearance. He was a short, square-built old fellow, with thick, bushy hair and a grizzled beard. His dress was of the antique Dutch fashion — a cloth jerkin strapped around the waist — several pairs of breeches, the outer ones of ample volume, decorated with rows of buttons down the sides and bunches at the knees. He bore on his shoulder a stout keg that seemed full of liquor, and made signs for Rip to approach and assist him with his load.
                —WASHINGTON IRVING: *Rip Van Winkle.*

27. Complete and Incomplete Images. — Some sentences have for their purpose the presentation of an image, and in order to form that image correctly and completely, we must be familiar with all the words used. If an unfamiliar word is introduced, the mind may omit this entirely, or may substitute something for it. Notice the image that the following sentence from Henry James presents: " Her dress was dark and rich; she had pearls around her neck and an old rococo fan in her hand." If the meaning of *rococo* is unknown to you, the image which you form will not be exactly the one that Mr. James had in mind. The pearls and the dress may stand out clearly in your image, but the fan will be lacking or indistinct. The whole may be compared to a photograph of which a part is blurred. If your attention is directed to the fan, you may recall the word *rococo*, but not the image represented by it. If your attention is not called to the fan, the mind is satisfied with the indistinct image, or substitutes for it an image of some other fan. Such an image is therefore either incomplete or inaccurate.

An oath in court provides that we shall "tell the truth, the whole truth, and nothing but the truth," but, in forming images, it is not always possible to hold our minds to such exactness. We are prone to picture more or less than the words convey. In fact, in some forms of prose, and often in poetry, the author purposely takes advantage of this habit of the mind and wishes us to enlarge with creations of our own imagination the bare image that his words convey. Such writing, however, aims to give pleasure or to arouse our emotions. It calls out something in the reader even more strongly than it sets forth something in the writer. This suggestiveness in writing will be considered later, but for the present it will be well for you to bear in mind that most language has for its purpose the exact expression of a definite idea. Much of the failure in school work arises from the careless substitution of one image for another, and from the formation of incomplete and inaccurate images.

EXERCISES

A. Make a list of the words in the following selections whose meanings you need to look up in order to make the images exact and complete. Do not attempt to memorize the language of the definition, but to form a correct image.

1. The sun stared brazenly down on a gray farmhouse, on ranges of whitewashed outbuildings, and on a goodly array of dark-thatched ricks.

2. In his shabby frieze jacket and mud-laden brogans, he was scarcely an attractive object.

3. In a sunlit corner of an old coquina fort they came suddenly face to face with a familiar figure.

4.
Somewhat back from the village street
Stands the old-fashioned country seat.
Across its antique portico
Tall poplar trees their shadows throw,
And from its station in the hall
An ancient timepiece says to all:
     " Forever — never !
     Never — forever ! "
     — LONGFELLOW: *The Old Clock on the Stairs.*

5. There was a room which bore the appearance of a vault. Four spandrels from the corners ran up to join a sharp cup-shaped roof. The architecture was rough, but very strong. It was evidently part of a great building.

6. The officer proceeded, without affecting to hear the words which escaped the sentinel in his surprise; nor did he again pause, until he had reached the low strand, and in a somewhat dangerous vicinity to the western water bastion of the fort.

7. She stood on the top step under the *porte-cochère*, on the extreme edge, so that the toes of her small slippers extended a little over it. She bent forward, and then tipped back on the high, exiguous heels again.

8. Before the caryatides of the fireplace, under the ancestral portraits, a valet moves noiselessly about, arranging the glistening silver service on the long table and putting in order the fruits, sweets, and ices.

9. No sooner is the heavy gate of the portal passed than one sees from afar among the leafage the court of honor, to which one comes along an alley decorated uniformly with upright square shafts like classic termæ in stone and bronze. The impression of the antique lines is striking: it springs at once to the eyes, at first in this portico with columns and a heavy entablature, but lacking a pediment.

B. Read again the selections beginning on page 46. Do you form complete images in every case?

C. Notice in each of your lessons for to-day what images are incomplete. Bring to class a list of the words you would need to look up in order to form complete images. Do not include all the words whose meanings are not clear, but only those that assist in forming images.

Theme XII. — *Form a clear mental image of some incident, person, or place. Write about it, using such words as will give your classmates complete and accurate images. The following may suggest a subject:* —

1. A party dress I should like.
2. My room.
3. A cozy glen.
4. In the apple orchard.
5. Going to the fire.
6. The hand-organ man.
7. A hornets' nest.
8. The last inning.
9. An exciting race.

(Consider what you have written with reference to the images which the *reader* will form. Do you think that when the members of the class hear your theme, each will form the same images that you had in mind when writing? Notice how many of your sentences begin in the same way. Can you rewrite them so as to give variety?)

28. Reproduction of Images. — If we were asked to tell about an accident which we had seen, we could recall the various incidents in the order of their occurrence. If the accident had occurred recently, or had made a vivid impression upon us, we could easily form mental images of each scene. If we had only read a description of the accident, it would be more difficult to recall the image, because that which we gain through language is less vitally a part of ourselves than is that which comes through experience.

When called upon to reproduce the images suggested to us by language, our memory is apt to concern itself with the words that suggested the image, and our expression is hampered rather than aided by this remembrance. The author has made, or should have made, the best possible selection of words and phrases. If we repeat his language, it is but memory drill or copy work; and if we do not, we are limited to such second-class language as we may be able to find.

Word memory has its uses, but it is less valuable than image memory. It is necessary to distinguish carefully between the images that a writer presents and the words that he uses. If a botany lesson should consist of a description of fifteen different leaves, a pupil deficient in image memory will attempt to memorize the language of the book. A better-trained pupil, on meeting such a term as *serrated*, will ask himself: "Have I ever seen such a leaf? Can I form an image of it?" If so, his only task will be to give the new name, *serrated*, to the idea that he already has. In a similar way he will form images for each of the fifteen leaves described in the lesson. The language of the book may help him form these images, or he may use it in describing them, but he will make no attempt to memorize it. With him, "getting the lesson" means forming images and naming them, and reciting the lesson will be but talking about an image that he has clearly in mind. Try this in your own lessons.

If we are called upon to reproduce the incidents and scenes of some story that has been read to us, our success will depend upon the clearness of the images that we have formed. Our efforts should be directed to making the images as definite and vivid as possible, and our memory will be concerned with the recalling of these images in their proper order, and not with the language that first caused them to appear.

EXERCISES

1. Report orally some interesting incident taken from a book which you have recently read. Do not reread the story. Use such language as will cause the class to form clear mental images.

2. Report orally upon some chapter selected from Cooper's *Last of the Mohicans* or Scott's *Ivanhoe*.

3. Read a portion of Scott's *Lady of the Lake*, and report orally what happened.

4. Report orally some incident that you have read about in a magazine. Select one that caused you to form images, and tell it so that the hearers will form like images.

Theme XIII. — *Reproduce a story read to you by the teacher.*

(Before writing, picture to yourself the scenes and recall the order of their occurrence. If it is necessary to condense, omit events of the least importance.)

29. Comparison. — Writing which contains unfamiliar words fails to call up complete and definite images. It is often difficult to form the correct mental picture, even though the words in themselves are familiar. Definitions, explanations, and descriptions may cause us to understand correctly, but this can usually be attained much more readily by means of a comparison. We can form an image of an object as soon as we know what it is like.

If I wished you to form an image of an okapi, a lengthy description would give you a less vivid picture than the statement that it was a horselike animal, having stripes similar to those of a zebra. If an okapi were as well known to you as is a horse, the name alone would call up the proper image, and no comparison would be necessary. By means of it we are enabled to picture the unfamiliar. In this case the comparison is literal.

If the comparison is imaginative rather than literal, our language becomes figurative, and usually takes the form of a simile or metaphor. Similes and metaphors are of great value in rendering thought clear. They make language forceful and effective, and they may add much to the beauty of expression.

We may speak of an object as being like another, or as acting like another. If the comparison is imaginative rather than literal, and is directly stated, the expression is a simile. Similes are introduced by *like*, *as*, *similar to*, etc.

> He fought like a lion.
> The river wound like a serpent around the mountains.

If two things are essentially different, but yet have a common quality, their *implied comparison* is a metaphor. It takes the form of a statement that one is the other.

> " He was a lion in the fight."
> " The river wound its serpent course."

Sometimes inanimate objects, abstract ideas, or the lower animals are given the attributes of human beings. Such a figure is called personification, and is in fact a modified metaphor, since it is based upon some resemblance of the lower to the higher.

> This music crept by me upon the waters.
>
> Time is a very bankrupt, and owes more than he is worth to season.
> Nay, he's a thief, too ; have you not heard men say,
> That time comes stealing on by night and day?
>
> — SHAKESPEARE.

30. Use of Figures of Speech. — The three figures of speech, simile, metaphor, and personification, are more frequently used than are the others. Figures of speech are treated in a later chapter, but some suggestions as to their use will be of value to beginners.

1. Never write for the purpose of using figures of speech. Nearly everything that we need to say can be well expressed in plain, bare English, and the ability to express our thoughts in this way is the essential thing. If a figure that adds to the force and clearness of your expression occurs to you, use it without hesitation. A figure may also add to the beauty of our expression. The examples to be found in literature are largely of this character. If well used, they are effective, but the beginner should beware of a figure that is introduced for decorative purposes only. An attempt to find figures of speech in ordinary prose writing will show how rarely they are used.

2. The figures should fit the subject in hand. Some comparisons are appropriate and some are not. If the writer is familiar with his subject and deeply in earnest, the appropriate figures will rise spontaneously in his mind. If they do not, little is gained by seeking for them.

3. The effectiveness of a comparison, whether literal or figurative, depends upon the familiarity of the reader with one of the two things compared. To say that a petrel resembled a kite would be of no value to one who knew nothing of either bird. Similarly a figure is defective if neither element of the comparison is familiar to the readers.

4. Suitable figures give picturesqueness and vivacity to language, but hackneyed figures are worse than none.

5. Elaborate and long-drawn-out figures, or an over-abundance of short ones, should be avoided.

6. A figure must be consistent throughout. A comparison once begun must be carried through without change; mixing figures often produces results which are ridiculous. The " mixed metaphor " is a common blunder of beginners. This fault may arise either from confusing different metaphors in the same sentence, or from blending literal language with metaphorical. The following will serve to illustrate : —

1. [Confused metaphor.] Let us pin our faith to the rock of perseverance and honest toil, where it may sail on to success on the wings of hope.

2. [Literal and figurative blended.] Washington was the father of his country and a surveyor of ability.

3. When the last awful moment came, the star of liberty went down with all on board.

4. The glorious work will never be accomplished until the good ship " Temperance " shall sail from one end of the land to the other, and with a cry of " Victory ! " at each step she takes, shall plant her banner in every city, town, and village in the United States.

5. All along the untrodden paths of the future we see the hidden footprints of an unseen hand.

6. The British lion, whether it is roaming the deserts of India, or climbing the forests of Canada, will never draw in its horns nor retire into its shell.

7. Young man, if you have the spark of genius in you, water it.

EXERCISES

Are the images which you form made more vivid by the use of the figures in the following selections ?

1. She began to screech as wild as ocean birds.

2. And when its force expended,
    The harmless storm was ended ;
    And as the sunrise splendid
          Came blushing o'er the sea —

3.　　　As a demon is hurled by an angel's spear,
Heels over head, to his proper sphere —
Heels over head and head over heels, —
Dizzily down the abyss he wheels, —
So fell Darius.

　　　　　　　　　　　　　　　— J. T. TROWBRIDGE.

4. In this republican country, amid the fluctuating waves of our social life, somebody is always at the drowning point.

　　　　　　　　　　　　　　　— HAWTHORNE.

5. Poverty, treading close at her heels for a lifetime, has come up with her at last.　　　　　　　　— HAWTHORNE.

6. Friendships begin with liking or gratitude — roots that can be pulled up.　　　　　　　　　　　— GEORGE ELIOT.

7. Nearing the end of the narrative, Ben paced up and down the narrow limits of the tent in great excitement, running his fingers through his hair, and barking out a question now and then.

8. A sky above,
Where one white cloud like a stray lamb doth move.

　　　　　　　　　　　　　　　— LOWELL.

9. In days of public commotion every faction, like an Oriental army, is attended by a crowd of camp followers, a useless and heartless rabble, who prowl round its line of march in the hope of picking up something under its protection, but desert it in the day of battle, and often join to exterminate it after a defeat.　　— MACAULAY.

10. It is to be regretted that the prose writings of Milton should, in our time, be so little read. As compositions, they deserve the attention of every man who wishes to become acquainted with the full power of the English language. They abound with passages compared with which the finest declamations of Burke sink into insignificance. They are a perfect field of cloth of gold. The style is stiff with gorgeous embroidery.　　　　— MACAULAY.

11.　　　　　　　And close behind her stood
Eight daughters of the plow, stronger than men,
Huge women blowzed with health, and wind, and rain,
And labor. Each was like a Druid rock,
Or like a spire of land that stands apart
Cleft from the main and wall'd about with mews.

　　　　　　　　　　　　　　　— TENNYSON.

12.   But bland the smile that, like a wrinkling wind
     On glassy water, drove his cheek in lines.   —TENNYSON.

13. The rush of affairs drifts words from their original meanings, as ships drag their anchors in a gale, but terms sheltered from common use hold to their moorings forever.   — MILL.

Theme XIV. — *Write a story suggested by the picture on page 59 or by one of the following subjects:* —

    1. A modern fable.
    2. The willow whistle.
    3. How I baked a cake.
    4. The delayed picnic.
    5. The missing slipper.
    6. A misdirected letter.
    7. A ride on a raft.
    8. The rescue of Ezekiel.
    9. A railway experience.
  10. A soldier's soldier.

(Do you think the reader will form the images you wish him to form? Consider what you have written with reference to climax. (See Section 7.) Have you needed to use figures? If so, have you used them in accordance with the suggestions on page 55? If you have used the word *only*, is it placed so as to give the correct meaning?)

31. Determination of Meaning Requires More than Image Making. — The emphasis laid upon image making should not lead to the belief that this is all that is necessary in order to determine what is meant by the language we hear or read. Image making is important, but much of our language is concerned with presenting ideas of which no mental pictures can be formed. This very paragraph

will serve as an illustration of such language. Our understanding of language of this kind depends upon our knowledge of the meanings of words, upon our understanding
of the relations between word groups, or parts of sentences, and especially upon our appreciation of the relations in thought that sentences bear to one another. Each
of these will be discussed in the following pages. Later
it will be necessary to consider the relations in thought
existing among paragraphs.

32. Word Relations. — In order to get the thought of
a sentence, we must understand the relations that exist
between the words and word groups (phrases and clauses)
that compose it. If the thought is simple, and expressed
in straightforward terms, we grasp it readily and without
any conscious effort to determine these relations. If the
thought is complex, the relations become more complicated,
and before we are sure that we know what the writer
intends to say it may be necessary to note with care which
is the main clause and which are the subordinate ones. In
either case our acquiring the thought depends upon our
understanding the relations between words and word
groups. This may occur without any knowledge of the
names that have been applied to them in grammar, but
a knowledge of the names will assist somewhat. These
relations are treated in the grammar review in the Appendix and need not be repeated here.

33. Incomplete Thoughts. — We have learned (Section
27) that the introduction of unfamiliar words may cause
us to form incomplete images. When the language is
not designed to present images, we may, in a similar way,
fail to get its real meaning if we are unfamiliar with the
words used. If you do not know the meaning of *fluent*

and *viscous*, you will fail to understand correctly the statement, "Fluids range from the peculiarly fluent to the peculiarly viscous." If we wish to think precisely what the writer intended us to think, we must know the meanings of the words he uses. Many of us are inclined to substitute other ideas than those properly conveyed by the words of the writer, and so get confused or incomplete or inaccurate ideas. The ability to determine exactly what images the writer suggests, and what ideas his language expresses, is the first requisite of scholarship and an important element of success in life.

EXERCISES

A. The first step in acquiring knowledge is to determine what it is that we do not know. Just which word or words in each of the following sentences keep you from understanding the full meaning of the sentence? Notice that a dictionary definition will not always make the meaning clear.

1. It is really more scientific to repeat a quotation from a political speech correctly, or to pass on a story undistorted, than it is to know of the rings of Saturn or the striation of diatoms.

2. The process of testing a hypothesis requires great caution in order to prevent mistakes.

3. The aërial foliage stem is the most favorable for studying stem structure.

4. Taken collectively, isotherms indicate the distribution of mean temperature over the region embraced in the map.

5. Vibrations of the membrane of the tympanum are "damped" by the ossicles of the middle ear, which also receive and pass on the auditory tremors to the membrane closing the oval window.

6. In the battle which followed, the mobile Roman legion, arranged in open order three ranks deep, proved its superiority over the massive Macedonian phalanx.

7. The narrow and dissected forms have been attributed to the scarcity of carbon dioxide and oxygen in the water.

B. Make a list of words in your lessons in other subjects for to-day that you need to look up in order to understand the lessons. This should be done daily, whether assigned or not.

34. Choice of Words Adapted to the Reader. — Words familiar to the reader should be used. Since the reader's ability to understand the thought of a paragraph depends to some extent upon his understanding of the words employed, it is necessary for the writer to choose words that will be understood by those whom he addresses. Of course we cannot tell whether a particular word will be understood by our readers, but, in case there is doubt, it is well to substitute one that is more likely to be understood. When you have written anything, it is well to ask yourself the question, Have I used words with which *the reader* is probably familiar?

Theme XV. — *Write a theme about one of the following subjects, using words that you think will be understood by your readers:* —

1. How we breathe.
2. How to make a kite.
3. The causes of the seasons.
4. Why wood floats on water.
5. The use of baking powder.
6. The difference between arithmetic and algebra.

(Have you said what you meant to say? Have you used words that your reader will understand? Find your longest sentence. Is its meaning clear? Notice the short sentences. Should some of them be united into a longer one?)

35. Word Selection. — There are many shades of meaning which differ but little from each other, and a careful writer will select just the word that best conveys his thought. The reader needs to be no less careful in determining the exact meaning, and it was to assist in this that exercises in synonyms were suggested (Section 21).

Another source of error, both in acquiring and expressing thought, arises from the confusion of similar words. Some similarity of spelling causes one word to be substituted for another. There are many words and expressions that are so often interchanged that some time may be spent with profit upon exercises in determining their correct usage. These usually consist of brief reports to the class that set forth the meanings of the words, show their uses, and illustrate their differences.

In preparing such reports, determine the meaning of the words from as many sources as are available. The usual meaning can be determined from the dictionary. A fuller treatment is given in some dictionaries in a chapter on faulty diction. Additional material may be found in many of the text-books on rhetoric, and in special books treating of word usage. After you are sure that you know the correct use, prepare a report for the class that shall make that use clear to others. In the simplest form this will consist of definitions and sentences in which the words are correctly used. The following examples, handed in by pupils, will serve to illustrate such reports: —

1. A *council* is an assembly of persons convened for consultation or deliberation. *Counsel* is used to indicate either (1) an opinion as the result of consultation or (2) a lawyer engaged to give advice or to act as advocate in court. Lewis furnishes the following example of the use of these two words: "The plaintiff's *counsel* held a *council* with his partners in law, and finally gave him as his best *counsel* the advice that he should drop the suit; but, as Swift says, 'No man will

take *counsel,* but every man will take money,' and the plaintiff refused to accept the advice unless the *counsel* could persuade the defendant to settle the case out of court by paying a large sum."

2. The correct meaning of *transpire* may perhaps be best understood by considering its derivations. It comes from *trans,* through, and *spiro,* to breathe, from which it gets its meaning, to escape gradually from secrecy. It is frequently used incorrectly in the sense of to happen, but both Webster and the Standard dictionary condemn this use of the word. The latter says that it is often so misused especially in carelessly edited newspapers, as in " Comments on the heart-rending disaster which transpired yesterday are unnecessary, but," etc. When *transpire* is correctly used, it is not a synonym of *happen.* A thing that happened a year ago may transpire to-day, that is, it may " become known through unnoticed channels, exhale, as it were, through invisible pores like a vapor or a gas disengaging itself." Many things which happen in school thus become known by being passed along in a semi-secret manner until nearly all know of them though few can tell just how the information was spread. *Transpire* may properly be applied to such a diffusion of knowledge.

Theme XVI. — *Report as suggested above on any one of the following groups of words :* —

1. Allude, mention.
2. Beside, besides.
3. Character, reputation.
4. Degrade, demean, debase.
5. Last, latest, preceding.
6. Couple, pair.
7. Balance, rest, remainder.

(Have you made clear the correct use of the words under discussion? Can you give examples which do not follow the dictionaries so closely as do the illustrative reports above?)

NOTE. — Lists of words suitable for exercises similar to the above are given in the Appendix. The teacher will assign them to such an extent and at such times as seems desirable. One such lesson a week will be found profitable.

36. Sentence Relations. — What we read or hear usually consists of several sentences written or spoken together. The meaning of any particular sentence may depend upon the sentence or sentences preceding. In order to determine accurately the meaning of the whole, we must understand the relation in thought that each sentence bears to the others. Notice the two sentences : " Guns are dangerous. Boys should not use them." Though the last sentence is independent, it gets its meaning from the first.

In the following selection consider each sentence apart from the others. Notice that the meaning of the whole becomes intelligible only when the sentences are considered in their relations to each other.

Once upon a time, a notion was started, that if all the people in the world would shout at once, it might be heard in the moon. So the projectors agreed it should be done in just ten years. Some thousand shiploads of chronometers were distributed to the selectmen and other great folks of all the different nations. For a year beforehand, nothing else was talked about but the awful noise that was to be made on the great occasion. When the time came, everybody had his ears so wide open, to hear the universal ejaculation of Boo, — the word agreed upon, — that nobody spoke except a deaf man in one of the Fiji Islands, and a woman in Pekin, so that the world was never so still since the creation. — HOLMES.

Gutenberg did a great deal of his work in secret, for he thought it was much better that his neighbors should know nothing of what he was doing. So he looked for a workshop where no one would be likely to find him. He was now living in Strasburg, and there was in that city a ruined old building where, long before his time, a number of monks had lived. There was one room in the building which needed only a little repairing to make it fit to be used. So he got the right to repair the room and use it as his workshop.

In all good writing we find a similar dependence in thought. Each sentence takes a meaning because of its relation to some other. The personal pronouns and pronominal adjectives, adverbial phrases indicating time or place, conjunctions, and such expressions as *certainly*, *however*, *on the other hand*, etc., are used to indicate more or less directly a relation in thought between the phrase or sentence in which they occur and some preceding one. If the reader cannot readily determine to what they refer, the meaning becomes obscure or ambiguous. The pronominal adjectives and the personal pronouns are especially likely to be used in such a way as to cause ambiguity. Care must be taken to use them so as to keep the meaning clear, and your own good sense will help you in this more than rules. Notice in your reading how frequently expressions similar to those mentioned above are used.

Theme XVII. — *Write a theme suggested by one of the following subjects:* —

1. The last quarter.
2. An excursion with the physical geography class.
3. What I saw while riding to town.
4. The broken bicycle.
5. An hour in the study hall.
6. Seen from my study window.

(Are your sentences so arranged that the relation in thought is clear? Are the personal pronouns and pronominal adjectives used so as to avoid ambiguity? Does your story relate real events or imaginary ones? If imaginary events are related, have you made them seem probable?)

37. Getting the Main Thought. — In many cases the relation in thought is not directly indicated, and we are left to determine it from the context, just as we decide upon the meaning of a word because of what precedes or follows it. In this case the meaning of a particular sentence may be made clear if we have in mind the main topic under discussion. Many pupils fail in recitations because they do not distinguish that which is more important from that which is less so. If a dozen pages of history are assigned, they cannot master the lesson because it is too long to be memorized, and they are not able to select the three or four things of importance with which it is really concerned. Thirty or forty minor details are jumbled together without any clear knowledge of the relations that they bear either to each other or to the main thoughts of the lesson.

In the following selection but three things are discussed. Determine what they are, but not what is said about them.

In all the ages the extent and value of flood plains have been increased by artificial means. Dikes or levees are built to regulate the spread and flow of the water and to protect the land from destructive floods. Dams and reservoirs are constructed for the storage of water, which is led by a system of canals and ditches to irrigate large tracts of land which would be otherwise worthless. By means of irrigation, the farmer has control of his water supply and is able to get larger returns than are possible where he depends upon the irregular and uncertain rainfall. It is estimated that in the arid regions of western United States there are 150,000 square miles of land which may be made available for agriculture by irrigation. Perhaps in the future the valley of the lower Colorado may become as productive as that of the Nile.

Streams are the easiest routes of travel and commerce. A river usually furnishes from its mouth well up toward its source a smooth, graded highway, upon which a cargo may be transported with much less effort than overland. If obstructions occur in the form of rapids or falls, boat and cargo are carried around them. It is often easy to pass by a short portage or "carry" from one stream system across the divide to another. In regions which are not very level the easiest grades in every direction are found along the streams, and the main routes of land travel follow the stream valleys. In traversing a mountainous region, a railroad follows the windings of some river up to the crest of the divide, which it crosses through a pass, or often by a tunnel, and descends the valley of some stream on the other side.

Man is largely indebted to streams for the variety and beauty of scenery. Running water itself is attractive to young and old. A landscape without water lacks its chief charm. A child instinctively finds its way to the brook, and the man seeks beside the river the pleasure and recreation which no other place affords. Streams have carved the surface of the land into an endless variety of beautiful forms, and a land where stream valleys are few or shallow is monotonous and tiresome. The most common as well as the most celebrated beauty of scenery in the world, from the tiny meanders of a meadow brook to the unequaled grandeur of the Colorado canyons, is largely due to the presence and action of streams.

— DRYER: *Lessons in Physical Geography.*

In the above selection we find that each group of sentences is related to some main topic. A more extended observation of good writing will give the same result. Men naturally think in sentence groups. A group of sentences related to each other and to the central idea is called a **paragraph**.

38. Topic Statement. — In the three paragraphs of the selection on page 67, notice that the first sentence in each tells what the paragraph is about. In a well-written paragraph it is possible to select the phrase or sentence that states the main thought. If such a sentence does not occur in the paragraph itself, one can be framed that will express clearly and concisely the chief idea of the paragraph. This brief, comprehensive summary of the contents of a paragraph is called the **topic statement**.

In order to master the thought of what we read we must be able to select or to make the successive topic statements, and in order to express our own thoughts clearly we must write our paragraphs so that our readers may easily grasp the topic statement of each.

When expressed in the paragraph, the topic statement may be a part of a sentence, a whole sentence, or it may extend through two sentences. It is usual to place the topic statement first, but it may be preceded by one or more introductory sentences, or even withheld until the end of the paragraph. For emphasis it may be repeated, though usually in a slightly different form.

EXERCISES

Determine the topic statements of the following paragraphs. If one is not expressed, make one.

1. No less valuable is the mental stimulus of play. The child is trained by it to quick perception, rapid judgment, prompt decision. His imagination cunningly suggests a thousand things to be done, and then trains the will and every power of body and mind in the effort to do them. The sports of childhood are admirably adapted to quicken the senses and sharpen the wits. Nature has effective ways in her school of securing the exercise which is needed to develop every mental and every bodily power. She fills the activity brimful of enjoyment, and then gives her children freedom, assured that they will be their own best teachers. —BRADLEY.

2. Our Common Law comes from England, and originated there in custom. It is often called the unwritten law, because unwritten in origin, though there are now many books describing it. Its principles originated as habits of the people, five hundred, eight hundred, years ago, perhaps some of them back in the time when the half-savage Saxons landed on the shores of England. When the time came that the government, through its courts, punished the breach of a custom, from that time the custom was a law. And so the English people acquired these laws, one after another, just as they were acquiring at the same time the habits of making roads, using forks at table, manufacturing, meeting in Parliament, using firearms, and all the other habits of civilization. When the colonists came to America, they brought the English Common Law with them, not in a book, but in their minds, a part of their life, like their religion.
—CLARK: *The Government.*

3. Accuracy is always to be striven for, but it can never be attained. This fact is only fully realized by scientific workers. The banker can be accurate because he only counts or weighs masses of metal which he assumes to be exactly equal. The Master of the Mint knows that two coins are never exactly equal in weight, although he strives by improving machinery and processes to make the differences as small as possible. When the utmost care is taken, the finest balances which have been constructed can weigh 1 lb. of a metal with an uncertainty less than the hundredth part of a grain. In other words, the weight is not accurate, but the inaccuracy is very small. No person is so stupid as not to feel sure that the height of a man he sees is between 3 ft. and 9 ft.; some are able by the eye to estimate the height as between 5 ft. 6 in. and 5 ft. 8 in.; measurement may show it to be between 5 ft. 6³ in. and 5 ft. 7 in., but to go closer than that requires many precautions. Training in observation and the use of delicate instruments thus narrow the limits of approximation. Similarly with regard to space and time, there are instruments with which one millionth of an inch, or of a second, can be measured, but even this approximation, although far closer than is ever practically necessary, is not accuracy. In the statement of measurements there is no meaning in more than six significant figures, and only the most careful observations can be trusted so far. The height of Mount Everest is given as 29,002 feet; but here the fifth figure is meaningless, the height of that mountain not being known so accurately that two feet more or less would be detected. Similarly, the radius of the earth is sometimes given as 3963.295833 miles, whereas no observation can get nearer the truth than 3963.30 miles.

— MILL: *The Realm of Nature.* (Copyright, 1892, by Charles Scribner's Sons.)

4. The chief cause which made the fusion of the different elements of society so imperfect was the extreme difficulty which our ancestors found in passing from place to place. Of all the inventions, the alphabet and the printing press alone excepted, those inventions which abridge distance have done most for the civilization of our species. Every improvement of the means of locomotion benefits mankind morally and intellectually as well as materially, and not only facilitates the interchange of the various productions of nature and art, but tends to remove national and provincial prejudices, and to bind together all the branches of the great human family. In the seventeenth century the inhabitants of London were for almost every prac-

tical purpose farther from Reading than they are now from Edinburgh, and farther from Edinburgh than they are now from Vienna.

— MACAULAY : *History of England.*

5. He touched New England at every point. He was born a frontiersman. He was bred a farmer. He was a fisherman in the mountain brooks and off the shore. He never forgot his origin, and he never was ashamed of it. Amid all the care and honor of his great place here he was homesick for the company of his old neighbors and friends. Whether he stood in Washington, the unchallenged prince and chief in the Senate, or in foreign lands, the kingliest man of his time in the presence of kings, his heart was in New England. When the spring came, he heard far off the fife bird and the bobolink calling him to his New Hampshire mountains, or plashing of the waves on the shore at Marshfield alluring him with a sweeter than siren's voice to his home by the summer sea.

— GEORGE F. HOAR : *Daniel Webster.*

6. Nor must I forget the suddenly changing seasons of the northern clime. There is no long and lingering spring, unfolding leaf and blossom one by one; no long and lingering autumn, pompous with many-colored leaves and the glow of Indian summer. But winter and summer are wonderful, and pass into each other. The quail has hardly ceased piping in the corn when winter, from the folds of trailing clouds, sows broadcast over the land snow, icicles, and rattling hail. The days wane apace. Erelong the sun hardly rises above the horizon, or does not rise at all. The moon and the stars shine through the day; only at noon they are pale and wan, and in the southern sky a red, fiery glow, as of a sunset, burns along the horizon and then goes out. And pleasantly under the silver moon, and under the silent, solemn stars, ring the steel shoes of the skaters on the frozen sea, and voices, and the sound of bells.

— LONGFELLOW : *Rural Life in Sweden.*

7. Extreme *busyness*, whether at school or college, kirk or market, is a symptom of deficient vitality; and a faculty for idleness implies a catholic appetite and a strong sense of personal identity. There is a sort of dead-alive, hackneyed people about, who are scarcely conscious of living except in the exercise of some conventional occupation. Bring these fellows into the country, or set them aboard ship, and you will see how they pine for their desk or their study. They have no curiosity; they cannot give themselves over to random provocations;

they do not take pleasure in the exercise of their faculties for its own sake; and unless Necessity lays about them with a stick, they will even stand still. It is no good speaking to such folk: they *cannot* be idle, their nature is not generous enough; and they pass those hours in a sort of coma, which are not dedicated to furious moiling in the gold mill. When they do not require to go to the office, when they are not hungry and have no mind to drink, the whole breathing world is a blank to them. If they have to wait an hour or so for a train, they fall into a stupid trance, with their eyes open. To see them, you would suppose there was nothing to look at and no one to speak with; you would imagine they were paralyzed or alienated; and yet very possibly they are hard workers in their own way, and have good eyesight for a flaw in a deed or a turn of the market. They have been to school and college, but all the time they had their eye on the medal; they have gone about in the world and mixed with clever people, but all the time they were thinking of their own affairs. As if a man's soul were not too small to begin with, they have dwarfed and narrowed theirs by a life of all work and no play; until here they are at forty, with a listless attention, a mind vacant of all material amusement, and not one thought to rub against another while they wait for the train. Before he was breeched, he might have clambered on the boxes; when he was twenty, he would have stared at the girls; but now the pipe is smoked out, the snuffbox is empty, and my gentleman sits bolt upright on a bench, with lamentable eyes. This does not appeal to me as being Success in Life.

—Robert Louis Stevenson. (Copyright, by Charles Scribner's Sons.)

B. Examine the themes which you have written. Does each paragraph have a topic statement? Have you introduced sentences which do not bear upon this topic statement? Are the paragraphs real ones treating of a single topic, or are they merely groups of sentences written together without any close connection in thought?

Theme XVIII. — *State two or three advantages of public high schools over private boarding schools. Use each as a topic statement and develop it into a short paragraph.*

(Add to each topic statement such sentences as will prove to a pupil of your own age that it is a real advantage. Include in each paragraph only that which bears upon the topic statement. Consider the definition of a paragraph on page 68. Does this definition apply to your paragraphs?)

39. Reproduction of the Thought of a Paragraph. — Our ability to reproduce the thought of what we read will depend largely upon our ability to select the topic statements. In preparing a lesson for recitation it is evident that we must first determine definitely the topic statement of each paragraph. These may bear upon one general subject or upon different subjects. The three paragraphs on page 67 are all concerned with one subject, the uses of rivers. A pupil preparing to recite them would have in mind, when he went to class, an outline about as follows: —

General subject : The uses of rivers.
First topic statement : The fertility of flood plains is improved by irrigation.
Second topic statement : Streams are the easiest routes of travel and commerce.
Third topic statement : Man is indebted to streams for beauty of scenery.

While such a clear statement is the first step toward a proper understanding of the lesson, it is not enough. In order to understand thoroughly a topic statement, we need explanation or illustration. The idea is not really our own until we have thought about it in its relations to other knowledge already in our possession. In order to know whether you understand the topic statements, the teacher will ask you to discuss them. This may be done by telling what the writer said about them, or by giving thoughts and illustrations of your own, but best of all, by doing both. It is necessary, then, to know in what way the writer develops each topic statement.

Read the following paragraph : —

The most productive lands in the world are flood plains. At every period of high water, a stream brings down mantle rock from the higher grounds, and deposits it as a layer of fine sediment over its flood plain. A soil thus frequently enriched and renewed is literally inexhaustible. In a rough, hilly, or mountainous country the finest farms and the densest population are found on the "bottom lands " along the streams. The flood plain most famous in history is that of the river Nile in Egypt. For a distance of 1500 miles above its mouth this river flows through a rainless desert, and has no tributary. The heavy spring rains which fall upon the highlands about its sources produce in summer a rise of the water, which overflows the valley on either side. Thus the lower Nile valley became one of the earliest centers of civilization, and has supported a dense population for 7000 years. The conditions in Mesopotamia, along the Tigris and Euphrates rivers, are similar to those along the lower Nile, and in ancient times this region was the seat of a civilization perhaps older than that of Egypt. The flood plains of the Ganges in India, and the Hoang in China, are the most extensive in the world, and in modern times the most populous. The alluvial valley of the Mississippi is extremely productive of corn, cotton, and sugar cane.

— DRYER: *Lessons in Physical Geography.*

Notice that the first sentence gives the topic statement, flood plains are productive. The second and third sentences tell why this is so, and the rest of the paragraph is given up to illustrations.

In preparing this paragraph for recitation the pupil would have in mind an outline about as follows : —

Topic statement : Flood plains are the most productive lands in the world.

1. Reasons.
2. Examples: (*a*) Bottom lands.
   (*b*) Nile.
   (*c*) Tigris and Euphrates.
   (*d*) Ganges.
   (*e*) Hoang.
   (*f*) Mississippi.

In order to make such an outline, the relative importance of the ideas in the paragraph must be mastered. A recitation that omitted the topic statement or the reasons would be defective, while one that omitted one or more of the examples might be perfect, especially if the pupil could furnish other examples from his own knowledge. The illustration about bottom lands is a general one, and should suggest specific cases that could be included in the recitation. The details in regard to the Nile might be included if they happened to be recalled at the time of the recitation, but even the omission of all mention of the Nile might not materially detract from the value of the recitation. The effort to remember minor details hinders real thought-getting power.

It is better not to write this outline. The use of notes or written outlines at the time of the recitation soon establishes a habit of dependence that renders real scholarship an impossibility. With such an analysis of the thought clearly in mind, the pupil need not attempt to remember the language of the writer.

EXERCISES

A. Complete the partial outline given for the paragraph below. Which of the illustrations might be omitted from a recitation? For which can you furnish different illustrations?

Mountain ranges have great influence upon climate, political geography, and commerce. Many of them form climatic boundaries. The Cordilleras of western America and the Scandinavian mountains arrest the warm, moist, western winds which rise along those great rock barriers to cooler altitudes, where their water vapor is condensed and falls as rain, so that the country on the windward side of the mountains is wet and that on the leeward side is dry. Mountain chains stretching east and west across central Asia protect the southern part of the continent from frigid arctic winds. The large winter tourist traffic of the Riviera is due to the mountains that shield this favored French-Italian coast from the north and northeast continental winds, giving it a considerably warmer winter's temperature than that of Rome, two and a half degrees farther south. As North America has no mountain barriers across the pathway of polar winds, they sweep southward even to the Gulf of Mexico and have twice destroyed Florida's orange groves within a decade. Mountain ranges are conspicuous in political geography because they are the natural boundary between many nations and languages, as the Pyrenees between France and Spain, the Alps between Austria and Italy, and the Himalayas between Tibet and India. Mountains sometimes guard nations from attack by the isolation they give, and therefore promote national unity. Thus the Swiss are among the few peoples in Europe who have maintained the integrity of their state. Commercially, mountains are of great importance as a source of water, which they store in snow, glaciers, and lakes. Snow and ice, melting slowly on the mountains, are an unfailing source of supply for perennial rivers, and thus promote navigation. Mountains are the largest source of water power, which is more valuable than ever now that electricity is employed to transmit it to convenient centers for use in the industries. A large part of the mining machinery in the United States is run by water power. Switzerland, which has no coal, turns the wheels of its mills with water. Mountains supply most of the metals and minerals, and are therefore the scene of the largest mining industry. They are also among the greatest sources of forest wealth. Though the slopes are not favorable for agriculture they afford good pasturage, and the débris of the rocks washed into the valleys and plains by mountain torrents supplies good soil. Thus the Appalachians have been worn down to a comparatively low level, and the soil formed from their rock particles is the basis of large husbandry.

The scenic attractions of many mountain regions is a source of large revenue. The Alps attract crowds of tourists, who spend about twenty million dollars a year in Switzerland and Austria, and give employment to many thousands of persons.

— ADAMS: *Commercial Geography.*

OUTLINE (to be completed)

Mountain ranges have a great influence upon —

    I.   Climate.
          Why ?
          Where ?
          a, b, etc.
   II.   Political geography.
          Why ?
          Where ?
          a, b, etc.
 III. Commerce.
          Why ?
          Where ?
          a, b, etc.

B. Make an outline of the following paragraph : —

1. The armor of the different classes was also accurately ordered by the law. The first class was ordered to wear for the defense of the body, brazen helmets, shields, and coats of mail, and to bear spears and swords, excepting the mechanics, who were to carry the necessary military engines and to serve without arms. The members of the second class, excepting that they had bucklers instead of shields and wore no coats of mail, were permitted to bear the same armor and to carry the sword and spear. The third class had the same armor as the second, excepting that they could not wear greaves for the protection of their legs. The fourth had no arms excepting a spear and a long javelin. The fifth merely carried slings and stones for use in them. To this class belonged the trumpeters and horn blowers.

— GILMAN: *Story of Rome.*

C. In preparing your other lessons for to-day, make outlines of the paragraphs.

Theme XIX. — *Reproduce the thought of some paragraph read to you by the teacher.*

(Do not attempt to remember the language. Try to get the main thought of what is read and then write a paragraph which sets forth that same idea. Use different illustrations if you can.)

NOTE. — This theme may be repeated as many times as seems desirable.

40. Importance of the Paragraph. — Emphasis needs to be laid upon the importance of the paragraph. Our ability to express our thoughts clearly depends, to a large extent, upon our skill in constructing paragraphs. The writing of correct sentences is not sufficient. Though each of a series of sentences may be correct, they may, as a whole, say but little, and that very poorly, while another set of sentences, which cluster around some central idea, may set it forth most effectively. It is only by giving our sentence groups that unity of thought which combines them into paragraphs that we make them most effective. A well-constructed paragraph will make clear some idea, and a series of such paragraphs, related to each other and properly arranged, will set forth the sum of our thoughts on any subject.

41. Paragraph Length. — The proper length of a paragraph cannot be determined by rule. Sometimes the thought that we wish to present will require several sentences; sometimes two or three will be sufficient. A single illustration may make a topic statement clear or it may require several. The writer must judge when he has included enough to make his meaning understood, and must avoid including so much that the reader becomes weary. Usually a paragraph that exceeds three hundred words will be found too long, or else it will contain more than one main idea, each of which could have been presented more effectively in a separate paragraph.

42. Indentation. — In written and printed matter the beginning of a paragraph is indicated by an indentation. Indentation does not make a paragraph, but we indent because we are beginning a new paragraph. Indentation thus serves the same purpose as punctuation. It helps the reader to determine when we have finished one main thought and are about to begin another. Beginners are apt to use indentations too frequently. There are some special uses of indentation in letter writing, printed conversation, and other forms, but for ordinary paragraph division the indentation is determined by the thought, and its correct use depends upon clear thinking. Can the following selection be improved by reparagraphing?

Outside in the darkness, gray with whirling snowflakes, he saw the wet lamps of cabs shining, and he darted along the line of hansoms and coupés in frantic search for his own.

"Oh, there you are," he panted, flinging his suit case up to a snow-covered driver. "Do your best now; we're late!" And he leaped into the dark coupé, slammed the door, and sank back on the cushions, turning up the collar of his heavy overcoat.

There was a young lady in the farther corner of the cab, buried to her nose in a fur coat. At intervals she shivered and pressed a fluffy muff against her face. A glimmer from the sleet-smeared lamps fell across her knees.

Down town flew the cab, swaying around icy corners, bumping over car tracks, lurching, rattling, jouncing, while its silent occupants, huddled in separate corners, brooded moodily at their respective windows.

Snow blotted the glass, melting and running down; and over the watery panes yellow light from shop windows played fantastically, distorting vision.

Presently the young man pulled out his watch, fumbled for a match box, struck a light, and groaned as he read the time.

At the sound of the match striking, the young lady turned her head. Then, as the bright flame illuminated the young man's face, she sat bolt upright, dropping the muff to her lap with a cry of dismay.

He looked up at her. The match burned his fingers; he dropped it and hurriedly lighted another; and the flickering radiance brightened upon the face of a girl whom he had never before laid eyes on.

"Good heavens!" he said, "where's my sister?"

The young lady was startled but resolute. "You have made a dreadful mistake," she said; "you are in the wrong cab —"

Theme XX. — *Write a theme using one of the subjects below:* —

1. A personal incident.
2. The advantages and disadvantages of recesses.
3. Complete the story commenced in the selection just preceding.

(Make a note of the different ideas you may discuss. Which are important enough to become topic statements? Which may be grouped together in one paragraph? In what order shall they occur? After your theme is written, consider the paragraphs. Does the definition apply to them? Are any of them too short or too long?)

43. Reasons for Studying Paragraph Structure. — A knowledge of the way in which a paragraph is constructed will aid us in determining the thought it contains. There are several methods of developing paragraphs, and usually one of these is better suited than another to the expression of our thought. Attention given to the methods used by others will enable us both to understand better what we read, and to employ more effectively in our own writing that kind of paragraph which best expresses our thought. Hence we shall give attention to the more common forms of paragraph development.

44. Development by Giving Specific Instances. — If you hear a general statement, such as, "Dogs are useful animals," you naturally think at once of some of the ways in which they are useful, or of some particular occasion on which a dog was of use. If a friend should say, " My dog, Fido, knows many amusing tricks," you would expect him to tell you some of them. A large share of our thinking consists of furnishing specific instances to illustrate general ideas which arise. Since the language we use is but the expression of the thoughts we have, it happens that many of our paragraphs are made up of general statements and the specific instances which illustrate them. When the topic sentence is a general statement, we naturally seek to supply specific instances, and the writer will most readily make his meaning clear by furnishing such illustrations. Either one or many instances may be used. The object is to explain the topic statement or to prove its truth, and a good writer will use that number of instances which best accomplishes his purpose.

In the following selection notice how the topic statement, set forth and repeated in the first part of the paragraph, is illustrated in the last part by means of several specific instances : —

Nine tenths of all that goes wrong in this world is because some one does not mind his business. When a terrible accident occurs, the first cry is that the means of prevention were not sufficient. Everybody declares we must have a new patent fire escape, an automatic engine switch, or a high-proof non-combustible sort of lamp oil. But a little investigation will usually show that all the contrivances were on hand and in good working order; the real trouble was that somebody didn't mind his business; he didn't obey orders; he thought he knew a better way than the way he was told; he said, " Just this once I'll take the risk," and in so doing, he made other people take the risk too; and the risk was too great. At Toronto, Canada, not long ago, a conductor, against orders, ran his train on a certain siding, which resulted in the death of thirty or forty people. The engineer of a mill, at Rochester, N.Y., thought the engine would stand a higher pressure than the safety valve indicated, so he tied a few bricks to the valve to hold it down; result—four workmen killed, a number wounded, and a mill blown to pieces. The *City of Columbus*, an iron vessel fitted out with all the means of preservation and escape in use on shipboard, was wrecked on the best-known portion of the Atlantic coast, on a moonlight night, at the cost of one hundred lives, because the officer in command took it into his head to save a few ship-lengths in distance by hugging the shore, in direct disobedience to the captain's parting orders. The best-ventilated mine in Colorado was turned into a death trap for half a hundred miners because one of the number entered with a lighted lamp the gallery he had been warned against. Nobody survived to explain the explosion of the dynamite-cartridge factory in Pennsylvania, but as that type of disaster almost always is due to heedlessness, it is probable that this instance is not an exception to the rule. — WOLSTAN DIXEY: *Mind Your Business.*

EXERCISES

A. Which sentences make the general statements, and which furnish specific instances, in the following paragraphs?

My contemplations were often interrupted by strangers who came down from Forsyth's to take their first view of the falls. A short, ruddy, middle-aged gentleman, fresh from Old England, peeped over the rock, and evinced his approbation by a broad grin. His spouse, a very robust lady, afforded a sweet example of maternal solicitude, being so intent on the safety of her little boy that she did not even glance at Niagara. As for the child, he gave himself wholly to the enjoyment of a stick of candy. Another traveler, a native American, and no rare character among us, produced a volume of Captain Hall's tour, and labored earnestly to adjust Niagara to the captain's description, departing, at last, without one new idea or sensation of his own. The next comer was provided, not with a printed book, but with a blank sheet of foolscap, from top to bottom of which, by means of an ever pointed pencil, the cataract was made to thunder. In a little talk which we had together, he awarded his approbation to the general view, but censured the position of Goat Island, observing that it should have been thrown farther to the right, so as to widen the American falls, and contract those of the Horseshoe. Next appeared two traders of Michigan, who declared that, upon the whole, the sight was worth looking at; there certainly was an immense water power here; but that, after all, they would go twice as far to see the noble stone works of Lockport, where the Grand Canal is locked down a descent of sixty feet. They were succeeded by a young fellow, in a homespun cotton dress, with a staff in his hand, and a pack over his shoulders. He advanced close to the edge of the rock, where his attention, at first wavering among the different components of the scene, finally became fixed in the angle of the Horseshoe falls, which is, indeed, the central point of interest. His whole soul seemed to go forth and be transported thither, till the staff slipped from his relaxed grasp, and falling down — down — down — struck upon the fragment of the Table Rock.

— HAWTHORNE: *My Visit to Niagara.*

No wonder he learned English quickly, for he was ever on the alert — no strange word escaped him, no unusual term. He would say it over and over till he met a friend, and then demand its meaning. One day he came to me with a very troubled face. "Madame," he said, "please tell me why shall a man, like me, like any man, be a 'bluenose'?"

"A what?" I asked.

"A 'bluenose.' So he was called in the restaurant, but he seemed not offended about it. I have looked in my books; I can't find any disease of that name."

With ill-suppressed laughter I asked, "Do you know Nova Scotia and Newfoundland?"

"I hear the laugh in your voice," he said; then added, "Yes, I know both these places."

"They are very cold and foggy and wet," I explained.

But with brightening eyes he caught up the sentence and continued: "And the people have blue noses, eh? Ha! ha! Excuse me, then, but is a milksop a man from some state, or some country, too?"

At tea some one used the word "claptrap." "What's that?" quickly demanded the student in our midst. "'Claptrap'—'clap' is so (he struck his hands together); 'trap' is for rats — what is, then, 'claptrap'?"

"It is a vulgar or unworthy bid for applause," I explained.

"Bah!" he contemptuously exclaimed. "I know him, — that cheap actor who plays at the gallery. He is, then, in English a 'clap-trapper,' is he not?"

It was hardly possible to meet him without having a word or a term offered thus for explanation.

—CLARA MORRIS: *Alessandro Salvini* ("McClure's").

B. Write six sentences which might be developed into paragraphs by giving specific instances.

Theme XXI. — *Write a paragraph by furnishing specific instances for one of the following topic statements:* —

1. Nine tenths of all that goes wrong in this world is because some one does not mind his business.

2. It requires a man of courage and perseverance to become a pioneer.

3. Even the wisest teacher does not always punish the boy who is most at fault.

4. It is impossible to teach a dog many amusing tricks.

5. Even so stupid a creature as a chicken may sometimes exhibit much intelligence.

6. Carelessness often leads into difficulty.

7. Our school clock must see many interesting things.

8. Our first impressions are not always our best ones.

9. I am a very busy lead pencil, for my duties are numerous.

10. Dickens's characters are taken from the lower classes of people.

11. Some portions of the book I am reading are very interesting.

(Do your specific instances really illustrate the topic statement? Have you said what you intended to say? Can you omit any words or sentences? Have you used *and* or *got* unnecessarily?

45. Development by Giving Details. — Many general statements lead to a desire to know the details, and the writer may make his idea clearer by giving them. The statement, "The wedding ceremony was impressive," at once arouses a desire to know the details. If a friend should say, "I enjoyed my trip to the city," we wish him to relate that which pleased him. These details assist us in understanding the topic statement, and increase our interest in it. Notice in the paragraphs below how much is added to our understanding of the topic statement by the sentences that give the details: —

1. I left my garden for a week, just at the close of a dry spell. A season of rain immediately set in, and when I returned the transformation was wonderful. In one week every vegetable had fairly jumped forward. The tomatoes, which I left slender plants, eaten of bugs and debating whether they would go backward or forward, had become stout and lusty, with thick stems and dark leaves, and some of them had blossomed. The corn waved like that which grows so rank out of the French-English mixture at Waterloo. The squashes — I will not speak of the squashes. The most remarkable growth was the asparagus. There was not a spear above ground when I went away; and now it had sprung up, and gone to seed, and there were stalks higher than my head.

— WARNER: *My Summer in a Garden.*

2. The wedding ceremony was solemn and beautiful, in the church on the estate. At the door of the palace stood the mother of the bride, to greet her return from the ceremony with the blessing, "May you always have bread and salt," as she served her from a loaf of black bread, with a salt cellar in the center, as is the Russian custom for prince and peasant. Just at this dramatic moment a courier dashed up with a telegram from the Czar and Czarina, and their gifts for the bride, — a magnificent tiara and necklace of diamonds. The other presents were already displayed in a magnificent room; but we saw their splendor through the glass of locked cases, — a precaution surprising to an Englishwoman. The large swan of forcemeat was the only reminder of boyar customs at the rather Parisian feast. Wine was served between the courses, with a toast;

while guests in turn left their seats to express their sentiments to bride and groom, who stood to receive them.

— MARY LOUISE DUNBAR: *The Household of a Russian Prince*

("Atlantic Monthly").

Theme XXII. — *Write a paragraph by giving details for one of the following topic statements:* —

1. There were many interesting things on the farm where I spent my summer vacation.

2. The sounds heard in the forest at night are somewhat alarming to one who is not used to the language of the woods.

3. I am always much amused when the Sewing Circle meets at my mother's house.

4. Good roads are of advantage to farmers in many ways.

5. A baseball game furnishes abundant opportunity to exercise good judgment.

6. I remember well the first time that I visited a large city.

7. I shall never forget my first attempt at milking a cow.

8. The haunted house is a square, old-fashioned one of the colonial type.

9. A mouse suddenly entering the class room caused much disturbance.

10. A freshman's trials are numerous.

(Do the details bear upon the main idea? If the paragraph is long and rambling, condense by omitting the least important parts. By changing the order of the sentences, can you improve the paragraph?)

46. Details Related in Time-Order. — The experiences of daily life follow each other in time, and when we read of a series of events we at once think of them as having occurred in a certain time-order. It will be of assistance in establishing the correct time-order, if the writer states the details of his story in the order in which they occurred. The method of showing time relations for simultaneous events has been discussed in Section 11.

If the narrative is of considerable length, it may be divided into paragraphs, each of which deals with some particular stage of its progress. The time relations among the sentences within the paragraph and among the paragraphs themselves should be such that the reader may readily follow the thread of the story to its main point. Narrative paragraphs often do not have topic sentences.

In the following selection from *Black Beauty* notice how the time relations give unity of thought both to the paragraphs and to the whole selection : —

He hung my rein on one of the iron spikes, and was soon hidden among the trees. Lizzie was standing quietly by the side of the road, a few paces off, with her back to me. My young mistress was sitting easily, with a loose rein, humming a little song. I listened to my rider's footsteps until he reached the house, and heard him knock at the door.

There was a meadow on the opposite side of the road, the gate of which stood open. As I looked, some cart horses and several young colts came trotting out in a very disorderly manner, while a boy behind was cracking a great whip. The colts were wild and frolicsome. One of them bolted across the road and blundered up against Lizzie. Whether it was the stupid colt or the loud cracking of the whip, or both together, I cannot say, but she gave a violent kick and dashed off into a headlong gallop. It was so sudden that Lady Anne was nearly unseated, but she soon recovered herself.

I gave a long, shrill neigh for help. Again and again I neighed, pawing the ground impatiently, and tossing my head to get the rein loose. I had not long to wait. Blantyre came running to the gate. He looked anxiously about, and just caught sight of the flying figure now far away on the road. In an instant he sprang to the saddle.

I needed no whip, no spur, for I was as eager as my rider.　He saw it; and giving me a free rein, and leaning a little forward, we dashed after them.

For about a mile and a half the road ran straight, then bent to the right; after this it divided into two roads.　Long before we came to the bend my mistress was out of sight.　Which way had she turned? A woman was standing at her garden gate, shading her eyes with her hand, and looking eagerly up the road.　Scarcely drawing rein, Lord Blantyre shouted, "Which way?" "To the right!" cried the woman, pointing with her hand, and away we went up the right-hand road. For a moment we caught sight of Lady Anne; another bend, and she was hidden again.　Several times we caught glimpses of the flying rider, only to lose her again.　We scarcely seemed to gain ground upon her at all.

An old road mender was standing near a heap of stones, his shovel dropped and his hands raised.　As we came near he made a sign to speak.　Lord Blantyre drew the rein a little.　"To the common, to the common, sir!　She has turned off there."

I knew this common very well.　It was, for the most part, very uneven ground, covered with heather and dark-green bushes, with here and there a scrubby thorn tree.　There were also open spaces of fine, short grass, with ant-hills and mole turns everywhere — the worst place I ever knew for a headlong gallop.

We had just turned on to the common, when we caught sight again of the green habit flying on before us.　My mistress's hat was gone, and her long brown hair was streaming behind her.　Her head and body were thrown back, as if she were pulling with all her remaining strength, and as if that strength were nearly exhausted.　It was clear that the roughness of the ground had very much lessened Lizzie's speed, and there seemed a chance that we might overtake her.

While we were on the highroad, Lord Blantyre had given me my head; but now, with a light hand and a practiced eye, he guided me over the ground in such a masterly manner that my pace was scarcely slackened, and we gained on them every moment.

About halfway across the common a wide dike had recently been cut and the earth from the cutting cast up roughly on the other side. Surely this would stop them!　But no; scarcely pausing, Lizzie took the leap, stumbled among the rough clods, and fell.

— ANNA SEWELL: *Black Beauty.*

Theme XXIII. — *Write a brief narrative giving unity to the paragraphs by means of the time relations.*

Suggested subjects : —
1. An adventure on horseback.
2. A trip with the engineer.
3. A day on the river.
4. Fido's mishaps.
5. An inquisitive crow.
6. The unfortunate letter carrier.
7. Teaching a calf to drink.
8. The story of a silver dollar.
9. A narrow escape.
10. An afternoon at the circus.
11. A story accounting for the situation shown in the picture on page 90.

(Do you need more than one paragraph ?   If so, is each a group of sentences treating of a single topic ?   Can the reader follow the thread of your story ?   Leave out details not essential to the main point.)

47. Order of Details Determined by Position in Space. — The order of presentation of details may be determined by the position that the details themselves occupy in space. In description we wish to give the reader both a correct general impression of the thing described, and to make certain details clear.   The general impression should be given in the first sentence or two and the details should follow.   The effectiveness of the details will depend upon their order of presentation.   In looking at a scene the eye passes from one object to another near it, and so in recalling the scene the image of one thing naturally recalls that of an adjoining one.   A skillful writer will take advantage of this habit of thinking, and will state the details in

his description in the order in which we would naturally see them if we were actually looking at them. By so doing he most easily presents to our minds the image he wishes to convey.

In the following paragraphs notice that we get first an impression of the general appearance, to which we are enabled to add new details as the description proceeds.

The companion of the church dignitary was a man past forty, thin, strong, tall, and muscular; an athletic figure, which long fatigue and constant exercise seemed to have left none of the softer part of the human form, having reduced the whole to brawn, bones, and sinews, which had sustained a thousand toils, and were ready to dare a thousand more. His head was covered with a scarlet cap, faced with fur, of that kind which the French call *mortier*, from its resemblance to the shape of an inverted mortar. His countenance was therefore fully displayed, and its expression was calculated to impress a degree of awe, if not of fear, upon strangers. High features, naturally strong and powerfully expressive, had been burnt almost into negro blackness by constant exposure to the tropical sun, and might, in their ordinary state, be said to slumber after the storm of passion had passed away; but the projection of the veins of the forehead, the readiness with which the upper lip and its thick black mustache quivered upon the slightest emotion, plainly intimated that the tempest might be again and easily awakened. His keen, piercing, dark eyes told in every glance a history of difficulties subdued and dangers dared, and seemed to challenge opposition to his wishes, for the pleasure of sweeping it from his road by a determined exertion of courage and of will; a deep scar on his brow gave additional sternness to his countenance and a sinister expression to one of his eyes, which had been slightly injured on the same occasion, and of which the vision, though perfect, was in a slight and partial degree distorted.

The upper dress of this personage resembled that of his companion in shape, being a long monastic mantle; but the color, being scarlet, showed that he did not belong to any of the four regular orders of monks. On the right shoulder of the mantle there was cut, in white cloth, a cross of a peculiar form. This upper robe concealed what at first view seemed rather inconsistent with its form, a shirt, namely, of linked mail, with sleeves and gloves of the same, curiously plaited and interwoven, as flexible to the body as those which are now wrought in the stocking loom out of less obdurate materials. The fore part of his thighs, where the folds of his mantle permitted them to be seen, were also covered with linked mail; the knees and feet were defended by splints, or thin plates of steel, ingeniously jointed upon each other; and mail hose, reaching from the ankle to the knee, effectually protected the legs, and completed the rider's defensive armor. In his girdle he wore a long and double-edged dagger, which was the only offensive weapon about his person.

He rode, not a mule, like his companion, but a strong hackney for the road, to save his gallant war horse, which a squire led behind, fully accoutered for battle, with a chamfron or plaited headpiece upon his head, having a short spike projecting from the front. On one side of the saddle hung a short battle-ax, richly inlaid with Damascene carving; on the other the rider's plumed headpiece and hood of mail, with a long two-handed sword, used by the chivalry of the period. A second squire held aloft his master's lance, from the extremity of which fluttered a small banderole, or streamer, bearing a cross of the same form with that embroidered upon his cloak. He also carried his small triangular shield, broad enough at the top to protect the breast, and from thence diminishing to a point. It was covered with a scarlet cloth, which prevented the device from being seen.

— SCOTT : *Ivanhoe.*

Notice also how the description proceeds in an orderly way from one thing to another, placing together in the description those which occur together in the person described. Just as we turn our eyes naturally from one thing to another near it in space, so in a paragraph should our attention be called from one thing to that which naturally accompanies it. If the first sentence describes a man's eyes, the second his feet, and a third his forehead, our mental image is likely to become confused. If a description covers several paragraphs, each may be given a unity by placing in it those things which are associated in space.

EXERCISES

A. If you were to write three paragraphs describing a man, which of the following details should be included in each?

(*a*) eyes, (*b*) shoes, (*c*) size, (*d*) complexion, (*e*) general appearance, (*f*) hair, (*g*) carriage, (*h*) trousers, (*i*) mouth, (*j*) coat, (*k*) nose.

B. Make a list of the details which might be mentioned in describing the outside of a church. Arrange them in appropriate groups.

C. In the following paragraphs which sentences give the general outline and which give details? Are the details arranged with reference to their position in space? Can the paragraph be improved by rearranging them?

1. We came finally to a brook more wild and mysterious than the others. There were a half dozen stepping-stones between the path we were on and the place where it began again on the opposite side. After a few missteps and much laughter we were landed at last, but several of the party had wet feet to remember the experience by. We found ourselves in a space that had once been a clearing. A tumbledown chimney overgrown with brambles and vines told of an abandoned hearthstone. The blackened remnants of many a picnic camp fire strewed the ground. A slight turn brought us to the spot where the Indian Spring welled out of the hillside. The setting was all that we could have hoped for, — great moss-grown rocks wet and slippery, deep shade which almost made us doubt the existence of the hot August sunshine at the edge of the forest, cool water dripping and tinkling. A half-dozen great trees had been so undermined by the action of the water long ago that they had tumbled headlong into the stream bed. There they lay, heads down, crisscross — one completely spanning the brook just below the spring — their tangled roots like great dragons twisting and thrusting at the shadows. The water trickled slowly over the smooth rocky bottom as if reluctant to leave a spot enchanted. A few yards below, the overflow from Indian

Spring joined the main stream, and their waters mingled in a pretty little cataract. We went below and looked back at it. How it wrinkled and paused over the level spaces, played with the bubbles in the eddies, and ran laughing and turning somersaults wherever the ledges were abrupt.

— MARY ROGERS MILLER: *The Brook Book.*
(Copyright, 1902, by Doubleday, Page & Co.)

2. Rowena was tall in stature, yet not so much so as to attract observation on account of superior height. Her complexion was exquisitely fair, but the noble cast of her head and features prevented the insipidity which sometimes attaches to fair beauties. Her clear blue eyes, which sat enshrined beneath a graceful eyebrow of brown, sufficiently marked to give expression to the forehead, seemed capable to kindle as well as to melt, to command as well as to beseech. Her profuse hair, of a color betwixt brown and flaxen, was arranged in a fanciful and graceful manner in numerous ringlets, to form which art had probably been aided by nature. These locks were braided with gems, and being worn at full length, intimated the noble birth and free-born condition of the maiden. A golden chain, to which was attached a small reliquary of the same metal, hung around her neck. She wore bracelets on her arms, which were bare. Her dress was an under gown and kirtle of pale sea-green silk, over which hung a long loose robe, which reached to the ground, having very wide sleeves, which came down, however, very little below the elbow. This robe was crimson, and manufactured out of the very finest wool. A veil of silk, interwoven with gold, was attached to the upper part of it, which could be, at the wearer's pleasure, either drawn over the face and bosom after the Spanish fashion, or disposed as a sort of drapery round the shoulders.

— SCOTT : *Ivanhoe.*

Theme XXIV. — *Write a paragraph and arrange the details with reference to their association in space.*

Suggested subjects : —

1. Ichabod Crane.
2. Rip Van Winkle.
3. The man who lives near us.
4. A minister I met yesterday.

5. Our family doctor.
6. The gymnasium.
7. A fire engine.
8. The old church.
9. The shoe factory.
10. Some character in the book you are reading.

(Which sentence gives the general impression and which sentences give the details? Are the details arranged with reference to their real space order? Should others be added? Can any be omitted? Will the reader form the mental image you wish him to form?)

48. Development by Comparison. — In Section 29 we found that comparison, whether literal or figurative, aided us in forming mental images of objects. In a similar way events and general principles may be explained by making suitable comparisons. We are continually comparing one thing with another. Every idea tends to recall other ideas that are similar to it or in contrast with it. When an unfamiliar idea is presented to us we at once seek to associate it with similar ones already known to us. A writer, therefore, will make his meaning clear by furnishing the desired comparisons. If these are familiar to us, they enable us to understand the new ones. Even when both ideas in the comparison are unfamiliar, each may gain in clearness by comparison with the other.

In comparing two objects, events, or principles we may point out that they are *not* alike in certain respects. A comparison that thus emphasizes differences, rather than likenesses, becomes a contrast. The contrast may be given in a single sentence or in a single paragraph, but often a paragraph or more may be required for each of the two ideas contrasted.

EXERCISE

Notice how comparisons and contrasts are used in the following paragraphs: —

1. Niagara is the largest cataract in the world, while Yosemite is the highest; it is the volume that impresses you at Niagara, and it is the height of Yosemite and the grand surroundings that make its beauty. Niagara is as wide as Yosemite is high, and if it had no more water than Yosemite has, it would not be of much consequence. The sound of the two falls is quite different: Niagara makes a steady roar, deep and strong, though not oppressive, while Yosemite is a crash and rattle, owing to the force of the water as it strikes the solid rock after its immense leap.

2. It is not only in appearance that London and New York differ widely. They also speak with different accents, for cities have distinctive accents as well as people. Tennyson wrote about " streaming London's central roar "; the roar is a gentle hum compared with the din which tingles the ears of visitors to New York. The accent of New York is harsh, grating, jarring. The rattle of the elevated railroad, the whir of the cable cars, the ringing of electric-car bells, the rumble of vehicles over the hard stones, the roar of the traffic as it reëchoes through the narrow canyons of down-town streets, produce an appalling combination of discords. The streets of New York are not more crowded than those of London, but the noise in London is subdued. It is more regular, less jarring and piercing. The muffled sounds in London are due partly to the wooden and asphalt pavements, which deaden the sounds. London must be soothing to the New Yorker, as the noise of New York is at first disconcerting to the Londoner. — *Outlook*.

3. Now their separate characters are briefly these. The man's power is active, progressive, defensive. He is eminently the doer, the creator, the discoverer, the defender. His intellect is for speculation and invention; his energy for adventure, for war, and for conquest wherever war is just, wherever conquest necessary. But the woman's power is for rule, not for battle, and her intellect is not for invention or creation, but for sweet ordering, arrangement, and decision. She sees the qualities of things, their claims, and their places.

— RUSKIN: Sesame and Lilies.

Theme XXV. — *Write a paragraph using comparison or contrast.*

Suggested topics: —

1. The school, a beehive.
2. The body, a steam engine.
3. Two generals about whom you have read.
4. Girls, boys.
5. Two of your studies.
6. Graded school work, high school work.
7. Animal life, plant life.
8. Two of your classmates.

(Have you used comparison or contrast? Have you introduced any of the other methods of development? Have you developed the paragraph so that the reader will understand fully your topic statement? Omit sentences not really needed.)

49. Development by Stating Cause and Effect. — We are better satisfied with our understanding of a thing if we know the causes which have produced it or the effects which follow it. Likewise we feel that another has mastered the topic statement of a paragraph if he can answer the question, Why is this so? or, What will result from this? When either is stated, we naturally begin to think about the other. The idea of a topic statement may, therefore, be satisfactorily developed by stating its causes or its effects. A cause may be stated and the effects given or the effects may be made the topic statement for which we account by giving its causes.

The importance of the relation of cause and effect to scientific study is discussed in the following paragraph from Mill: —

The relation of cause and effect is the fundamental law of nature. There is no recorded instance of an effect appearing without a previous cause, or of a cause acting without producing its full effect. Every change in nature is the effect of some previous change and the cause of some change to follow; just as the movement of each carriage near the middle of a long train is a result of the movement of the one in front and a precursor of the movement of the one behind. Facts or effects are to be seen everywhere, but causes have usually to be sought for. It is the function of science or organized knowledge to observe all effects, or phenomena, and to seek for their causes. This twofold purpose gives richness and dignity to science. The observation and classifying of facts soon become wearisome to all but the specialist actually engaged in the work. But when reasons are assigned, and classification explained, when the number of causes is reduced and the effects begin to crystallize into essential and clearly related parts of one whole, every intelligent student finds interest, and many, more fortunate, even fascination in the study.

— MILL: *The Realm of Nature.* (Copyright, 1892, by Charles Scribner's Sons.)

EXERCISES

A. In your reading, notice how often the effects are indicated by the use of some one of the following expressions: *as a result, accordingly, consequently, for, hence, so, so that, thus.*

B. Which sentences state causes and which state effects in the following paragraphs?

1. The power of water to dissolve most minerals increases with its temperature and the amount of gases it contains. Percolating water at great depths, therefore, generally dissolves more mineral matter than it can hold in solution when it reaches the surface, where it cools, and, being relieved of pressure, much of its carbonic acid gas escapes to the atmosphere or is absorbed by aquatic plants or mosses. Hence, deep-seated springs are usually surrounded by a deposit of the minerals with which the water is impregnated. Sometimes this deposit may even form large hills; sometimes it forms a mound around the spring, over the sides of which the water falls, while the spray, evaporating from surrounding objects, leaves them also incrusted

with a mineral deposit. Percolating water evaporating on the sides and roof of limestone caverns, leaves the walls incrusted with carbonate of lime in beautiful masses of crystals. Water slowly evaporating as it drips from the roof of caverns to the floor beneath leaves a deposit on both places, which gradually grows downward from the roof as a *stalactite*, and upward from the floor as a *stalagmite*, until these meet and form one continuous column of stone.

—HINMAN: *Eclectic Physical Geography.*

2. The frequent use of cigars or cigarettes by the young seriously affects the quality of the blood. The red blood corpuscles are not fully developed and charged with their normal supply of life-giving oxygen. This causes paleness of the skin, often noticed in the face of the young smoker. Palpitation of the heart is also a common result, followed by permanent weakness, so that the whole system is enfeebled, and mental vigor is impaired as well as physical strength. Observant teachers can usually tell which of the boys under their care are addicted to smoking, simply by the comparative inferiority of their appearance, and by their intellectual and bodily indolence and feebleness. After full maturity is attained the evil effects of commencing the use of tobacco are less apparent; but competent physicians assert that it cannot be safely used by those under the age of forty.

—MACY-NORRIS: *Physiology for High Schools.*

3. In many other ways, too, the Norman Conquest affected England. For example, before long all the best places in the Church were filled with foreigners. But most of the new bishops and abbots were far superior in morals and education to the Englishmen whom they succeeded. They were also devoted to the Pope of Rome, and soon made the English National Church a part of the Roman Catholic Church. But William, while willing to bow to the Pope as his chief in religious matters, refused to give way to him in things which concerned only this world. No former English king had done that, he knew, and no more would he. This union with the Roman Catholic Church was of the greatest benefit to England, as it brought her once more into connection with the educated men of Europe. Indeed, Lanfranc, the Conqueror's Archbishop of Canterbury, was one of the best and wisest men of his day.

—HIGGINSON AND CHANNING: *English History for American Readers.*

Theme XXVI. — *Develop one of the following topic statements into paragraphs by stating causes or effects :* —

1. A government which had no soldiers to call upon in an emergency would not last long.

2. One of the first needs of a new country is roads.

3. The number of people receiving public support is smaller in this country than in Europe.

4. An efficient postal system is a great aid to civilization.

5. A straight stream is an impossibility in nature.

6. Mountain ranges have great influence upon climate.

7. The United States holds first place as a manufacturing nation.

8. There are many swift rivers in New England.

9. Towns or cities are located at the mouths of navigable rivers.

(Which sentences state causes and which state effects? Would the effects which you have stated really follow the given causes ?)

50. Development by Repetition. — The repetition of a thought in different form will often make plain that which we do not at first understand. This is especially true if the repetitions are accompanied by new comparisons. In every school the teacher furnishes daily illustrations of this in her efforts to explain to the pupils that which they do not understand. In a similar way a writer makes use of this tendency of ours, and will develop the idea of the topic sentence by repetition. Each sentence should, however, do more than merely repeat. It should add something to the central idea, making it clearer, more definite, or more emphatic. If repetition is excessive and purposeless, it becomes a fault.

Repetition may extend through the whole paragraph, or it may be used to explain any sentence or any part of a sentence. It may tell what the thing is or what it is not, and in effect becomes a definition setting limits to the original idea.

EXERCISE

Notice how the idea in the topic statement of each of the following paragraphs is repeated in those which follow : —

1. No man ever made a complete new system of law and gave it to a people. No monarch, however absolute or powerful, ever had the power to change the habits of a people to that extent. Revolution generally means, not a change of law, but merely a change of government officials; even when it is a change from monarchy to democracy. Our Revolution made practically no changes in the criminal and civil laws of the colonies. — CLARK : *The Government.*

2. People talk of liberty as if it meant the liberty to do just what a man likes. I call that man free who fears doing wrong, but fears nothing else. I call that man free who has learned the most blessed of all truths, — that liberty consists in obedience to the power, and to the will, and to the law that his higher soul reverences and approves. He is not free because he does what he likes; but he is free because he does what he ought, and there is no protest in his soul against the doing. — FREDERICK WILLIAM ROBERTSON.

3. This dense forest was to the Indians a home in which they had lived from childhood, and where they were as much at ease as a farmer on his own acres. To their keen eyes, trained for generations to more than a wild beast's watchfulness, the wilderness was an open book. Nothing at rest or in motion escaped them. They had begun to track game as soon as they could walk ; a scrape on a tree trunk, a bruised leaf, a faint indentation of the soil, which no white man could see, all told them a tale as plainly as if it had been shouted in their ears. — THEODORE ROOSEVELT : *The Winning of the West.*

4. Public enterprises, whether conducted by the municipality or committed to the public service corporation, exist to render public

services. Streets are public highways. They exist for the people's use. Nothing should be placed in them unless required to facilitate their use by or for the people. Only the general need of water, gas, electricity, and transportation justifies the placing of pipes and wires and tracks in the streets. The public need is the sole test and measure of such occupation. To look upon the streets as a source of private gain, or even municipal revenue, except as incidents of their public use, is to disregard their public character. Adequate service at the lowest practicable rates, not gain or revenue, is the test. The question is, not how much the public service corporation may gain, but what can be saved to the people by its employment.

— EDWIN BURRETT SMITH : *The Next Step in Municipal Reform*
("Atlantic Monthly").

Theme XXVII. — *Develop one of the following topic statements into a paragraph, using the method of repetition as far as possible:* —

1. It is difficult to become angry with one who is always good-natured.

2. It is gloomy in the woods on a rainy day.

3. The government is always in need of honest men.

4. Rural free delivery of mail will have a great effect on country life.

5. Not every boy in school uses his time to the best advantage.

6. Haste is waste.

7. Regular exercise is one of the essentials of good health.

(Have the repetitions really made the idea of the topic sentence clearer or more emphatic or more definite ? What other methods of development have you used ?)

51. Development by a Combination of Methods. — A paragraph should have unity of thought, and, so long as this unity of thought is kept, it does not matter what methods of development are used. A dozen paragraphs taken at random will show that combinations are very frequent. Often it will be difficult to determine just how a paragraph has been developed. In general, however, it may be said that an indiscriminate mixture of methods is confusing and interferes with unity of thought. If more than one is used, it requires skillful handling to maintain such a relation between them that both contribute to the clear and emphatic statement of the main thought.

The paragraph from Dryer, page 74, shows a combination of cause and effect with specific illustrations; that from Wolstan Dixey, page 81, shows a combination of repetition with specific instances.

EXERCISES

What methods of paragraph development, or what combinations of methods, are used in the following selections?

1. I believe the first test of a truly great man is his humility. I do not mean, by humility, doubt of his power, or hesitation in speaking of his opinions; but a right understanding of the relation between what he can do and say and the rest of the world's sayings and doings. All great men not only know their business, but usually know that they know it; and are not only right in their main opinions, but they usually know that they are right in them; only they do not think much of themselves on that account. Arnolfo knows he can build a good dome at Florence; Albert Dürer writes calmly to one who had found fault with his work, "It cannot be better done"; Sir Isaac Newton knows that he has worked out a problem or two that would have puzzled anybody else; only they do not expect their fellow-men therefore to fall down and worship them; they have a curious undersense of powerlessness, feeling that the greatness is not *in* them, but *through* them; that they could not do or be anything else than God made them. And they see something divine and God-made in every other man they meet, and are endlessly, foolishly, and incredibly merciful. — Ruskin.

2. The first thing to be noted about the dress of the Romans is that its prevalent material was always woolen. Sheep raising for wool was practiced among them on an extensive scale, from the earliest historic times, and the choice breeds of that animal, originally imported from Greece or Asia Minor, took so kindly to the soil and climate of Italy that home-grown wool came even to be preferred to the foreign for fineness and softness of quality. Foreign wools were, however, always imported more or less, partly because the supply of native wools seems never to have been quite sufficient, partly because the natural colors of wools from different parts varied so considerably as to render the art of the dyer to some extent unnecessary. Thus, the wools of Canusium were brown or reddish, those of Pollentia in Liguria were black, those from the Spanish Bætica, which comprised Andalusia and a part of Granada, had either a golden brown or a grayish hue; the wools of Asia were almost red; and there was a Grecian fleece, called the crow colored, of which the natural tint was a peculiarly deep and brilliant black.

— PRESTON AND DODGE: *The Private Life of the Romans.*

3. Art has done everything for Munich. It lies on a large flat plain sixteen hundred feet above the sea and continually exposed to the cold winds from the Alps. At the beginning of the present century it was but a third-rate city, and was rarely visited by foreigners; since that time its population and limits have been doubled, and magnificent edifices in every style of architecture erected, rendering it scarcely secondary in this respect to any capital in Europe. Every art that wealth or taste could devise seems to have been spent in its decoration. Broad, spacious streets and squares have been laid out; churches, halls, and colleges erected, and schools of painting and sculpture established which drew artists from all parts of the world.

— TAYLOR: *Views Afoot.*

4. In all excursions to the woods or to the shore the student of ornithology has an advantage over his companions. He has one more avenue of delight. He, indeed, kills two birds with one stone and sometimes three. If others wander, he can never get out of his way. His game is everywhere. The cawing of a crow makes him feel at home, while a new note or a new song drowns all care. Audubon, on the desolate coast of Labrador, is happier than any king ever was; and on shipboard is nearly cured of his seasickness when a new gull appears in sight.   — BURROUGHS: *Wake Robin.*

Theme XXVIII. — *Write a paragraph, using any method or combination of methods which best suits your thought. Use any of the subjects hitherto suggested that you have not already used.*

(Is every sentence related to the topic statement so that your paragraph possesses unity? What methods of development have you used?)

52. The Topical Recitation. — In conducting a recitation the teacher may ask direct questions about each part of a paragraph or she may ask a pupil to discuss some topic. Such a topical recitation should be an exercise in clear thinking rather than in word memory, and in order to prepare for it, the pupil should have made a careful analysis of the thought in each paragraph similar to that discussed on page 74. When this analysis has been made he will have clearly in mind the topic statement and the way it has been developed, and can distinguish the essential from the non-essential elements.

A topical recitation demands that the pupil know the main idea and be able to develop it in one of the following methods, or by a combination of them : (1) by giving specific instances, (2) by giving details, (3) by giving comparisons or contrasts, (4) by giving causes or effects, and (5) by repetition.

Thoughts so mastered are our own. We understand them, we believe them, and so can explain them, or describe them, or prove them to others. We can furnish details or instances, originate comparisons, or state causes and effects. *When ideas gained from language have thus become our own, we do not need to remember the language in which they were expressed, and not until then do they become proper material for composition purposes.*

53. Outlining Paragraphs. — Making an outline of a paragraph that we have read brings the thought clearly before our mind. In a similar way we may make our own thoughts clear and definite by attempting to prepare in advance an outline of a paragraph that we are about to write. Arranging the material that we have in mind and deciding upon the order in which we shall present it, will both help us to understand the thought ourselves, and enable us to present it more effectively to others.

EXERCISES

A. Prepare for recitation the following selection from Newcomer's introduction to Macaulay's *Milton and Addison:* —

There were two faculties of Macaulay's mind that set his work far apart from other work in the same field, — the faculties of organization and illustration. He saw things in their right relation and he knew how to make others see them thus. If he was describing, he never thrust minor details into the foreground. If he was narrating, he never "got ahead of his story." The importance of this is not sufficiently recognized. Many writers do not know what organization means. They do not know that in all great and successful literary work it is nine tenths of the labor. Yet consider a moment. History is a very complex thing: divers events may be simultaneous in their occurrence; or one crisis may be slowly evolving from many causes in many places. It is no light task to tell these things one after another and yet leave a unified impression, to take up a dozen new threads in succession without tangling them and without losing the old ones, and to lay them all down at the right moment and without confusion. Such is the narrator's task, and it was at this task that Macaulay proved himself a past master. He could dispose of a number of trivial events in a single sentence. Thus, for example, runs his account of the dramatist Wycherley's naval career: "He embarked, was present at a battle, and celebrated it, on his return, in a copy of verses too bad for the bellman." On the other hand, when it is a question of a great crisis, like the impeachment of Warren Hastings, he knew how to prepare for it with elaborate ceremony and to portray it in a scene of the highest dramatic power.

This faculty of organization shows itself in what we technically name structure; and logical and rhetorical structure may be studied at their very best in his work. His essays are perfect units, made up of many parts, systems within systems, that play together without clog or friction. You can take them apart like a watch and put them together again. But try to rearrange the parts and the mechanism is spoiled. Each essay has its subdivisions, which in turn are groups of paragraphs. And each paragraph is a unit. Take the first paragraph of the essay on Milton: the word *manuscript* appears in the first sentence, and it reappears in the last; clearly the paragraph deals with a single very definite topic. And so with all. Of course the unity manifests itself in a hundred ways, but it is rarely wanting. Most frequently it takes the form of an expansion of a topic given in the first sentence, or a preparation for a topic to be announced only in the last. These initial and final sentences — often in themselves both aphoristic and memorable — serve to mark with the utmost clearness the different stages in the progress of the essay.

Illustration is of more incidental service, but as used by Macaulay becomes highly organic. For his illustrations are not farfetched or laboriously worked out. They seem to be of one piece with his story or his argument. His mind was quick to detect resemblances and analogies. He was ready with a comparison for everything, sometimes with half a dozen. For example, Addison's essays, he has occasion to say, were different every day of the week, and yet, to his mind, each day like something — like Horace, like Lucian, like the "Tales of Scheherezade." He draws long comparisons between Walpole and Townshend, between Congreve and Wycherley, between Essex and Villiers, between the fall of the Carlovingians and the fall of the Moguls. He follows up a general statement with swarms of instances. Have historians been given to exaggerating the villainy of Machiavelli? Macaulay can name you half a dozen who did so. Did the writers of Charles's faction delight in making their opponents appear contemptible? "They have told us that Pym broke down in a speech, that Ireton had his nose pulled by Hollis, that the Earl of Northumberland cudgeled Henry Marten, that St. John's manners were sullen, that Vane had an ugly face, that Cromwell had a red nose." Do men fail when they quit their own province for another?

Newton failed thus; Bentley failed; Inigo Jones failed; Wilkie failed. In the same way he was ready with quotations. He writes in one of his letters: "It is a dangerous thing for a man with a very strong memory to read very much. I could give you three or four quotations this moment in support of that proposition; but I will bring the vicious propensity under subjection, if I can." Thus we see his mind doing instantly and involuntarily what other minds do with infinite pains, bringing together all things that have a likeness or a common bearing.

It is precisely these talents that set Macaulay among the simplest and clearest of writers, and that accounts for much of his popularity. People found that in taking up one of his articles they simply read on and on, never puzzling over the meaning of a sentence, getting the exact force of every statement, and following the trend of thought with scarcely a mental effort. And his natural gift of making things plain he took pains to support by various devices. He constructed his sentences after the simplest normal fashion, subject and verb and object, sometimes inverting for emphasis, but rarely complicating, and always reducing expression to the barest terms. He could write, for example, "One advantage the chaplain had," but it is impossible to conceive of his writing, "Now, amid all the discomforts and disadvantages with which the unfortunate chaplain was surrounded, there was one thing which served to offset them, and which, if he chose to take the opportunity of enjoying it, might well be regarded as a positive advantage." One will search his pages in vain for loose, trailing clauses and involved constructions. His vocabulary was of the same simple nature. He had a complete command of ordinary English and contented himself with that. He rarely ventured beyond the most abridged dictionary. An occasional technical term might be required, but he was shy of the unfamiliar. He would coin no words and he would use no archaisms. Foreign words, when fairly naturalized, he employed sparingly. "We shall have no disputes about diction," he wrote to Napier, Jeffrey's successor; "the English language is not so poor but that I may very well find in it the means of contenting both you and myself."

B. Recite upon some topic taken from your other lessons for the day. Let the class tell what method of development you have used.

C. Make a collection of well-written paragraphs illustrating each of the methods of development.

Theme XXIX. — *Write two paragraphs using the same topic statement, but developing each by a different method.*

Suggested topic statements : —

1. The principal tools of government are buildings, guns, and money.
2. The civilized world was never as orderly as now.
3. Law suits take time, especially in cities; sometimes they take years.
4. There is a difference between law and justice.
5. We cry for a multitude of reasons of surprising variety.
6. In the growth of a child nothing is more surprising than his ceaseless activity.
7. Education for the children of a nation is a benefit to the whole nation.

(Have you said what you intended to say? What methods of development have you used? Is the main thought of the two paragraphs the same even though they begin with the same sentence?)

SUMMARY

1. Language is (1) a means of expressing ideas, and (2) a medium through which ideas are acquired.
2. The acquisition of ideas by means of language requires : —
    a. That we know the meanings of words, and so avoid forming incomplete images (Section 27) and incomplete thoughts (Section 33).

      b. That we understand the relations in thought existing among words, phrases, clauses, sentences, and paragraphs (Section 32).

3. Ideas acquired through language may be used for composition purposes —

      a. Provided we form complete and accurate images and do not confuse the image with the language that suggested it (Section 28).

      b. Provided we make the main thoughts so thoroughly our own that we can furnish details and instances, originate comparisons, or state causes and effects, thus enabling us to describe them or explain them, or prove them to others (Section 52).

      Until both of the above are done, ideas acquired through language are undesirable for composition purposes.

4. Comparisons aid in the forming of correct images. They may be literal or imaginative. If imaginative, they become figures of speech.

5. Figures of speech. (Complete list in the Appendix.)

      a. A simile is a direct comparison.

      b. A metaphor is an implied comparison.

      c. Personification is a modified metaphor, assigning human attributes to objects, abstract ideas, or the lower animals.

6. Suggestions as to the use of figures of speech.

      a. Never write for the purpose of using them.

      b. They should be appropriate to the subject.

      c. One of the two things compared must be familiar to the reader.

      d. Avoid hackneyed figures.

      e. Avoid long figures.

  f. Avoid mixed metaphors.

7. Choice of words.

  a. Use words presumably familiar to the reader.

  b. Use words that express your exact meaning. Do not confuse similar words.

  c. Avoid the frequent use of the same word (Section 17).

8. Ambiguity of thought must be avoided. Care must be exercised in the use of the forms which show relations in thought between sentences, especially with pronouns and pronominal adjectives (Section 36).

9. A paragraph is a group of sentences related to each other and to one central idea.

10. The topic statement of a paragraph is a brief comprehensive summary of the contents of the paragraph.

11. Methods of paragraph development. A paragraph may be developed —

  a. By giving specific instances (Section 44).

  b. By giving details (Section 45). The order in which the details are told may be determined by —

   (1) The order of their occurrence in time (Section 46).

   (2) Their position in space (Section 47).

  c. By comparison or contrast (Section 48).

  d. By stating cause and effect (Section 49).

  e. By repetition (Section 50).

  f. By any suitable combination of the above.

12. The topical recitation demands —

  a. That the pupil get the central idea of the

paragraph and be able to make the topic statement.

b. That he be able to determine the relative importance of the remaining ideas in the paragraph.

c. That he know by which of the five methods named above the paragraph has been developed.

d. That he be able to furnish details, instances, and comparisons of his own. (See Sections 37, 38, 39, 52, 53.)

IV. THE PURPOSE OF EXPRESSION

54. Kinds of Composition. — When considered with reference to the purpose in the mind of the writer, there are two general classes of writing, — that which informs, and that which entertains. The language that we use should make our meaning clear, arouse interest, and give vividness. Writing that informs will lay greater emphasis on clearness, though it may at the same time be interesting and vivid. We do not add to the value of an explanation by making it dull. On the other hand, writing that entertains, though it must be clear, will lay greater emphasis on interest and vividness. That language is best which combines all three of these characteristics. The writer's purpose will determine to which the emphasis shall be given.

Composition is also divided into description, narration, exposition, and argument (including persuasion). These are called forms of discourse. It will be found that this division is also based upon the purpose for which the composition is written. You all have occasion to use each of these daily; you describe, you narrate, you explain, you argue, you persuade. You have used language for these purposes from your infancy, and you are now studying composition in order to acquire facility and effectiveness in that use. When this chapter is completed, you will have considered each in an elementary way. A more extended treatment of each is given in later chapters.

A. To which of the two general classes of composition would each of the following belong?

1. A business letter.
2. The story of a runaway.
3. A description of a lake written by a geologist.
4. A description of a lake written by a boy who was camping near it.
5. A letter to a friend describing a trip.
6. A text-book on algebra.
7. An application for a position as stenographer.
8. A recipe for making cake.
9. How I made a cake.
10. How to make a kite.
11. A political speech.
12. A debate.

B. Could a description be written for the purpose of entertaining?   Could the same object be described for the purpose of giving information? ·

C. To which general class do narratives belong?   Explanations?   Arguments?

55. Discourse Presupposes an Audience. — The object of composition is communication, and communication is not concerned with one's self alone.   It always involves two,— the one who gives and the one who receives.   If its purpose is to inform, it must inform *somebody;* if to entertain, it must entertain *somebody*.   To be sure, discourse may be a pleasure to us, because it is a means of self-expression, but it is *useful* to us because it conveys ideas to that other somebody who hears or reads it.   We describe in order that another may picture that which we have experienced; we narrate events for the entertainment of others; we explain to others that which we understand; and we argue in order to prove to some one the truth of a proposition or to persuade him to action. Thus all discourse, to be useful, demands an audience. Its effective use requires that the writer shall give quite as much attention to the way in which that reader will receive his ideas as he gives to the ideas themselves. "Speaking or writing is, therefore, a double-ended process. It springs from me, it penetrates him; and both of these ends need watching. Is what I say precisely what I mean? That is an important question. Is what I say so shaped that it can readily be assimilated by him who hears? This is a question of quite as great consequence and much more likely to be forgotten. . . . As I write I must unceasingly study what is the line of least intellectual resistance along which my thought may enter the differently constituted mind; and to that line I must subtly adjust, without enfeebling my meaning. Will this combination of words or that make the meaning clear? Will this order of presentation facilitate swiftness of apprehension or will it clog the movement?"[1]

In the preceding chapters emphasis has been laid upon the care that a writer must give to saying exactly what he means. This must never be neglected, but we need to add to it a consideration of how best to adapt what we say to the interest and intelligence of our readers. It will become clear in writing the following theme that the discussion of paragraph development in Chapter III was in reality a discussion of methods of adapting our discourse to the mental habits of our readers.

[1] Professor George Herbert Palmer: *Self-cultivation in English.*

Theme XXX. — *Write a theme showing which one of the five methods of paragraph development proceeds most nearly in accordance with the way the mind usually acts.*

(This theme will furnish a review of the methods of paragraph development treated in Chapter III. If possible, write your theme without consulting the chapter. "Think it out" for yourself. After the theme has been written, review paragraph development treated in Chapter III. Can you improve your theme? What methods of development have you used?)

56. Selecting a Subject. — Sometimes our theme subjects are chosen for us, but usually we shall need to choose our own subjects. What we shall choose depends both upon ourselves and upon those for whom we write. The elements which adapt a subject to the reader will be considered later. In so far as the writer is concerned, two things will determine the suitableness of a subject: —

First, the writer's knowledge of the subject. We cannot make ideas clear to others that are not clear to us. Our information must be clearly and definitely our own before we can hope to present it effectively. This is one of the advantages possessed by subjects arising from experience. Any subject about which we know little or nothing, should be rejected. We must not, however, reject a subject too soon. When it is first thought of we may find that we have but few ideas about it, but by thinking we may discover that our information is greater than it at first seemed. We may be able to assign reasons or give instances or originate comparisons or add details, and so amplify our knowledge. Even if we find that we know but little about the subject from our own experience, we may still be able to use it for a composition subject by getting our information from others. We may from conversation or from reading gain ideas which we can make our own and so be able to write intelligently. Care must be taken that this "reading up" on a subject does not fill our minds with smatterings of ideas that we think we understand because we can remember the language in which they were expressed; but reading, *supplemented by thinking*, may enable us to write well about a subject concerning which on first thought we seem to know but little.

Second, the writer's interest in the subject. It will be found difficult for the writer to present vividly that in which he himself has no special interest. Enthusiasm is contagious, and if the writer has a real interest in his subject, he is likely to present his material in such a manner as to arouse interest in others. In our earlier years we are more interested in the material presented by experience and imagination than in that presented by reading, but as we grow older our interest in thoughts conveyed to us by language increases. As we enlarge our knowledge of a subject by reading and by conversation, so we are likely to increase our interest in that subject. A boy may know but little about Napoleon, but the effort to inform himself may cause him to become greatly interested. This interest will lead him to a further search for information about Napoleon, and will at the same time aid in making what he writes entertaining to others.

EXERCISES

A. About which of the following subjects do you now possess a sufficient knowledge to enable you to write a paragraph? In which of them are you interested? Which would you need to "read up" about?

1. Golf.	11. Birds.
2. Examinations.	12. Pyrography.
3. Warships.	13. Photography.
4. Wireless telegraphy.	14. Beavers.
5. Radium.	15. Making calls.
6. Tennis.	16. Stamp collecting.
7. Automobiles.	17. The manufacture of tacks.
8. Picnics.	18. The manufacture of cotton.
9. Printing.	19. The smelting of zinc.
10. Bees.	20. The silver-plating process.

B. Make a list of thirty things about which you know something.

C. Bring to class a list of five subjects in which you are interested.

D. Make a list of five subjects about which you now possess a sufficient knowledge to enable you to write a paragraph.

Theme XXXI. — *Write a short theme. Select a suitable subject from the lists in the preceding exercise.*

(What method or methods of paragraph development have you used? Have your paragraphs unity of thought?)

57. Subject Adapted to Reader. — We may be interested in a subject and possess sufficient knowledge to enable us to treat it successfully, but it may still be unsuitable because it is not adapted to the reader. Some knowledge of a subject and some interest in it are quite as necessary on the part of the reader as on that of the writer, though in the beginning this knowledge and interest may be meager. The possibility of developing them must exist, however, or the writing will be a failure. It would be difficult to make "Imperialism" interesting to third grade pupils, or "Kant's Philosophy" to high school pupils. Even if you know enough to write a valuable "Criticism" of *Silas Marner*, or a real "Review" of the *Vicar of Wakefield*, the work is waste time if your readers do not have a breadth of knowledge sufficient to insure a vital and appreciative interest in the subject. A subject must be of present, vital interest to your readers, and care must be taken to select one that possesses these qualities.

58. Sources of Subjects. — Thought goes everywhere, and human interest touches everything. The sources of subjects are therefore unlimited; for anything about which we think and in which we are interested may become a suitable subject for a paragraph, an essay, or a book. Such subjects are everywhere — in what we see and do, in what we think and feel, in what we hear and read. We relate to our parents what a neighbor said; we discuss for the teacher an event in history, or a character in literature; we show a companion how to make a kite or work a problem in algebra; we consider the advantages of a commercial course or relate the pleasures of a day's outing, — in each case we are interested, we think, we express our thoughts, and so are practicing oral composition with *subjects that may be used for written exercises*.

59. Subjects should be Definite. — Both the writer and the reader are more interested in definite and concrete subjects than in the general and abstract ones, and we shall make our writing more interesting by recognizing this fact. One might write about "Birds," or "The Intelligence of Birds," or "How Birds Protect their Young," or

"A Family of Robins." The last is a specific subject, while the other three are general subjects. Of these, the first includes more than the second; and the second, more than the third. A person with sufficient knowledge might write about any one of these general subjects, but it would be difficult to give it adequate treatment in a short theme. Though a general subject may suggest more lines of thought, our knowledge about a specific subject is less vague, and so is more usable. We really know more about the specific subject, and we have a greater interest in it. The subject, "A Family of Robins," indicates that the writer knows something interesting that he intends to tell. Such a subject compels expectant attention from the reader, and so aids in arousing an appreciative interest on his part.

On first thought, it would seem easier to write about a general subject than about a specific one, but this is not the case. A general subject presents so many lines of thought that the writer is confused, rather than aided, by the abundance of material. A skilled and experienced writer possessing a large fund of information may treat general subjects successfully, but for the beginner safety lies only in selecting definite subjects and in keeping within the limits prescribed. The "Women of Shakespeare" might be an interesting subject for a book by a Shakespearean scholar, but it is scarcely suitable for a high school pupil's theme.

60. Narrowing the Subject. — It is often necessary to narrow a subject in order to bring it within the range of the knowledge and interest of ourselves and of our readers. A description of the transportation of milk on the electric roads around Toledo would probably be more interesting than an essay on "Freight Transportation by Electricity," or on "Transportation." The purpose that the writer has in mind, and the length of the article he intends to write, will affect the selection of a subject. "Transportation" might be the subject of a book in which a chapter was given to each important subdivision of it; but it would be quite as difficult to treat such a subject in three hundred words as it would to use three hundred pages for the "Transportation of Milk at Toledo."

A general subject may suggest many lines of thought, and it is the task of the writer to select that one about which he knows something or can learn something, in which both he and his readers are interested, or can become interested, and which can be adequately treated in the time and space at his disposal.

EXERCISES

A. Arrange the subjects in each of the following groups so that the most general ones shall come first : —
1. The intelligence of wild animals.
   How a fox escaped from the hounds.
   How animals escape destruction by their enemies.
   Animals.
2. The benefits that arise from war.
   The defeat of the Cimbri and Teutons by Marius.
   War.
   The value of military strength to the Romans.
3. Pleasure.
   A summer outing in the Adirondacks.
   Value of vacations.
   Catching bass.

B. Narrow ten of the following subjects until the resulting subject may be treated in a single paragraph: —

1. Fishing.	6. Houses.	11. Sympathy.
2. Engines.	7. Games.	12. Sailboats.
3. Literature.	8. Basket ball.	13. Baseball.
4. Heroes of fiction.	9. Cats.	14. Rivers.
5. Cooking.	10. Canaries.	15. Trees.

C. A general subject may suggest several narrower subjects, each of which would be of interest to a different class of persons; for example —

General subject, — Education.

Specific subjects, —

1. Methods of conducting recitations. (Teachers.)
2. School taxes. (Farmers.)
3. Ventilation of school buildings. (Architects.)

In a similar way, narrow each of the following subjects so that the resulting subjects will be of interest to two or more classes of persons: —

SUBJECTS	CLASSES
1. Vacations.	1. Farmers.
2. Mathematics.	2. High school pupils.
3. Picnics.	3. Ministers.
4. Civil service.	4. Merchants.
5. Elections.	5. Sailors.
6. Botany.	6. Girls.
7. Fish.	7. Boys.

Theme XXXII. — *Write a paragraph about one of the narrowed subjects.*

(Does your paragraph have unity of thought? What methods of development have you used? Have you selected a subject which will be of interest to your readers?)

61. Selecting a Title. — The subject and the title may be the same, but not necessarily so. The statement of the subject may require a sentence of considerable length, while a title is best if short. In selecting this brief title, it is well to get one which will attract the attention and arouse the curiosity of a reader without appearing obviously to do so. A peculiar or unusual title is not at all necessary, though if properly selected such a title may be of value. Care must be taken not to have the title make a promise that the theme cannot fulfill. If it does, the effect is unsatisfactory.

EXERCISES

A. Discuss the appropriateness of the titles for the subjects in the following: —

1. Title : " My Kingdom for a Horse."
   Subject : An account of a breakdown of an automobile at an inconvenient time.
2. Title: A Blaze of Brilliance.
   Subject : Description of a coaching parade.
3. Title: A Brave Defense.
   Subject: An account of how a pair of birds drove a snake away from their nest.
4. Title : The Banquet Book.
   Subject : Quotations designed for general reference, and also as an aid in the preparation of the toast list, the after-dinner speech, and the occasional address.
5. Title : Dragons of the Air.
   Subject : An account of extinct flying reptiles.
6. Title : Rugs and Rags.
   Subject: A comparison of the rich and the poor, from a socialistic point of view.

7. Title: Lives of the Hunted.
   Subject: A true account of the doings of five quadrupeds and three birds.
8. Title: The Children of the Nations.
   Subject: A discussion of colonies and the problems
   of colonization.

B. Supply an appropriate title for a story read by the teacher.

C. Suggest a title, other than the one given it, for each magazine article you have read this month.

62. Language Adapted to the Reader. — A writer may select a subject with reference to the knowledge and interest of his readers; he may develop his paragraphs in accordance with the methods studied in Chapter III, and yet he may fail to make his meaning clear, because he has not used language suited to the reader. Fortunately, the language that we understand and use is that which is most easily understood by those of equal attainments with ourselves. It therefore happens that when writing for those of our own age and attainments, or for those of higher attainments, we usually best express for them that which we make most clear and pleasing to ourselves. But if we write for younger people, or for those of different interests in life, we must give much attention to adapting what we write to our readers. Before writing it is well to ask, For whom am I writing? Then, if necessary, you should modify your language so that it will be adapted to your readers. Can you tell for what kind of an audience each of the following is intended?

In the field both teams played faultless ball, not the semblance of an error being made. Besides backing up their pitchers in this fashion, both local and visiting athletes turned sensational plays.

The element of luck figured largely in the result. In the first inning Dougherty walked and Collins singled. Dougherty had third base sure on the drive, but stumbled and fell down between second and third, and he was an easy out.

Boston got its only run in the second. Parent sent the ball to extreme left for two bases. He stole third nattily when catcher Sugden tried to catch him napping at the middle station. Ferris scored him with a drive to left. St. Louis promptly tied the score in its half. Wallace opened with a screeching triple to the bulletin board. At that he would not have scored if J. Stahl had not contributed a passed ball, Heidrick, Friel, and Sugden, the next three batters, expiring on weak infield taps. The Browns got the winning run in the sixth on Martin's triple and Hill's swift cut back of first. Lachance knocked the ball down and got his man at the initial sack, but could not prevent the tally. — *Boston Herald.*

His name was Riley, and although his parents had called him Thomas, to the boys he had always been "Dennis," and by the time he had reached his senior year in college he was quite ready to admit that his "name was Dennis," with all that slang implied. He had tried for several things, athletics particularly, and had been substitute on the ball nine, one of the immortal second eleven backs of the football squad, and at one time had been looked upon as promising material for a mile runner on the track team.

But it was always his luck not quite to make anything. He couldn't bat up to 'varsity standard, he wasn't quite heavy enough for a 'varsity back, and in the mile run he always came in fresh enough but could not seem to get his speed up so as to run himself out, and the result was that, although he finished strong and with lots of running in him, the other fellows always reached the tape first, even though just barely getting over and thoroughly exhausted.

Now "Dennis" had made up his mind at Christmas time that he actually would have one more trial on the track, and that his family, consisting of his mother and a younger brother, both of them great believers in and very proud of Thomas, should yet see him possessed of a long-coveted "Y."

So he went out with the first candidates in the spring, and the addition of the two-mile event to the programme of track contests gave him a distance better suited to his endurance. There were a half-dozen other men running in his squad, and Dennis, from his former failures, was not looked upon with much favor, or as a very likely man. But he kept at it. When the first reduction of the squad was made, some one said, " Denny's kept on just to pound the track." With the middle of March came some class games, and Dennis was among the " also rans," getting no better than fourth place in the two-mile. The worst of it was that he knew he could have run it faster, for he felt strong at the finish, but had no burst of speed when the others went up on the last lap. But in April he did better, and it soon developed that he was improving. The week before the Yale-Harvard games he was notified that he was to run in the two-mile as pace maker to Lang and Early, the two best distance men on the squad. Nobody believed that Yale would win this event, although it was understood that Lang stood a fair chance if Dennis and Early could carry the Harvard crack, Richards, along at a fast gait for the first mile.

So it was all arranged that Early should set the pace for the first half mile, and Dennis should then go up and carry the field along for a fast second half. Then, after the first mile was over, Early and Dennis should go out as fast as they could, and stay as long as they could in the attempt to force the Harvard man and exhaust him so that Lang could come up, and, having run the race more to his liking, be strong enough to finish first.

The day of the games came, and with it a drenching rain, making the track heavy and everybody uncomfortable. But as the inter-collegiates were the next week, it was almost impossible to postpone the games, and consequently it was decided to run them off. As the contest progressed, it developed that the issue would hang on the two-mile event, and interest grew intense. When the call for starters came, Dennis felt the usual trepidation of a man who is before the public for the first time in a really important position. But the feel-ing did not last long, and by the time he went to his mark he had made up his mind that that Harvard runner should go the mile and a half fast at any rate, or else be a long way behind.

At the crack of the pistol the six men went off, and, according to orders, during the first mile Early and Dennis set the pace well up. Richards, the Harvard man, let them open up a gap on him in the first half-mile, and, being more or less bothered by the conditions of the wet track, he seemed uncertain whether the Yale runners were setting the pace too high or not, and in the second half commenced to move up. In doing this his team mates gradually fell back until they were out of it, and the order was Dennis, Early, Richards, and Lang. At the beginning of the second mile, Early, whose duty it was to have gone up and helped Dennis make the pace at the third half-mile, had manifestly had enough of it, and, after two or three desperate struggles to keep up, was passed by Richards. When, therefore, they came to the mile and a half, Dennis was leading Richards by some fifteen yards, and those who knew the game expected to see the Harvard man try to overtake Dennis, and in so doing exhaust himself, so that Lang, who was running easily in the rear, could come up and in the last quarter finish out strong. Dennis, too, was expecting to hear the Harvard man come up with him pretty soon, and knew that this would be the signal for him to make his dying effort in behalf of his comrade, Lang. As they straightened out into the back stretch Richards did quicken up somewhat, and Dennis let himself out. In fact, he did this so well that as they entered upon the last quarter Richards had not decreased the distance, and indeed it had opened up a little wider. But where was Lang? Dennis was beginning to expect one or the other of these two men to come up, and, as he turned into the back stretch for the last time, it began to dawn upon him, as it was dawning upon the crowd, that the pace had been too hot for Lang, and, moreover, that Yale's chance depended on the despised Dennis, and that the Harvard runner was finding it a big contract to overhaul the sturdy pounder on the wet track. But Richards was game, and commenced to cut the gap down. As they turned into the straight, he was within eight yards of Dennis. But Dennis knew it, and he ran as he had never run before. He could fairly feel the springing tread of Richards behind him, and knew it was coming nearer every second. But into the straight they came, and the crowd sprang to its feet like one man with wild yells for Dennis. Twenty yards from home Richards, who had picked up all but two yards of the lead, began to stagger and waver, while Dennis hung to it true and steady, and breasted the tape three yards in advance, winning his " Y " at last! .

— WALTER CAMP: *Winning a " Y "* ("Outlook").

In which of the preceding accounts were you most interested? Which made the most vivid impression? Which would be best suited for a school class composed of boys and girls? Which for a newspaper report? In attempting to relate a contest it is essential that the writer know what really happened, and in what order it happened, but his successful presentation will depend to some extent upon the consideration given to adapting the story to the audience. A person thoroughly conversant with the game will understand the technical terms, and may prefer the first account to the second, but those to whom the game is not familiar would need to have so much explanation of the terms used that the narration would become tedious to those already familiar with the terms. In order to make an account of a game interesting to persons unfamiliar with that game, we must introduce enough of explanation to make clear the meaning of the terms we use.

Theme XXXIII. — *Write a theme telling some one who does not understand the game about some contest which you have seen.*

Suggested subjects : —

1. A basket ball game.
2. A football game.
3. A tennis match.
4. A baseball game.
5. A croquet match.
6. A golf tournament.
7. A yacht race.
8. A relay race.

(Have you introduced technical terms without making the necessary explanations? Have you explained so many terms that your narrative is rendered tedious? Have you related what really happened, and in the proper time order? Have your paragraphs unity? Can you shorten the theme without affecting the clearness or interest? Does *then* occur too frequently?)

Theme XXXIV. — *Write a theme, using the same subject that you used for Theme XXXIII. Assume that the reader understands the game.*

(Will the reader get the whole contest clearly in mind? Can you shorten the account? Compare this theme with Theme XXXIII.)

63. Explanation of Terms. — Any word that alone or with its modifiers calls to mind a single idea, is a term. When applied to a particular object, quality, or action, it is a specific term; but when applied to any one of a class of objects, qualities, or actions, it is a general term. For example : *The Lake*, referring to a lake near at hand, is a specific term; but *a lake*, referring to any lake, is a general term. In Theme XXXIII you had occasion to explain some of the terms used. If, in telling about a baseball game, you mentioned a particular " fly," it was description or narration; but if some one should ask what you meant by " a fly," your answer would be general in character; that is, it would apply to all " flies," and would belong to that division of composition called exposition. Exposition is but another name for explanation. It is always concerned with that which is general, while description and narration deal with particular cases. We may describe a particular lake; but if we answer the question, What is a lake? the answer would apply to any lake, and would be exposition. Explanation of the meaning of general terms is one form of exposition.

64. Definition by Synonyms. — If asked to explain the meaning of a general term, our reply in many cases will be a brief definition. Often it will be sufficient to give a synonym. For example, in answer to the question, What is exposition? we make its meaning clearer by saying, Exposition is explanation.

Definition by synonym is frequently used because of its brevity. In the smaller dictionaries the definitions are

largely of this kind.   For example : to desert, *to abandon ;*
despot, *tyrant;* contemptible, *mean or vile ;* to fuse, *to blend;*
inviolable, *sacred*.   Synonyms are, however, seldom exact,
but a fair understanding of a term may be gained by comparing it with its synonyms and discussing the different
shades of meaning.   Such a discussion, especially if supplemented by examples showing the correct use of each term,
is a profitable exercise in exposition.   For example : —

Both *discovery* and *invention* denote generally something new that
is found out in the arts and sciences.   But the term *discovery* involves
in the thing discovered not merely novelty, but curiosity, utility, difficulty, and consequently some degree of importance.   All this is less
strongly involved in invention.   But there are yet wider differences.
One can only discover what has in its integrity existed before the discovery, while invention brings a thing into existence.   America was
discovered.   Printing was invented.   Fresh discoveries in science often
lead to new inventions in the industrial arts.   Indeed, discovery belongs more to science ; invention, to art.   Invention increases the store
of our practical resources, and is the fruit of search.   Discovery extends
the sphere of our knowledge, and has often been made by accident.
                                        — SMITH : *Synonyms Discriminated.*

If exactness is desired, this is obtained by means of the
logical definition, which will be discussed in a later chapter.

Theme XXXV. — *Explain the meaning of the words
in one of the following groups:* —

1. Caustic, satirical, biting.
2. Imply, signify, involve.
3. Martial, warlike, military, soldierlike.
4. Wander, deviate, err, stray, swerve, diverge.
5. Abate, decrease, diminish, lessen, moderate.
6. Emancipation, freedom, independence, liberty.
7. Old, ancient, antique, antiquated, obsolete.
8. Adorn, beautify, bedeck, decorate, ornament.
9. Active, alert, brisk, lively, spry.

65. Use of Simpler Words. — In defining terms by giving a synonym we must be careful to choose that which will be most likely to be understood by our listeners, or our explanation is of no avail. For instance, in explaining the term *abate* to a child, if we say it means *to diminish*, and he is unfamiliar with that word, he is made none the wiser by our explanation. If we tell him that it means *to grow less*, he will, in all probability, understand our explanation. Very many words in our language have equivalents that may be substituted the one for the other. Much of our explanation to children and to those whose attainments are less than our own consists in substituting common, everyday words for less familiar ones.

EXERCISE

Give familiar equivalents for the following words : —

1. emancipate.	14. edifice.	27. cohere.
2. procure.	15. collide.	28. athwart.
3. opportunity.	16. suburban.	29. clavicle.
4. peruse.	17. repugnance.	30. omnipotent.
5. elapsed.	18. grotesque.	31. enumerate.
6. approximately.	19. equipage.	32. eradicate.
7. abbreviate.	20. exaggerate.	33. application.
8. constitute.	21. ascend.	34. constitute.
9. simultaneous.	22. financial.	35. employer.
10. familiar.	23. nocturnal.	36. rendezvous.
11. deceased.	24. maternal.	37. obscure.
12. oral.	25. vision.	38. indicate.
13. adhere.	26. affinity.	39. prevaricate.

66. Definitions Need to be Supplemented. — The purpose of exposition is to make clear to others that which we understand ourselves. If the mere statement of a definition does not accomplish this result, it may often be brought about by supplementing the definition with suitable comparisons and examples. In making use of comparisons and examples we must choose those with which our readers are familiar, and we must be sure that they fairly represent the term that we wish to illustrate.

Theme XXXVI. — *Explain any one of the following terms. Begin with as exact a definition as you can frame.*

1. A "fly" in baseball.
2. A "foul" in basket ball.
3. A "sneak."
4. A hero.
5. A "spitfire."
6. A laborer.
7. A capitalist.
8. A coward.
9. A freshman.
10. A "header."

(Is your definition exact, or only approximately so? How have you made its meaning clear? Can you think of a better comparison or a better example? Can your meaning be made clearer, or be more effectively presented, by arranging your material in a different order?)

67. General Description. — We may often make clear the meaning of a term by giving details. In describing a New England village we might enumerate the streets, the houses, the town pump, the church, and other features. This would be specific description if the purpose was to have the reader picture some particular village; but if the purpose was to give the reader a clear conception of the general characteristics of all New England villages, the paragraph would become a general description.

Such a general description would include all the characteristics common to all the members of the class under discussion, but would omit any characteristic peculiar to

some of them. For example, a general description of a
windmill would include the things common to all windmills. If an object is described more for the purpose of
giving a clear conception of the class of which this is a
type than for the purpose of picturing the object described,
we have a general description, which is in effect an enlarged
definition, and so becomes exposition rather than description. It is sometimes called scientific description because
it is so commonly employed by writers of scientific books.
Notice the following examples of general description : —

1. Around every house in Broeck are buckets, benches, rakes, hoes,
and stakes, all colored red, blue, white, or yellow. The brilliancy
and variety of colors and the cleanliness, brightness, and miniature
pomp of the place are wonderful. At the windows there are em·
broidered curtains with rose-colored ribbons. The blades, bands, and
nails of the gayly painted windmills shine like silver. The houses
are brightly varnished and surrounded with red and white railings
and fences.

The panes of glass in the windows are bordered by many lines of
different hues. The trunks of all the trees are painted gray from root
to branch. Across the streams are many little wooden bridges, each
painted as white as snow. The gutters are ornamented with a sort of
wooden festoon perforated like lace. The pointed façades are surmounted with a small weathercock, a little lance, or something resem-
bling a bunch of flowers. Nearly every house has two doors, one in
front and one behind, the last for everyday entrance and exit, the
former opened only on great occasions, such as births, deaths, and
marriages. The gardens are as peculiar as the houses. The paths
are hardly wide enough to walk in. One could put his arms around
the flower beds. The dainty arbors would barely hold two persons
sitting close together. The little myrtle hedges would scarcely reach
to the knees of a four-year-old child.

2. Ginseng has a thick, soft, whitish, bulbous root, from one to three
inches long, — generally two or three roots to a stalk, — with wrinkles
running around it, and a few small fibers attached. It has a peculiar,
pleasant, sweetish, slightly bitter, and aromatic taste. The stem or

stalk grows about a foot high, is smooth, round, of a reddish green color, divided at the top into three short branches, with three to five leaves to each branch, and a flower stem in the center of the branches. The flower is small and white, followed by a large, red berry. It is found growing in most of the states in rich, shady soils.

3. As a general proposition, the Scottish hotel is kept by a benevolent-looking old lady, who knows absolutely nothing about the trains, nothing about the town, nothing about anything outside of the hotel, and is non-committal regarding matters even within her jurisdiction. Upon arrival you do not register, but stand up at the desk and submit to a cross-examination, much as if you were being sentenced in an American police court.

Your hostess always wants twelve hours' notice of your departure, so that she can make out your bill — a very arduous, formidable undertaking. The bill is of prodigious dimensions, about the size of a sheet of foolscap paper, lined and cross-lined for a multitude of entries. When the account finally reaches you, it closely resembles a design for a cobweb factory. Any attempt to decipher the various hieroglyphics is useless — it can't be done. The only thing that can be done is to read the total at the foot of the page and pay it.

— *Hotels in Scotland* (" Kansas City Star ").

Theme XXXVII. — *Write a general description of one of the following :* —

1. A bicycle.
2. A country hay barn.
3. A dog.
4. A summer cottage.
5. An Indian wigwam.
6. A Dutch windmill.
7. A muskrat's house.
8. A robin's nest.
9. A blacksmith's shop.
10. A chipmunk.
11. A threshing machine.
12. A sewing circle.

(The purpose is not to picture a particular object, but to give a general notion of a class of objects. Cross out everything in your theme that applies only to some particular object. Have you included enough to make your meaning clear ?)

Theme XXXVIII. — *Using the same title as for Theme XXXVII, write a specific description of some particular object.*

(How does it differ from the general description? What elements have you introduced which you did not have in the other? Which sentence gives the general outline? Are your details arranged with regard to their proper position in space? Will the reader form a vivid picture — just the one you mean him to have?)

68. General Narration. — Explanations of a process of manufacture, methods of playing a game, and the like, often take the form of generalized narration. Just as we gain a notion of the appearance of a sod house from a general description, so may we gain a notion of a series of events from a general narration. Such a narration will not tell what some one actually did, but will relate the things that are characteristic of the process or action under discussion whenever it happens. Such general narration is really exposition.

EXERCISES

A. Notice that the selection below is a generalized narration, showing what a hare does when hunted. In it no incident peculiar to some special occasion is introduced.

She [the hare] generally returns to the beat from which she was put up, running, as all the worlds knows, in a circle, or sometimes something like it, we had better say, that we may keep on good terms with the mathematical. At starting, she tears away at her utmost speed for a mile or more, and distances the dogs halfway; she then turns, diverging a little to the right or left, that she may not run into the mouths of her enemies — a necessity which accounts for what we call the circularity of her course. Her flight from home is direct and precipitate; but on her way back, when she has gained a little time for consideration and stratagem, she describes a curious labyrinth of short turnings and windings as if to perplex the dogs by the intricacy of her track.

— RICHARD AYTON.

B. The selection below narrates an actual hunt. Notice in what respects it differs from the preceding selection.

Sir Roger is so keen at this sport that he has been out almost every day since I came down; and upon the chaplain's offering to lend me his easy pad, I was prevailed on yesterday morning to make one of the company. I was extremely pleased, as we rid along, to observe the general benevolence of all the neighborhood towards my friend. The farmers' sons thought themselves happy if they could open a gate for the good old knight as he passed by; which he generally requited with a nod or a smile, and a kind inquiry after their fathers and uncles.

After we had rid about a mile from home, we came upon a large heath, and the sportsmen began to beat. They had done so for some time, when, as I was at a little distance from the rest of the company, I saw a hare pop out from a small furze brake almost under my horse's feet. I marked the way she took, which I endeavored to make the company sensible of by extending my arm; but to no purpose, till Sir Roger, who knows that none of my extraordinary motions are insignificant, rode up to me and asked me if puss was gone that way? Upon my answering "Yes," he immediately called in the dogs, and put them upon the scent. As they were going off, I heard one of the country fellows muttering to his companion, that 'twas a wonder they had not lost all their sport, for want of the silent gentleman's crying, "Stole away."

This, with my aversion to leaping hedges, made me withdraw to a rising ground, from whence I could have the pleasure of the whole chase, without the fatigue of keeping in with the hounds. The hare immediately threw them above a mile behind her; but I was pleased to find, that instead of running straight forwards, or, in hunter's language, "flying the country," as I was afraid she might have done, she wheeled about, and described a sort of circle round the hill, where I had taken my station, in such manner as gave me a very distinct view of the sport. I could see her first pass by, and the dogs some time afterwards, unraveling the whole track she had made, and following her through all her doubles. I was at the same time delighted in observing that deference which the rest of the pack paid to each particular hound, according to the character he had acquired among them: if they were at a fault, and an old hound of reputation opened but once, he was immediately followed by the whole cry; while a raw dog, or one who was a noted liar, might have yelped his heart out without being taken notice of.

The hare now, after having squatted two or three times, and been put up again as often, came still nearer to the place where she was at first started. The dogs pursued her, and these were followed by the jolly knight, who rode upon a white gelding, encompassed by his tenants and servants, and cheering his hounds with all the gayety of five and twenty. One of the sportsmen rode up to me, and told me that he was sure the chase was almost at an end, because the old dogs, which had hitherto lain behind, now headed the pack. The fellow was in the right. Our hare took a large field just under us, followed by the full cry in view. I must confess the brightness of the weather, the cheerfulness of everything around me, the chiding of the hounds, which was returned upon us in a double echo from two neighboring hills, with the hallooing of the sportsmen, and the sounding of the horn, lifted my spirits into a most lively pleasure, which I freely indulged because I was sure it was innocent. If I was under any concern, it was on account of the poor hare, that was now quite spent, and almost within the reach of her enemies; when the huntsman getting forward, threw down his pole before the dogs. They were now within eight yards of that game which they had been pursuing for almost as many hours; yet on the signal before mentioned they all made a sudden stand, and though they continued opening as much as before, durst not once attempt to pass beyond the pole. At the same time Sir Roger rode forward, and alighting, took up the hare in his arms; which he soon after delivered up to one of his servants with an order, if she could be kept alive, to let her go in his great orchard; where it seems he has several of these prisoners of war, who live together in a very comfortable captivity. I was highly pleased to see the discipline of the pack, and the good nature of the knight, who could not find in his heart to murder a creature that had given him so much diversion.

—BUDGELL: *Sir Roger de Coverley Papers.*

Theme XXXIX. — *Explain one of the following by the use of general narration:* —

1. Baking bread.
2. How paper is made.
3. How to play tennis (or some other game).
4. Catching trout.
5. Life at school.
6. How to pitch curves.

(Have you arranged your details with reference to their proper time-order? Have you introduced unnecessary details? Have your paragraphs unity? Underscore *then* each time you have used it.)

69. Argument. — Especially in argument is it evident that language presupposes an audience. The fact that we argue implies that some one does not agree with us. The purpose of our argument is to convince some one else of the truth of a proposition which we ourselves believe, and he who wishes to succeed in this must give careful attention to his audience. The question which must always be in the mind of the writer is, What facts shall I select and in what order shall I present them in order to convince my reader? The various ways of doing this are more fully treated in a later chapter, but a few of them are given here.

70. The Use of Explanation in Argument. — In preparing an argument we must consider first the amount of explanation that it will be necessary to make. We cannot expect one to believe a proposition the meaning of which he does not understand. Often the explanation alone is sufficient to convince the hearer. Suppose you are trying to gain your parents' consent to take some course of study. They ask for an explanation of the different courses, and

when they know what each contains they are already
convinced as to which is best for you.

If you are trying to convince a member of your school
board that it would be well to introduce domestic science
into the high school, and he already understands what is
meant by that term, you not only waste time in explaining it, but you make him appear ignorant of what he
already understands.   With him you should proceed at
once to give your reasons for the advisability of the introduction of this branch into your school.   On the other
hand, if you are talking with a member who does not
understand the term, an explanation will be the first
thing necessary.   It is evident, therefore, that the amount
of explanation that we shall make depends upon the previous knowledge of the audience addressed.   If we explain too much, we prejudice our case; and if we explain
too little, the reader may fail to appreciate the arguments
that follow.

The point of the whole matter, then, is that explanation
is the first step in argument, and that in order to determine the amount necessary we must consider carefully the
audience for which our argument is intended.

71. Statement of Advantages and Disadvantages. — An
argument is often concerned with determining whether it
is expedient to do one thing or another.   Such an argument frequently takes the form of a statement of the
advantages that will follow the adoption of the course we
recommend, or of the disadvantages that the following of
the opposite course will cause.

If a corporation should ask for a franchise for a street
railway, the city officials might maintain that a double
track should be laid.   In proof of this they would name

the advantageous results that would follow from the use of a double track, such as the avoidance of delays on turnouts, the lessening of the liability of accidents, the greater rapidity in transportation, etc. To this the persons seeking the franchise might reply that a double track would occupy too much of the street and so hinder teams, or that the advantages were not sufficient to warrant the extra expense.

Concerning such a question there can be no absolute decision. We are not discussing what is right, but what is expedient, and the determination of what is expedient is based upon a consideration of advantages or disadvantages. In deciding, we must balance the advantages against the disadvantages and determine which has the greater weight. If called upon to take one side or the other, we must consider carefully the value of the facts counting both for and against the proposition before we can make up our mind which side we favor.

You must bear in mind that a thing may not be an advantage because you believe it to be. That which seems to you to be the reason why you should take some high school subject, may seem to your father or your teacher to be the very reason why you should not. In writing arguments of this kind you must take care to select facts that will appeal to your readers as advantages.

Notice the following editorial which appeared in the *Boston Latin School Register* shortly after a change was made whereby the pupils instead of the teachers moved from room to room for their various recitations : —

The new system of having the classes move about from room to room to their recitations has been in use for nearly a month, and there has been sufficient opportunity for testing its practicability and its advantages. There is no doubt that the new system alters the old form of recesses, shortening the two regular ones, but giving three minutes between recitations as a compensation for this loss. Although theoretically we have more recess time than formerly, in the practical working out of the system we find that the three minutes between recitations is occupied in gathering up one's books, and reaching the next recitation room; besides this, that there is often some confusion in reaching the various classrooms, and that there are many little inconveniences which would not occur were we sitting at our own desks. On the other hand, as an offset to these disadvantages, there is the advantage of a change of position, and a respite from close attention, with a breathing spell in which to get the mind as well as the books ready for another lesson. The masters have in every recitation their own maps and reference books, with which they can often make their instruction much more forceful and interesting. Besides that, they have entire control of their own blackboards, and can leave work there without fear of its being erased to make room for that of some other master. The confusion will doubtless be lessened as time goes on and we become more used to the system. Even the first disadvantage is more or less offset by the fact that the short three-minute periods, although they cannot be used like ordinary recesses, yet serve to give us breathing space between recitations and to lessen the strain of continuous application; so that, on the whole, the advantages seem to counterbalance the disadvantages.

EXERCISES

What advantages and disadvantages can you think of for each of the following? State them orally to the class.

1. All telephone and telegraph wires in cities should be put under ground.
2. The speed of bicycles and automobiles should be limited to eight miles per hour.
3. High school football teams should not play match games on regular school days.
4. High school pupils should not attend evening parties excepting on Fridays and Saturdays.

5. Monday would be a better day for school holiday than Saturday.

6. The school session should be lengthened.

Theme XL. — *Write two paragraphs, one of which shall give the advantages and the other the disadvantages that would arise from the adoption of any one of the following:*

1. This school should have a longer recess.

2. This school should have two hours for the noon recess.

3. This school should be in session from eight o'clock until one o'clock.

4. All the pupils in this school should be seated in one room.

5. The public library should be in the high school building.

6. The football team should be excused early in order to practice.

7. This school should have a greater number of public entertainments.

72. Explanation and Argument by Specific Instances. — Often we may make the meaning of a general proposition clear by citing specific instances. If these instances are given for the purpose of explanation merely, the paragraph is exposition. If, however, the aim is not merely to cause the reader to understand the proposition, but also to believe that it is true, we have argument. In either case we have a paragraph developed by specific instances as discussed in Section 44. Notice how in the following paragraph the author brings forward specific cases in order to prove the proposition : —

Nearly everything that an animal does is the result of an inborn instinct acted upon by an outward stimulus. The margin wherein intelligent choice plays a part is very small. . . . Instinct is undoubtedly often modified by intelligence, and intelligence is as often guided or prompted by instinct, but one need not hesitate long as to which side of the line any given act of man or beast belongs. When the fox resorts to various tricks to outwit and delay the hound (if he ever consciously does so), he exercises a kind of intelligence — the lower form of which we call cunning — and he is prompted to this by an instinct of self-preservation. When the birds set up a hue and cry about a hawk, or an owl, or boldly attack him, they show intelligence in its simpler form, the intelligence that recognizes its enemies, prompted again by the instinct of self-preservation. When a hawk does not know a man on horseback from a horse, it shows a want of intelligence. When a crow is kept away from a corn-field by a string stretched around it, the fact shows how masterful is its fear and how shallow its wit. When a cat or a dog or a horse or a cow learns to open a gate or a door, it shows a degree of intelligence — power to imitate, to profit by experience. A machine could not learn to do it. If the animal were to close the door or gate behind it, that would be another step in intelligence. But its direct wants have no relation to the closing of the door, only to the opening of it. To close the door involves an afterthought that an animal is not capable of. A horse will hesitate to go upon thin ice or frail bridges. This, no doubt, is an inherited instinct which has arisen in its ancestors from their fund of general experience with the world. How much with them has depended upon a secure footing! A pair of house-wrens had a nest in my well-curb; when the young were partly grown and heard any one enter the curb, they would set up a clamorous calling for food. When I scratched against the sides of the curb beneath them like some animal trying to climb up, their voices instantly hushed; the instinct of fear promptly overcame the instinct of hunger! Instinct is intelligence, but it is not the same as acquired individual intelligence; it is untaught.

JOHN BURROUGHS: *Some Natural History Doubts* ("Harper's").

EXERCISES

What facts or instances do you know which would lead you to believe either the following propositions or their opposites?

1. Dogs are intelligent.

2. Only excellent pupils can pass the seventh grade examination.

.3. Some teachers do not ask fair questions on examination.

4. Oak trees grow to be larger than maples.

5. Strikes increase the cost to the consumer.

6. A college education pays.

7. Department stores injure the trade of smaller stores.

8. Advertising pays.

Theme XLI. — *Write a paragraph, proving by one or more examples one of the propositions in the preceding exercise.*

(Do your examples really illustrate what you are trying to prove? Do they show that the proposition is always true or merely that it is true for certain cases? Would your argument cause another to believe the proposition?)

73. The Value of Debate. — Participation in oral debate furnishes excellent practice in accurate and rapid thinking. We may choose one side of a question and may write out an argument which, considered alone, and from our point of view, seems convincing, but when this is submitted to the criticism of some one of opposite views, or when the arguments in favor of the other side of the question are brought forward, we are not so sure that we have chosen the side which represents the truth. The ability to think "on one's feet," to present arguments concisely and effectively, and to reply to opposing arguments, giving due weight to those that are true, and detecting and pointing out those that are false, is an accomplishment of great practical value. Such ability comes only from practice, and the best preparation for it is the careful writing out of arguments.

74. Statement of the Question. — The subject of debate may be stated in the form of a resolution, a declarative sentence, or a question ; as, " Resolved that the recess should be lengthened," or " The recess should be lengthened," or, "Should the recess be lengthened ? " In any case, the affirmative must show why the recess should be lengthened, and the negative why it should not be lengthened.

In a formal debate the statement of the question and its meaning should be definitely determined in advance. Care must be taken to state it so that no mere quibbling over the meanings of terms can take the place of real arguments. Even if the subject of debate is so stated that this is possible, any self-respecting debater will meet the question at issue fairly and squarely, preferring defeat to a victory won by juggling with the meanings of terms.

75. Is Belief Necessary in Debate ? — If we are really arguing for a purpose, we should believe in the truth of the proposition which we support. If the members of the school board were discussing the desirability of building a new schoolhouse, each would speak in accordance with his belief. But if a class in school should debate such a question, having in mind not the determination of the question, but merely the selection and arrangement of the arguments for and against the proposition in the most effective way, each pupil might present the side in which he did not really believe.

EXERCISES

Consider each of the following propositions. Do you believe the affirmative or the negative ?

1. This city needs a new high school building.
2. All the pupils in the high school should be members of the athletic association.
3. The school board should purchase an inclosed athletic field.
4. The street railway should carry pupils to and from school for half fare.
5. There should be a lunch room in this school.
6. Fairy stories should not be told to children.

Theme XLII. — *Write a paragraph telling why you believe one of the propositions in the preceding exercise.*

(What questions should you ask yourself while correcting your theme?)

76. Order of Presentation. — If you were preparing to debate one of the propositions in the preceding exercise, you would need to have in mind both the reasons for and against it. Next you would consider the order in which these reasons should be discussed. This will be determined by the circumstances of each debate, but generally the emphatic positions, that is, the first and the last, will be given to those arguments that seem to you to have the greatest weight, while those of less importance will occupy the central portion of your theme.

77. The Brief. — If, after making a note of the various advantages, examples, and other arguments that you wish to use in support of one of the propositions in Section 75, you arrange these in the order in which you think they can be most effectively presented, the outline so formed is called a brief. Its preparation requires clear thinking, but when it is made, the task of writing out the argument is not difficult. When the debate is to be spoken, not read, the brief, if kept in mind, will serve to suggest the arguments we wish to make in the order in which we wish to present them. The brief differs from the ordinary outline in that it is composed of complete sentences. Notice the following brief: —

Manual Training should be substituted for school athletics.

Affirmative

1. The exercise furnished by manual training is better adapted to the developing of the whole being both physical and mental; for —
    a. It requires the mind to act in order to determine what to do and how to do it.
    b. It trains the muscles to carry out the ideal of the mind.
2. The effect of manual training on health is better, for —
    a. Excessive exercise, harmful to growing children, is avoided.
    b. Dangerous contests are avoided.
3. The final results of manual training are more valuable, for —
    a. The objects made are valuable.
    b. The skill of hand and eye may become of great practical value in after life.
4. The moral effect of manual training is better, for —
    a. Athletics develops the "anything to win" spirit, while manual training creates a wholesome desire to excel in the creation of something useful or beautiful.
    b. Dishonesty in games may escape notice, but dishonesty in workmanship cannot be concealed.

      c. Athletics fosters slovenliness of dress and man-
           ners, while manual training cultivates the
           love of the beautiful.

5. The beneficial results of manual training have a wider
    effect upon the school, for —
      a. But comparatively few "make the team" and
           so get the maximum athletic drill, while all
           pupils can take manual training.

78. Refutation or Indirect Argument. — In debate we
need to consider not only the arguments in favor of our
own side, but those presented by our opponents. That
part of our theme which states our own arguments is called
direct argument, and that part in which we reply to our
opponents is called indirect argument or refutation. It
is often very important to show that the opposing argument is false or, if true, has been given an exaggerated
importance that it does not really possess. If, however,
it is true and of weight, it should be frankly acknowledged.
Our desire for victory should not cause us to disregard the
truth. If the argument of our opponent has been so strong
that it seems to have taken possession of the audience, we
must reply to it in the beginning. If it is of less weight,
each separate point may be discussed as we take up related
points in our own argument. Often it will be found best
to give the refutation a place just preceding our own last
and strongest argument.

From this it will be seen that each case cannot be determined by rule, but must be determined for itself, and
it is because of the exercise of judgment required, that
practice in debating is so valuable. A dozen boys or girls
may, with much pleasure and profit, spend an evening a
week as a debating club.

Theme XLIII. — *Prepare a written argument for or against one of the propositions in Section 75.*

(Make a brief. Re-arrange the arguments that you intend to use until they have what seems to you the best order. Consider the probable arguments on the other side and what reply can be made. Answer one or two of the strongest ones. If you have any trivial arguments for your own side, either omit them or make their discussion very brief.)

79. Cautions in Debating. — When we have made a further study of argument we shall need to consider again the subject of debating. In the meantime a few cautions will be helpful.

1. Be fair. A debate is in the nature of a contest, and is quite as interesting as any other contest. The desire to win should never lead you to take any unfair advantage or to descend to mere quibbling over the statement of the proposition or the meanings of the terms. Win fairly or not at all.

2. Be honest with yourself. Do not present arguments which you know to be false, in the hope that your opponent cannot prove their falsity. This does not mean that you cannot present arguments in favor of a proposition unless you believe it to be true, but that those you do present should be real arguments for the side that you uphold, even though you believe that there are weightier ones on the other side. Do not use an example that seems to apply if you know that it does not. You are to "tell the truth and nothing but the truth," but in debate you may tell only that part of the "whole truth" which favors your side of the proposition.

3. Do not allow your desire for victory to overcome your desire for truth. Do not argue for the sake of winning, nor develop the habit of arguing in season and out. In the school and outside there are persons who, like Will Carleton's Uncle Sammy, " were born for arguing." They use their own time in an unprofitable way, and what is worse, they waste the time of others. They are not seeking for truth, but for controversy. It is quite as bad to doubt everything you hear as it is to believe it all.

4. Remember that mere statement is not argument. The fact that you believe a proposition does not make it so. In order to have weight, a statement must be related to some proposition which *the audience* believes.

5. Remember that exhortation is not argument. Entreaty may persuade one to action, but in debate you should aim to convince the intellect. Clear, accurate thinking on your own part, so that you may present sound, logical arguments, is the first essential.

Theme XLIV. — *Prepare a written argument for or against one of the following propositions:* —

1. Boys who cannot go to college should take a commercial course in the high school.
2. Novel reading is a waste of time.
3. Asphalt paving is more satisfactory than brick.
4. Foreign skilled labor should be kept out of the United States.
5. Our own town should be lighted by electricity.
6. Athletic contests between high schools should be prohibited.

(Consider your argument with reference to the cautions given in Section 79.)

SUMMARY

1. The purpose of discourse may be to inform or to entertain.
2. The forms of discourse are —
   - *a.* Description.
   - *b.* Narration.
   - *c.* Exposition.
   - *d.* Argument (Persuasion).
3. Discourse presupposes an audience, and we must select a subject and use language adapted to that audience.
4. The suitableness of a subject is determined —
   - *a.* By the writer's knowledge of the subject.
     - (1) This may be based on experience, or
     - (2) It may be gained from others through conversation and reading.
   - *b.* By the writer's interest in the subject.
     - (1) This may exist from the first, or
     - (2) It may be aroused by our search for information.
   - *c.* By its adaptability to the reader. It should be of present, vital interest to him.
5. Subjects.
   - *a.* The sources of subjects are unlimited.
   - *b.* Subjects should be definite. This often requires that they be narrowed.
   - *c.* The title should be brief and should aim to arouse a desire to hear the theme.
6. Exposition is explanation.
7. We may make clear the meaning of a term —
   - *a.* By using synonyms.
   - *b.* By using simpler words.
   - *c.* By supplementing our definitions with examples or comparisons.

8. General description includes the characteristics common to all members of a class of objects.

9. General narration is one form of exposition. It relates the things that characterize a process or action whenever it occurs.

10. Argument.

   a. Explanation is the first step in argument.

   b. A statement of advantages and disadvantages may assist in determining which side of a question we believe.

   c. Specific instances may be used either for explanation or argument.

11. Debate.

   a. The subject of the debate may be stated in the form of a resolution, a declarative sentence, or a question.

   b. The most important arguments should be given the first and last positions.

   c. A brief will assist in arranging our arguments in the most effective order.

   d. The refutation of opposing arguments may usually be best done just preceding our own last and strongest argument.

   e. Cautions in debating.

      (1) Be fair.

      (2) Be honest with yourself.

      (3) Do not allow your desire for victory to overcome your desire for truth.

      (4) Remember that mere statement is not argument.

      (5) Remember that exhortation is not argument.

V. THE WHOLE COMPOSITION

80. General Principles of Composition. — There are three important principles to be considered in every composition: unity, coherence, and emphasis. Though not always named, each of these has been considered and used in our writing of paragraphs. The consideration of methods of securing unity, coherence, and emphasis in the composition as a whole is the purpose of this chapter. It will serve also as a review and especially as an enlarged view of paragraph development as treated in Chapter III, for the methods discussed with regard to the whole composition are the same that are used in applying the three principles to single paragraphs.

81. Unity. — A composition possesses unity if all that it contains bears directly upon the subject. It is evident that the title of the theme determines to a large extent what should be included. Much that would be appropriate to a theme on " Bass Fishing " would be unnecessary in a theme entitled " How I caught a Bass." It is easier to secure unity in a theme treating of a narrow, limited subject than in one treating of a broad, general subject. The first step toward unity is, therefore, the selection of a limited subject and a suitable title (see Sections 58–61); the second is the collection of all facts, illustrations, and other material which may appropriately be used in a theme having the chosen title.

82. Coherence. — A composition is given coherence by placing the ideas in such an order that each naturally suggests the one which follows. If the last paragraph is more closely related in thought to the first paragraph than it is to the intervening ones, the composition lacks coherence. Similarly, that paragraph is coherent in which the thought moves forward in an orderly way with each sentence growing out of the preceding one.

A boy in describing the capture of a large trout might state that he broke his pole. This would suggest the telling of what kind of pole he had, why he did not have a better one, what poles are best adapted to trout fishing, etc. Though each idea has been suggested by the preceding, the story lacks coherence because the boy would need later to go back and tell us what happened to him or to the trout when the pole broke. If a knowledge of the kind of pole is necessary to an appreciation of the narrative, it should have been introduced earlier. To stop at the moment of vital interest to discuss fishing poles spoils the effect of the story. Good writers are very skillful in the early introducing of details that will enable the reader to appreciate the events as they happen, and they are equally skillful in omitting details that are unnecessary to the understanding of the situation. The proper selection of these details gives unity and their introduction at the proper place gives coherence to a narrative. To say, " I am getting ahead of my story," indicates that coherence is lacking. Read again the selection on page 106.

83. Emphasis. — If it is the purpose to make one part of a theme more emphatic than another, it may be done by giving a prominent position to that part. In debating we give the first place and the last to the strongest arguments. In simple narration the order in which incidents must be related is fixed by the time-order of their occurrence, but even in a story the point gains in force if it is near the close. Because these two positions are the ones of greatest emphasis, a poor beginning or bad ending will ruin an otherwise good story.

Emphasis may also be affected by the proportional amount of attention and space given to the different parts of a theme. The extent to which any division of a theme shall be developed will depend upon the purpose and the total length of the theme. A biography of Grant might appropriately devote two or three chapters to his boyhood, while a short sketch of his life would reduce this to a single paragraph. In determining the amount of space to be given to the different parts of a composition, care must be taken to keep the space assigned to each proportional to its importance, giving the largest amount of space to that which is of greatest worth.

Emphasis is sometimes given by making a single sentence into a paragraph. This method should be used with care, for such a paragraph may be too short for unity because it does not include all that should be said about the topic statement, and though it makes that statement emphatic, fails to make its meaning clear.

Clearness, unity, and coherence are of more importance than emphasis, and usually, if a theme possesses the first three qualities, it will possess the fourth in sufficient measure.

84. The Outline. — An outline will assist in securing unity, coherence, and emphasis.

1. The first step in making an outline will be concerned with unity. Unity demands that a theme include only

that which pertains to the subject.   There are always many more ideas that seem to bear upon a subject than can be included in the theme.   It will be well to jot down brief notes that will suggest these ideas and then to reject from this list all that seem irrelevant or trivial. Even those ideas which do pertain directly to the subject may be omitted if we have already said all that needs to be said in order to fulfill the purpose of the theme.

Which items in the following should be omitted as not being necessary to the complete treatment of the subject indicated by the title ?   Should anything be added ?

My First Partridge

My eagerness to go hunting.

Kinds of game : partridge, quail, squirrels.

Partridge drumming.

Other boys went hunting often.

Birch brush near hemlock ; partridge often found in such localities.

Borrowing the gun ; loading it; a muzzle loader.

Going to the woods.

Why partridge live near birch brush.

Fall season.

Hunting for partridge allowed from September to December.

Tramping through the woods.

Something moving.

Creeping up.

How I felt ; excited; hand shook.

Partridge on log.

Gun failed to go off ; repriming it.

The shot ; the recoil.

The flurry of the bird.

How partridges fly.

How they taste when cooked.

Getting the bird.

Going home.

Partridges are found in the woods ; quail in the fields.

How proud I was.

What my sister said.

My brother's interest.

My father's story about shooting three partridges with one shot.

What mother did.

2. The second step in outline making will be concerned with coherence. After we have rejected from our notes all items whose introduction would interfere with the unity of our theme, we should next arrange the remaining items in a coherent order. One method of securing coherence is illustrated by simple narration. Here coherence may be obtained by following the time-order. We naturally group together in our memory those events which occurred at a given time, and in recalling a series of events we pass in order from one such group to another. These groups form natural paragraph units, and the placing of them in their actual time-order gives coherence to the composition.

After rejecting the items in the preceding list not necessary for unity re-arrange the remaining ones in a coherent order. How many paragraphs would you make and what would you include in each ?

3. The third step in making an outline will be concerned with emphasis. Consider your outline with reference to emphasis. In some outlines emphasis would be given by placing the more important points either first or last. In this particular outline we have a natural time-order to

follow, and emphasis will be determined mainly by the relative proportion to be given to different paragraphs. Do not give the unimportant ones too much space. Be sure that the introduction and conclusion are short.

Theme XLV. — *Write a personal narrative at least three paragraphs in length.*

Suggested subjects : —

> 1. How I was saved from drowning.
> 2. The largest string of fish I ever caught.
> 3. An incident of the skating season.
> 4. What I did on Christmas day.
> 5. A Saturday with my grandmother.
> 6. To the city and back.

(Make an outline. Keep in mind unity, coherence, and emphasis. Consider each paragraph with reference to unity, coherence, and emphasis.)

85. Development of a Composition with Reference to the Time-Order. — Of the several methods of developing a composition let us consider first that of giving details in the natural time-order. (See Section 46.) If a composition composed of a series of paragraphs possesses coherence, each paragraph is so related to the preceding ones that the thought goes steadily forward from one to another. Often the connection in thought is so evident that no special indication of it is made, but if the paragraphs are arranged with reference to a time-order, this is usually indicated.

Notice how the relation in time of each paragraph to the preceding is shown by the following sentences or parts of sentences taken in order from a magazine article entitled " Yachting at Kiel," by James B. Connolly : —

1. It was slow waiting in Travemunde. The long-enduring twilight of a summer's day at fifty-four north began to settle down . . .
2. The dusk comes on, and on the ships of war they seem to be getting nervous . . .
3. The dusk deepens . . .
4. It is getting chilly in the night air, with the rations running low, and the charterers of some of the fishing boats decide to go home . . .
5. It is eleven o'clock — dark night — and the breeze is freshening, when the first of the fleet heaves in sight . . .
6. After that they arrive rapidly . . .
7. At midnight there is still no *Meteor* . . .
8. Through the entire night they keep coming . . .
9. Next morning . . .

Theme XLVI. — *Write a narrative, four or more paragraphs in length, showing the time-order.*

Suggested subjects : —
1. The race up the river.
2. The life of some well-known man.
3. The cake that fell.
4. Retell some incident that you have recently read.
5. Relate some personal experience.
6. A story suggested by the picture on page 160.

(Make an outline. Consider the unity, coherence, and emphasis of each paragraph separately and of the whole composition. Notice what expressions you have used to indicate the relations in time. Have you used the same one too often?)

86. Development of a Composition with Reference to Position in Space. — A second method of development is relating details with reference to their position in space. Just as we may give either a paragraph or a whole theme

coherence by following a given time-order, so may we make a paragraph or a whole theme coherent by stating the parts in an order determined by their position in space. This is nothing more than the application to a whole theme of the principles discussed for the development of a paragraph by relating details with reference to their position in space (Section 47).

In a description consisting of several paragraphs, each should contain a group of details closely related to each other in space. The paragraphs should be constructed so that each shall possess unity and coherence within itself, and they should be so arranged that we may pass most easily from the group of images presented by one paragraph to the images presented by the next. In narration, the space arrangement may supplement time-order in giving coherence.

If the most attractive features of the art room were its wall decorations, five paragraphs describing the room might be as follows : —

1. Point of view : general impression.
2. The north wall : general impression ; details.
3. The east wall : general impression ; details.
4. The south wall : general impression ; details.
5. The west wall : general impression ; details.

It is easy to imagine a room in the description of which the following paragraphs would be appropriate : —

1. Point of view.
2. The fireplace.
3. The easy-chair.
4. The table.
5. The bookcase.
6. The cozy nook.

Such an arrangement of paragraphs would give coherence. Unity would be secured by including in each only that which properly belonged to it.

There are many words and expressions which indicate the relative position of objects. The paragraph below is an illustration of the method of development described in Section 47. Notice the words which indicate the location of the different details in the scene. If each of these details should be developed into a paragraph the italicized expressions would serve to introduce these paragraphs and would show the relative positions of the objects described.

The beauty of the sea and shore was almost indescribable: *on one side* rose Point Loma, grim, gloomy as a fortress wall; *before* me stretched away to the horizon the ocean with its miles of breakers curling into foam; *between* the surf and the city, wrapped in its dark blue mantle, lay the sleeping bay; *eastward* the mingled yellow, red, and white of San Diego's buildings glistened in the sunlight like a bed of coleus; *beyond* the city heaved the rolling plains rich in their garb of golden brown, *from which* rose the distant mountains, tier on tier, wearing the purple veil which Nature here loves oftenest to weave for them; while *in the foreground,* like a jewel in a brilliant setting, stood the Coronado.

—STODDARD: *California.*

Theme XLVII. — *Write a description three or more paragraphs in length.*

Suggested subjects : —

     1. Some well-known building (exterior).
     2. A prominent person.
     3. An attractive room.
     4. The interior of a church.

(Consider your outline with reference to unity, coherence, and proportion of parts. When the theme is completed, consider the unity, coherence, and emphasis of each paragraph and of the composition as a whole.)

87. Paragraph Relations. — Relations in thought other than those of time and space may be indicated by the use of certain words and phrases. Such expressions as, *however*, *nevertheless*, *consequently*, *indeed*, *moreover*, *at all events*, etc., are often used to indicate a relation in thought between paragraphs. Notice how *nevertheless*, at the beginning of the selection below, serves to connect it in thought with a preceding paragraph not printed here. Notice also the relations in thought shown by the italicized words. These and similar words are used to make the transition from one paragraph to the next.

Nevertheless, Howe was at last in possession of Philadelphia, the object of his campaign, and with his communications by water open. He had consumed four months in this business since he left New York, three months since he landed near the Elk River. His prize, now that he had got it, was worth less than nothing in a military point of view, and he had been made to pay a high price for it, not merely in men, but in precious time, for while he was struggling sluggishly for Philadelphia, Burgoyne, who really meant something very serious, had gone to wreck and sunk out of sight in the northern forests. *Indeed*, Howe did not even hold his dearly bought town in peace. After the fall of the forts, Greene, aided by Lafayette, who had joined the army on its way to the Brandywine, made a sharp dash and broke up an outlying party of Hessians. *Such things* were intolerable, they interfered with personal comfort, and they emanated from the American army which Washington had now established in strong lines at Whitemarsh. *So* Howe announced that in order to have a quiet winter, he would drive Washington beyond the mountains. Howe did not often display military intelligence, but that he was profoundly right in this particular intention must be admitted. In pursuit of his plan, *therefore*, he marched out of Philadelphia on December 4th, drove off some Pennsylvania militia on the 5th, considered the American position for four days, did not dare to attack, could not draw his opponent out, returned to the city, and left Washington to go into winter quarters at Valley Forge, whence he could easily strike if any move was made by the British army.

— HENRY CABOT LODGE.

88. The Transition Paragraph. — Just as a word or phrase may serve to denote the relation in thought between paragraphs, so may a whole paragraph be used to carry over the thought from one group of paragraphs to another in the same theme. It makes a transition from one general topic or method of treating the subject of the theme to some other general topic or to the consideration of the subject from a different point of view. Such a transitional paragraph may summarize the thought of the preceding paragraph in addition to announcing a change of topic ; or it may mark the transition to the new topic and set it forth in general terms.

89. The Summarizing Paragraph. — Frequently we give emphasis to our thought by concluding what we have written with a paragraph summarizing the main points of the theme. Such a summary is in effect a restatement of the topic sentences of our paragraphs. If our theme has been coherent, these sentences stated in order will need but little changing to make a coherent paragraph. It is similarly of advantage to close a long paragraph with a sentence which repeats the topic statement or summarizes the thought of the paragraph.

90. Development of a Composition by Comparison or Contrast. — The third method of development is that of comparison or contrast. Nearly every idea which we have suggests one that is similar to it or in contrast with it. We are thus led to make comparisons or to state contrasts. When these are brief, we have a single paragraph (Section 48). If our comparisons or contrasts are extended, it may be better to make several paragraphs, and thus develop a whole theme by this method.

In outlining such a theme we have no fixed order of

presentation determined by the actual occurrence in time or space of that which we present. It therefore happens that more attention must be given to arranging our paragraphs in an order that shall give coherence and emphasis.

Theme XLVIII. — *Write a theme of three or more paragraphs developed by comparison.*

Suggested subjects : —

1. Compare men with verbs (active, passive, transitive, intransitive, defective, redundant, auxiliary, copulative, etc.).
2. Show that the body resembles a machine.
3. In what way is the school like a factory ?
4. How do two books that you have read differ ?
5. Compare Lincoln and McKinley. How alike ? How different ?
6. How can you tell an oak tree from an elm tree ?
7. Without naming them, compare two of your friends with each other.
8. Compare the advantages and disadvantages of public high schools with those of private academies.

91. Development of a Composition by Use of Generalization and Facts. — By the fourth method of development an entire composition may be given to the explanation of the meaning or to the demonstration of the truth of some general proposition. This is often accomplished by stating facts or instances that illustrate the meaning of the proposition or that show it to be true. In such a composition each important fact or instance may be given a separate paragraph, while several minor facts or illustrations may be properly combined in the same paragraph.

(See Section 44.) Greater emphasis may also be given the more important facts by assigning them to the emphatic positions.

Notice how by specific instances the following selection illustrates the truth of the generalization set forth in the second sentence and restated in the last sentence.

DEGENERATION THROUGH QUIESCENCE

While parasitism is the principal cause of degeneration among animals, yet it is not the sole cause. It is evident that if for any other reason animals should become fixed, and live inactive lives, they would degenerate. There are not a few instances of degeneration due simply to a quiescent life, unaccompanied by parasitism.

The Tunicata, or sea squirts, are animals which have become simple through degeneration, due to the adoption of a sedentary life, the withdrawal from the crowd of animals and from the struggle which it necessitates. The young tunicate is a free-swimming, active, tadpolelike, or fishlike creature, which possesses organs very like those of the adult of the simplest fishes or fishlike forms. That is, the sea squirt begins life as a primitively simple vertebrate. It possesses in its larval stage a notochord, the delicate structure which precedes the formation of a backbone, extending along the upper part of the body below the spinal cord. The other organs of the young tunicate are all of vertebral type. But the young sea squirt passes a period of active and free life as a little fish, after which it settles down and attaches itself to a shell or wooden pier by means of suckers, and remains for the rest of its life fixed. Instead of going on and developing into a fishlike creature, it loses its notochord, its special sense organs, and other organs; it loses its complexity and high organization, and becomes a " mere rooted bag with a double neck," a thoroughly degenerate animal.

A barnacle is another example of degeneration through quiescence. The barnacles are crustaceans related most nearly to the crabs and shrimps. The young barnacle just from the egg is a six-legged, free-swimming nauplius, very like a young prawn or crab, with a single eye. In its next larval stage it has six pairs of swimming feet, two compound eyes, and two antennæ or feelers, and still lives an independent free-swimming life. When it makes its final change to the adult condition, it attaches itself to some stone, or shell, or pile, or ship's bottom, loses its compound eyes and feelers, develops a protecting shell, and gives up all power of locomotion. Its swimming feet become changed into grasping organs, and it loses most of its outward resemblance to the other members of its class.

Certain insects live sedentary or fixed lives. All the members of the family of scale insects (Coccidæ), in one sex at least, show degeneration that has been caused by quiescence. One of these coccids, called the red orange scale, is very abundant in Florida and California and in other fruit-growing regions. The male is a beautiful, tiny, two-winged midge, but the female is a wingless, footless, little sack, without eyes or other organs of special sense, which lies motionless under a flat, thin, circular, reddish scale composed of wax and two or three cast skins of the insect itself. The insect has a long, slender, flexible, sucking beak, which is thrust into the leaf or stem or fruit of the orange on which the " scale bug " lives, and through which the insect sucks the orange sap, which is its only food. It lays eggs under its body, and thus also under the protecting wax scale, and dies. From the eggs hatch active little larval "scale bugs," with eyes and feelers, and six legs. They crawl from under the wax scale and roam about over the orange tree. Finally, they settle down, thrusting their sucking beak into the plant tissue, and cast their skin. The females lose at this molt their legs and eyes and feelers. Each becomes a mere motionless sack capable only of sucking up sap and laying eggs. The young males, however, lose their sucking beak and can no longer take food, but they gain a pair of wings and an additional pair of eyes. They fly about and fertilize the sacklike females, which then molt again and secrete the thin wax scale over them.

Throughout the animal kingdom loss of the need of movement is followed by the loss of the power to move and of all structures related to it.

—JORDAN AND KELLOGG: *Animal Life.*

Has the principle of unity been observed in the above selection; that is, of the many things that might be told about a sea squirt, a barnacle, or a scale bug, have the authors selected only those which serve to illustrate degeneration through quiescence ?

Instead of one generalization supported by a series of

facts to each of which a paragraph is given, we may have several subordinate generalizations relating to the subject of the theme. Each of these subordinate generalizations may become the topic statement of a paragraph which is further developed by giving specific instances or by some other method of paragraph development. Such an order, that is, generalization followed by the facts which illustrate it, is coherent ; but care must be taken to give each fact under the generalization to which it is most closely related. On the other hand, our theme may be made coherent by giving the facts first, and then the generalization that they establish.

Theme XLIX. — *Write a theme of three or more paragraphs illustrating or proving some general statement by means of facts or specific instances.*

Suggested subjects : —

1. Young persons should not drink coffee.
2. Reasons for the curfew bell.
3. Girls wear their hair in a variety of ways.
4. There are several kinds of boys in this school.
5. Civilization increases as the facilities for transportation increase.
6. Trolley roads are of great benefit to the country.
7. Presence of mind often averts danger.

92. Development of a Composition by Stating Cause and Effect. — The statement of the causes of an event or condition may be used as a fifth method of development. The principle, however, is not different from that applied to the development of a paragraph by stating cause and effect (Section 49). If several causes contribute to the same effect, each may be given a separate paragraph, or several minor ones may be combined in one paragraph.

For the sake of unity we shall include each fact, principle, or statement in the paragraph to which it really belongs. The coherent order is usually that which proceeds from causes to effects rather than that which traces events backward from effects to causes.

Theme L. — *Write a theme of three or more paragraphs, stating causes and effects.*

Suggested subjects: —

1. Why hospitals are necessary.
2. Why cigarette smoking is dangerous.
3. Why girls should take music lessons.
4. The effect of climate upon health.
5. The effect of rainfall upon the productivity and industries of a country.
6. The effect of mountains, lakes, or rivers upon exploration and travel.
7. What connection is there between occupation and height above the sea level, and why?
8. Why our city is located where it is.
9. Why I came late to school.

93. Combination of Methods of Development. — Frequently the presentation of our thought is made more effective by using some combination of the methods of development discussed in this chapter than it can be if we use but a single method. Time and place are often interwoven, comparisons and contrasts flash into mind, general statements need specific illustration, or results demand immediate explanation — all in the same theme. Even the order of coherence will be in dispute, for cause and effect demand a different order of statement from that which would be given if we follow either time-order or position in space. So the writer must choose whether it is most important to tell first *why* or *when* or *where*. There can be no other rule than that we shall do that which makes our meaning most clear, for it is for the sake of the clear presentation of our thought that we seek unity, coherence, and emphasis.

Theme LI. — *Write a theme of several paragraphs. Use any method of development or any combination of methods.*

(Choose your own subject. After the theme is written make a list of all the questions you should ask yourself about it. Correct the theme with reference to each point in your list of questions.)

SUMMARY

1. General principles of composition.
   - *a.* Unity.
   - *b.* Coherence.
   - *c.* Emphasis.
     - (1) By position.
     - (2) By proportion of parts.
2. An outline assists in securing unity, coherence, and emphasis.
3. Methods of composition development: A composition may be developed —
   - *a.* With reference to time-order.
   - *b.* With reference to position in space.
   - *c.* By use of comparison and contrast.
   - *d.* By stating generalization and facts.
   - *e.* By stating cause and effect.
   - *f.* By any suitable combination of the above methods.
4. Transition and summary paragraphs may occur in compositions.

VI. LETTER WRITING

94. Importance of Good Letter Writing. — This form of written language is used by most of us more frequently than any other form, and its importance must be obvious. Business, personal, and social relations necessitate the writing of letters. We are judged by those letters ; and in order that we be considered businesslike, educated, and cultured, it is necessary that we write good letters, both as regards the form and the subject-matter. The ability to write good letters is often the means of securing desirable positions and of keeping up pleasant and helpful friendships. Since this form of composition plays so important a part in our lives and the lives of those about us, it is worthy of careful study.

The subject-matter is the most important part of the letter, but adherence to usages generally adopted is an essential of successful letter writing. Some of these usages may seem trivial in themselves, but a lack of attention to them shows either ignorance or carelessness on the part of the writer, and the consequences resulting from this inattention are often anything but trivial. Applicants for good positions have been rejected either because they did not know the correct usages of letter writing, or because they did not heed them. In no other form of composition are the rules concerning form so rigid ; hence the need of knowledge and carefulness concerning them.

95. Paper. — The nature of the letter determines to some extent our choice of paper. Business letters are usually written on large paper, about ten by eight inches in size, while letters of friendship and notes of various kinds are written on paper of smaller size. White or delicately tinted paper is always in good taste for all kinds of letters. The use of highly tinted paper sometimes comes into use for a short time, but we are always sure not to transgress the laws of good taste if we do not make use of it. It is customary now to use unruled paper for all kinds of letters as well as for other forms of compositions. For letters of friendship four-page paper is preferred to that in tablet form. The order in which the pages are used may vary; but whatever the order, it should be such as shall not be confusing to the reader.

Black ink should always be used. The writing should be neat and legible. Attention should be paid to margin, paragraphs, and indentation. In fact, all the rules of theme writing apply to letter writing, and to these are added several others.

96. The Beginning of a Letter. — Certain forms for beginning letters have been agreed upon, and these forms should be followed. The beginning of a letter usually includes the heading, the address of the person or persons to whom the letter is sent, and the salutation.

Notice the following examples of the beginnings of a letter : —

(1)

> 171 Miles Ave.,
> Cleveland, Ohio.
> Oct. 21, 1905.

Marshall Field & Co.,
    State St., Chicago, Ill.

    Gentlemen :

(2)

Ottawa, Ill.
Nov. 9, 1905.

Dear Harold,

(3)

1028 Jackson Boulevard,
Chicago, Ill.
Nov. 10, 1905.

Messrs. Johnson & Foote,
120 Main St.,
Pittsfield, Mass.

Dear Sirs,

(4)

120 P Street,
Lincoln, Neb.
Oct. 17, 1905.

My dear Mrs. Scott,

(5)

Boston, Mass., Nov. 23, 1905.

Dear Mother,

(6)

33 Front St.,
Adrian, Mich.
Nov. 30, 1905.

Miss Gertrude Brown,
228 Warren Ave., Chicago, Ill.

Dear Madam:

(7)

New Hartford, Conn.
Nov. 3, 1905.

My dear Henry,

The heading of a letter includes the address of the writer and the date of the writing. When numerous letters are sent from one place to another, the street and number may after a time be omitted from the heading. Example (5) illustrates this. A son living in Boston has written to his mother frequently and no longer considers it necessary to write the street and number in every letter. If there is any doubt in the writer's mind as to whether his address will be remembered or not, he should include it in the letter. If the writer lives in a small place where the street and number will not be needed in a reply sent to him, it is unnecessary for him to make use of it in his letter. When the street and number are omitted, the heading may be written on one line, as in example (5), but the use of two lines is preferable.

Custom has decreed that the proper place for the heading is in the right-hand upper corner of the first page. Sometimes, especially in business letters, we find the writer's address at the close of the letter, but for the sake of convenience it is preferably placed at the beginning. The first line should be about one inch and a half from the top of the page. The second line should be commenced a little to the right of the first line, and the third line, a little to the right of the second line. Attention should be paid to proper punctuation in each line.

In a comparatively few cases we may find that the omission of the date of the letter will make no difference to the recipient, but in most cases it will cause annoyance at least, and in many cases result in serious trouble both to ourselves and to those who receive our letters. We should not allow ourselves to neglect the date even in letters of apparently no great importance. This date should include the day, month, and year. It is better to write out the entire year, as 1905, not '05. Omitting dates shows carelessness at least, and this habit of carelessness may become so strong that we shall be liable to omit the date when matters of great importance depend upon it.

In business letters it is customary to write the address of the person or persons addressed at the left-hand side of the page, using either two or three lines. The first line of this address should be one line lower than the last line of the heading. Notice examples (1), (3), and (6). When the address is thus written, the salutation is commonly written one line below it. Sometimes the salutation is commenced at the margin, and sometimes a little to the right of the address. Where there is no address, the salutation is written a line below the date and begins with the margin, as in examples (2), (4), (5), and (7).

The form of salutation naturally depends upon the relations existing between the correspondents. The forms *Dear Sir*, *My dear Sir*, *Madam*, *My dear Madam*, *Dear Sirs*, *Gentlemen*, are used in formal business letters. The forms *Dear Miss Robinson*, *My dear Mrs. Hobart*, *Dear Mr. Fraser*, *My dear Mr. Scott*, are used in business letters when the correspondents are acquainted with each other. The same forms are also used in letters of friendship when the correspondents are not well enough acquainted with each other to warrant the use of the more familiar forms, *My dear Mary*, *Dear Edmund*, *My dear Friend*, *Dear Cousin*, *My dear little Niece*.

There is no set rule concerning the punctuation of the

salutation. The comma, the colon, or the semicolon may be used either alone or in connection with the dash. The comma alone seems to be the least formal of all, and the colon the most so. Hence the former is used more frequently in letters of friendship, and the latter more frequently in business letters.

97. Body of the Letter. — The body of the letter is the important part; in fact, it is the letter itself, since it contains the subject-matter. It will be discussed under another head later, and is only mentioned here in order to show its place in connection with the beginning of a letter. As a rule, it is best to begin the body of our letters one line below, and either directly underneath or to the right of the salutation. It is not improper, however, especially in business letters, to begin it on the same line with the salutation. A few examples will be sufficient to show the variations of the place for beginning the main part of the letter.

(1)

> 1694 Cedar Ave.,
> Cleveland, Ohio.
> June 23, 1905.
>
> Messrs. Hanna, Scott & Co.,
>   Aurora, Ill.
>
> Gentlemen: — I inclose a money order for $10.00, etc.

(2)

> Everett, Washington.
> Oct. 20, 1905.
>
> My dear Robert,
>   We are very glad that you have decided to make us a visit, etc.

(3)

Greenwich, N.Y.
Sept. 19, 1905.

My dear Miss Russ,
Since I have been Miss Clark's assistant, etc.

(4)

2 University Ave.,
Nashville, Tenn.
April 19, 1905.

The American Book Co.
300 Pike St.,
Cincinnati, O.

Dear Sirs; Please send me by express two copies of Halleck's English Literature, etc.

98. Conclusion of a Letter. — The conclusion of a letter includes what is termed the complimentary close and the signature. Certain forms have been agreed upon, which should be closely followed.

Our choice of a complimentary close, like that of a salutation, depends upon the relations existing between us and those to whom we are writing. Such forms as *Your loving daughter, With love, Ever your friend, Your affectionate mother*, should be used only when intimate relations exist between correspondents. In letters where existing relations are not so intimate and in some kinds of business letters the forms *Sincerely yours, Yours very sincerely,* may be used appropriately. The most common forms in business letters are *Yours truly* and *Very truly yours.* The forms *Respectfully yours,* or *Yours very respectfully,* should be used only when there is occasion for some special respect such as writing to a person of high rank or position.

The complimentary close should be written one line below the last line of the main part of the letter, and toward the right-hand side of the page. Its first word should commence with a capital, and a comma should be placed at its close.

The signature properly belongs below and a little to the right of the complimentary close. Except in cases of familiar relationship, the name should be signed in full. It is difficult to determine the spelling of unfamiliar proper names if they are carelessly written. It is therefore important in writing to strangers that the signature be made plainly legible in order that those who receive the letter will know how to address the writer in their reply. A lady should make it plain whether she is to be addressed as *Miss* or *Mrs.* This can be done either by placing the title *Miss* or *Mrs.* in parentheses before the name, or by writing the whole address below and to the left of the signature. Boys and men may often avoid confusion by signing their first name instead of using only initials.

Notice the following examples of the complimentary close and signature : —

(1)

Appleton, Wisconsin.
Sept. 3, 1905.

My dear Cousin,

(Body of letter.)

Yours with love,
Gertrude Edmonds.

(2)

192 Lincoln Ave.,
Worcester, Mass.
Nov. 25, 1905.

L. B. Bliss & Co.,
109 Summer St.,
Boston, Mass.

Dear Sirs;

(Body of letter.)

Very truly yours,
Walter A. Cutler.

(3)

Paxton, Ill.
July 3, 1905.

American Typewriter Co.,
263 Broadway, New York.

Gentlemen:

(Body of letter.)

Very truly yours,
(Miss) Jennie R. McAllister.

(4)

May 5, 1905.

Daniel Low & Co.,
232 Essex St., Salem, Mass.

Dear Sirs;

(Body of letter.)

Mary E. Ball.

Mrs. George W. Ball,
415 Fourth St.,
La Salle, Ill.

(5)

Marshalltown, Iowa.
Oct. 3, 1905.

My dear Miss Meyer,

(Body of letter.)

Sincerely yours,
Dorothy Doddridge.

EXERCISE

Write suitable headings, salutations, complimentary endings, and signatures for the following letters : —

1. To Spaulding & Co., Wabash Ave., Chicago, Ill., ordering their rules for basket ball.
2. To your older brother.
3. To the school board, asking for a gymnasium.
4. To some business house, making application for a position.
5. To the governor of your state.
6. From one stranger to another.
7. From an older brother to his little sister.
8. From a boy living in New Orleans to the father of his most intimate friend.

99. The Envelope. — The direction on the envelope, commonly called the superscription, consists of the name and address of the person or persons to whom the letter is sent. It should include all that is necessary to insure promptness in its reaching its destination, and this should be written in a careful and *courteous manner.*

The superscription may be arranged in three or four lines, each line beginning a little to the right of the preceding line. The name should be written about midway between the upper and lower edges of the envelope, and there should be nearly an equal amount of space left at each side. If there is any difference, there should be less space at the right than at the left. The street and number may be written below the name, and the city or town and state below. The street and number may be properly written in the lower left-hand corner. This is also the place for any special direction that may be necessary for the speedy transmission of the letter ; for example, " In care of Mr. Charles R. Brown."

Women should be addressed as *Miss* or *Mrs*. In case the woman is married, her husband's first name and middle initial are commonly used, unless it is known that she prefers to have her own first name used. Men should be addressed as *Mr.*, and a firm may in many cases be addressed as *Messrs*. It is considered proper to use the titles *Dr.*, *Rev.*, etc., in directing an envelope to a man bearing such a title, but it would be entirely out of place to address the wife of a physician or clergyman as *Mrs. Dr.* or *Mrs. Rev.*

Abbreviations for states may be used, but care should be taken that they be plainly written, especially when there are others similar to the one used. In compound names, as North Dakota and West Virginia, do not abbreviate one part of the compound and write out the other. Either abbreviate both or write out both. If any punctuation besides the period after abbreviations is used, it consists of a comma after each line. It is the custom now to omit such punctuation. Either form is in good taste, but whichever form is used, it should be used throughout the entire superscription. The comma should not be used in one line and omitted in another.

Notice the following forms of correct superscriptions : —

(1)

Mr. Milo R. Maltbie

85 West 118th St.

New York.

(2)

Mr. John D. Clark

New York

Teachers College   N. Y.
Columbia University.

(3)

Mrs. Edgar N. Foster

South Haven

Mich.

Avery Beach Hotel.

(4)

Miss Louise M. Baker

Nottingham

Ohio.

Box 129.

(5)

Dr. James M. Postle

De Kalb

Ill.

(6)

Miss Ida Morrison

Chicago

Ill.

1048 Warren Ave.

EXERCISE

Write proper superscriptions to letters written to the following : —

1. Thaddeus Bolton, living at 524 Q Street, Lincoln, Nebraska.
2. The wife of a physician of your acquaintance.
3. James B. Angell, President of the University of Michigan, Ann Arbor, Michigan.
4. Your mother, visiting some relative or friend.
5. The publishers Allyn and Bacon, 378 Wabash Avenue, Chicago, Ill.
6. Edward Harrington, living at 1962 Seventh Avenue, New York.
7. To a friend at a seaside resort.
8. To a friend visiting your uncle in Oakland, California.

100. The Great Rule of Letter Writing. — The great rule of letter writing is never to send a letter which you would not be willing to see in print over your own signature. That which you *say* in anger may be discourteous and of little credit to you, but it may in time be forgotten, but that which you *write* may be in existence a hundred years. Thousands of letters are now on exhibition whose authors never had such a use of them in mind. If you ever feel like writing at the end of a letter, " Burn this as soon as you read it," do not send it, but burn the letter yourself. Before you sign your name to any letter read it over and ask yourself, " Is this letter in form and contents one which would do me credit if it should be published ? "

101. Business Letters. — Since the purpose of business letters is to inform, they should, first of all, be characterized by clearness. In asking for information, be sure that you state your questions so that there will be no doubt in the mind of the recipient concerning the information that you desire. In giving information, be equally sure to state facts so clearly that there can be no possibility of a mistake.

Brevity is the soul of business letters as well as of wit. Business men are busy men. They have no time to waste in reading long letters, but wish to gain their information quickly. Hence we should aim to state the desired facts in as concise a manner as possible, and we should give only pertinent facts. Short explanations may sometimes be necessary, but nothing foreign to the subject-matter should ever be introduced. While we should aim to make our letters short, they should not be so brief as to appear abrupt and uncourteous. It shows lack of courtesy to omit important words or to make too frequent use of abbreviations.

We should answer a business letter as soon as possible. This answer, besides giving the desired information, should include a reference to the letter received and an acknowledgment of inclosures, if there be any. All questions should receive courteous replies. The facts should be arranged in a form that will be convenient for the recipient. As a rule it is best to follow the same order which the writer has used in his letter, but in some cases we may be able to state our facts more definitely and concisely if we follow some other order.

What has been said in general about attention to forms in letter writing might well be emphasized here, for business men are keen critics concerning letters received. Be careful to use the correct forms already suggested. Also pay attention to punctuation, spelling, and grammar.

Write only on one side of the paper and fold the letter correctly. In fact, be businesslike in everything connected with the writing of business letters.

A few examples are here given for your notice: —

(1)

Ypsilanti, Mich.
April 4, 1905.

Mr. William Wylie,
    807 Linn St., Peoria, Ill.

Dear Mr. Wylie;
        Inclosed is a letter from Superintendent Rogers of Rockford, Ill. The position of teacher of mathematics is vacant. The salary may not be so much as you now receive, but in many respects the position is a desirable one. I advise you to apply for it.

Sincerely yours,
Charles M. Gates.

(2)

586 State St.,
Chicago, Ill.
July 20, 1905.

Mrs. Charles H. McNett,
    2345 Franklin St.,
        Denver, Colorado.

Dear Madam: — Your card of July 9th is at hand. We beg to say that we sent you the books by express, prepaid, July 9th, and they have probably reached you by this time. If you have not received them, please notify us, and we will send a tracer after them.

Very truly yours,
Brown and Sherman.

(3)

Elgin High School,
Elgin, Ill.
Sept. 4, 1905.

Miss Ella B. Walker,
Herkimer, New York.

My dear Miss Walker:

I am very sorry to have to trouble you, but I am desirous of obtaining some information concerning the High School Library. Will you kindly let me know whether the card catalogue was kept up to date prior to your departure and also whether the accession book was in use up to that time?

I shall be greatly indebted to you if you will give me this information.

Very sincerely yours,
Edward J. Taylor.

EXERCISE

Write at least three of the following suggested letters, paying attention to the rules for writing business letters: —

1. Write to a dry goods firm, asking them to send you one of their catalogues.
2. Write to the manager of a football team of some town near yours, proposing a game.
3. Write the reply.
4. In reply to an advertisement, write an application for the position of clerk or bookkeeper.
5. Write to the publishers of some magazine, asking them to change your address from 27 K Street, Toledo, Ohio, to 2011 Prospect Avenue, Beatrice, Nebraska.

6. Suppose yourself doing postgraduate work in your high school. Write to the president of some college, asking him concerning advanced credit.

102. Letters of Friendship. — While a great deal of information may be obtained from some letters of friendship, the real purpose of such letters is, usually, not to give information, but to entertain. You will notice that the information derived from letters of friendship differs from that found in business letters. Its nature is such that of itself it gives pleasure. Our letters to our relatives, friends, and acquaintances are but visits on paper, and it should be our purpose to make these visits as enjoyable as possible.

So much depends upon the circumstances attendant upon the writing of letters of friendship, that it is impossible to make any definite statement as to what they should contain. We may say in general that they should contain matter interesting to the recipient, and that they should be characterized by vividness and naturalness. Interesting material is a requisite, but that of itself is not sufficient to make an entertaining letter. Interesting material may be presented in so unattractive and lifeless a manner that much of its power to please is lost. Let your letters be full of life and spirit. In your descriptions, narrations, and explanations, express yourself so clearly and so vividly that those who read your letters will be able to understand exactly what you mean.

EXERCISES

1. Write a letter to a classmate who has moved to another town, telling him of the school of which he was once a member.

2. Write to a friend, describing your visit to the World's Fair at St. Louis.

3. Suppose yourself away from home. Write a letter to your little brother or sister at home.

4. If you have ever been abroad, describe in a letter some place of interest that you have visited.

5. Write to a friend who is fond of camping, about your camping experience.

6. Suppose your mother away from home on a visit. Write her about the home life.

7. Write to a friend, describing a party that you recently attended.

8. Suppose you have moved from one town to another. In a letter compare the two towns.

103. Adaptation to the Reader. — The golden rule of letter writing is to adapt the letter to the reader. While the letter is an expression of yourself, yet it should be that kind of expression which shall most interest and please your correspondent. In business letters the necessity of brevity and clearness forces attention to the selection and arrangement of details. In letters to members of the family or to intimate friends we must include many very minor things, because we know that our correspondent will be interested in them, but a rambling, disjointed jumble of poorly selected and ill-arranged details becomes tedious. What we shall mention is determined by the interests of the readers, and the successful letter writer will endeavor to determine what they wish to know. In writing letters to our friends we should show that sympathetic interest in them and their affairs which we would have if we were visiting with them. On occasion, our congratulations should be prompt and sincere.

In reading letters we must not be hasty to take offense. Many good friendships have been broken because some statement in a letter was misconstrued. The written words convey a meaning very different from that which would have been given by the spoken word, the tone of voice, the smile, and the personal presence. So in our writing we must avoid all that which even borders on complaint, or which may seem critical or fault-finding to the most sensitive.

104. Notes. — Notes may be divided in a general way into two classes, formal and informal. Formal notes include formal invitations, replies, requests, and announcements. Informal notes include informal invitations and replies, and also other short communications of a personal nature on almost every possible subject.

105. Formal Notes. — A formal invitation is always written in the third person. The lines may be of the same length, or they may be so arranged that the lines shall be of different lengths, thus giving the page a somewhat more pleasing appearance. The heading, salutation, complimentary close, and signature are all omitted. The address of the sender may be written below the body of the letter. Many prefer it a little to the left, and the date is sometimes written below it. Others, however, prefer it directly below or a little to the right.

Replies to formal invitations should always be written in the third person, and should in general follow the style of the invitation. The date and the hour of the invitation should be repeated in the reply, and this reply should be sent immediately after receiving the invitation.

A few examples are here given to show the correct forms of both invitations and replies : —

(1)

Mr. and Mrs. Frederick William Thompson
request the pleasure of your company
on Monday evening, December thirtieth,
at half-past eight o'clock.

(2)

Miss Barrows accepts with pleasure Mr. and
Mrs. Thompson's invitation for Monday evening,
December thirtieth, at half-past eight o'clock.

(3)

Mr. Morris regrets that a previous engagement
prevents his accepting Mr. and Mrs. Thompson's
kind invitation for Monday evening, December
the thirtieth.

(4)

Mr. and Mrs. Albert W. Elliott request the
pleasure of Mr. John Barker's company at dinner
on Wednesday, December sixth, at seven o'clock.

1068 Euclid Ave.

(5)

> Mr. Barker regrets his inability to accept Mr. and Mrs. Albert W. Elliott's invitation to dinner at seven o'clock, Wednesday, December sixth.

EXERCISE

1. Write an invitation to a golden wedding.
2. Mrs. Homer A. Payne invites Miss Eva Milton to dine with her next week Thursday at eight o'clock. Write out a formal invitation.
3. Write regrets to Mrs. Payne's invitation.
4. Write an acceptance of the same invitation.
5. Write a formal invitation to a party to be given in honor of your guest, Miss Grace Mason.

106. Informal Notes. — Informal invitations and replies may contain the same subject-matter as formal invitations and replies. The only difference is in the form in which they are written. The informal invitation is in form similar to a letter except that the same exactness about the heading is not required. Sometimes the heading is written and sometimes it is omitted entirely. The address of the one sending the invitation and the date may be written below the body of the note to the left of the signature. The reply to an informal invitation should always be informal, but the date and hour should be repeated as in replies to formal invitations.

A great many informal notes not included in invitations and replies are constantly written. These are simply brief letters of friendship, and the purposes for which they are written are exceedingly varied. When we write congratulations or words of condolence, when we introduce one friend to another, when we thank some one for a gift, and when we give words of advice, and in many other instances, we make use of informal notes. They should be simple, personal, and as a rule confined to but one subject. Notice the following examples of informal notes : —

(1)

My dear Mrs. Lathrop,

Will you not give us the pleasure of your company at dinner, on next Friday evening at seven o'clock? Miss Todd of Philadelphia is visiting us, and we wish our friends to meet her.

Very sincerely yours,

Ethel M. Trainor.

840 Forest Avenue,

Dec. 5, 1905.

(2)

Dec. 6, 1905.

My dear Mrs. Trainor,

I sincerely regret that I cannot accept your invitation to dinner next Friday evening, for I have made a previous engagement which it will be impossible for me to break.

Yours most sincerely,

Emma Lathrop.

(3)

My dear Blanche,

Mr. Gilmore and I are planning for a little party Thursday evening of this week. I hope you have no other engagement for that evening, as we shall be pleased to have you with us.

Very cordially yours,

Margaret Gilmore.

(4)

> My dear Margaret,
>
>   Fortunately I have no other engagement for this week Thursday evening, and I shall be delighted to spend an evening with you and your friends.
>
>   Very sincerely yours,
>   Blanche A. Church.

EXERCISE

Write the following informal notes : —

1. Write to a friend, asking him or her to lend you a book.
2. Write an invitation to an informal trolley, tennis, or golf party.
3. Write the reply.
4. Invite one of your friends to spend his or her vacation with you.
5. Write a note to your sister, asking her to send you your theme that you left at home this morning.
6. Mrs. Edgar A. Snow invites Miss Mabel Minard to dine with her. Write out the invitation.
7. Write the acceptance.

VII. POETRY

107. Purpose of Poetry. — All writing aims to give information or to furnish entertainment (Section 54). Often the same theme may both inform and entertain, though one of these purposes may be more prominent than the other. Prose may merely entertain, or it may so distinctly attempt to set forth ideas clearly that the giving of pleasure is entirely neglected. In poetry the entertainment side is never thus subordinated. Poetry always aims to please by the presentation of that which is beautiful. All real poetry produces an æsthetic effect by appealing to our æsthetic sense; that is, to our love of the beautiful.

In making this appeal to our love of the beautiful, poetry depends both upon the ideas it contains and upon the forms it uses. Like prose, it may increase its æsthetic effect by appropriate phrasing, effective arrangement, and subtle suggestiveness, but it also makes use of certain devices

To the Teacher. — Since the expression of ideas in metrical form is seldom the one best suited to the conditions of modern life, it has not seemed desirable to continue the themes throughout this chapter. The study of this chapter, with suitable illustrations from the poems to which the pupils have access, may serve to aid them in their appreciation of poetry. This appreciation of poetry will be increased if the pupils attempt some constructive work. It is recommended, therefore, that one or more of the simpler kinds of metrical composition be tried. For example, one or two good ballads may be read and the pupils asked to write similar ones. Some pupils may be able to write blank verse.

of language such as rhythm, rhyme, etc., which, though they may occur in writings that would be classed as prose, are characteristic of poetry. Much depends upon the ideas that poetry contains; for mere nonsense, though in perfect rhyme and rhythm, is not poetry. But it is not the idea alone which makes a poem beautiful; it is the form as well. The merely trivial cannot be made beautiful by giving it poetical form, but there are many poems containing ideas of small importance which please us because of the perfection of form. We enjoy them as we do the singing of the birds or the murmuring of the brooks. In fact, poetry is inseparable from its characteristic forms. To sort out, re-arrange, and paraphrase into second-class prose the ideas which a poem contains is a profitless and harmful exercise, because it emphasizes the intellectual side of a work which was created for the purpose of appealing to our æsthetic sense.

108. Rhythm. — There are several special forms peculiar to poetry, by the use of which it adds to the beauty of its effect. Of these, rhythm is the most prominent one, without which no poetry is possible. In its widest sense, rhythm indicates a regular succession of motions, impulses, sounds, accents, etc., producing an agreeable effect. Rhythm in poetry consists of the recurrence of accented and unaccented syllables in regular succession. In writing poetry, care must be taken to make the accented syllable of a word come at the place where the rhythm demands an accent. The regular recurrence of accented and unaccented syllables produces a harmony which appeals to our æsthetic sense and thus enhances for us the beauty of poetry. Read the following selections so as to show the rhythm: —

1. We were crowded in the cabin;
    Not a soul would dare to speak;
  It was midnight on the waters
    And a storm was on the deep.
                                        — JAMES T. FIELDS.

2. Break, break, break,
    At the foot of thy crags, O sea!
  But the tender grace of a day that is dead
    Will never come back to me.
                                        — TENNYSON.

3. Ah, distinctly I remember, it was in the bleak December,
  And each separate dying ember wrought its ghost upon the floor.
                                        — POE.

4. Sweet and low, sweet and low,
    Wind of the western sea,
  Low, low, breathe and blow,
    Wind of the western sea!

  Over the rolling waters go,
    Come from the dying moon and blow,
  Blow him again to me;
    While my little one, while my pretty one sleeps.
                                        — TENNYSON.

5. Stone walls do not a prison make,
    Nor iron bars a cage;
  Minds innocent and quiet take
    That for a hermitage.
                                        — LOVELACE.

6. Merrily swinging on brier and weed,
    Near to the nest of his little dame,
  Over the mountain side or mead,
    Robert of Lincoln is telling his name :
  Bob-o'-link, bob-o'-link,
    Spink, spank, spink,
  Snug and safe is this nest of ours,
    Hidden among the summer flowers.
                    Chee, chee, chee.
                                        — BRYANT.

7. Grow old along with me!
    The best is yet to be,
  The last of life, for which the first was made:
    Our times are in His hand
  Who saith, " A whole I planned,
    Youth shows but half; trust God: see all, nor be afraid!"
                                — BROWNING.

109. Feet. — The metrical effect of the preceding selections is given by the regular recurrence of accented and unaccented syllables. A group of accented and unaccented syllables is called a foot. There are four regular feet in English verse, the iambus, the anapest, trochee, and dactyl. Three irregular feet, the pyrrhic, the spondee, the amphibrach, are occasionally found in lines, but not in entire poems, and are often considered merely as substitutes for regular feet. For the sake of convenience the accented syllables are indicated thus: —, and the unaccented syllables thus: ◡.

An iambus is a foot consisting of two syllables with the accent on the last.

◡ —| ◡ —| ◡ — | ◡ —|◡ — |
Let not ambition mock their useful toil. — GRAY.

◡ —| ◡ —| ◡ —|◡ —|
He prayeth best who loveth best
  ◡ — | ◡ — | ◡ — |
  All things both great and small;
— ◡| ◡ —| ◡ —|◡ —|
For the dear God who loveth us,
  ◡ — | ◡ — |◡ —|
  He made and loveth all. — COLERIDGE.

An anapest is a foot consisting of three syllables with the accent on the last.

◡◡ — |◡ ◡ ◡—|◡◡ —|
I am monarch of all I survey.

⏑ ⏑   _ | ⏑ ⏑   _ | ⏑ ⏑   _ |
I would hide with the beasts of the chase.

A trochee is a foot consisting of two syllables with the accent on the first.

_ ⏑ | _ ⏑ | _ ⏑ | _ ⏑ |
Double, double, toil and trouble.
— SHAKESPEARE.

_ ⏑ | _   ⏑ | _ ⏑ | _ ⏑ |
Let us then be up and doing,
_   ⏑ | _   ⏑ | _ ⏑ | _ |
With a heart for any fate,
_ ⏑ | _ ⏑ | _   ⏑ | _ ⏑ |
Still achieving, still pursuing,
_   ⏑ | _ ⏑ | _ ⏑ | _ |
Learn to labor and to wait.
— LONGFELLOW.

A dactyl is a foot consisting of three syllables with the accent on the first.

_   ⏑ ⏑ | _ ⏑ ⏑ |
Cannon to right of them,
_   ⏑ ⏑ | _ ⏑ ⏑ |
Cannon to left of them,
_   ⏑ ⏑ | _ ⏑ ⏑ |
Cannon in front of them,
_ ⏑   ⏑ | _   ⏑ |
Volleyed and thundered.
— TENNYSON.

It will be convenient to remember that two of these, the iambus and the anapest, have the accent on the last syllable, and that two, the trochee and the dactyl, have the accent on the first syllable.

A spondee is a foot consisting of two syllables, both of which are accented about equally. It is an unusual foot in English poetry.

⏑   _ | _   _ | ⏑   _ | ⏑ _ |
Come now, blow, Wind, and waft us o'er.

A *pyrrhic* is a foot consisting of two syllables both of which are unaccented. It is frequently found at the end of a line.

$$\cup \ \_|\cup \ \_ \ |\cup \ \_|\cup \cup$$

Life is so full of misery.

An *amphibrach* is a foot consisting of three syllables, with the accent on the second.

$$\cup \_\cup \ | \ \cup \_ \ \cup | \ \cup \_ \_ \cup | \ \cup \ \_ \ |$$

Creator, Preserver, Redeemer and friend.

110. Names of Verse. — A single line of poetry is called a verse. A stanza is composed of several verses. When a verse consists of one foot, it is called a monometer; of two feet, a dimeter; of three feet, a trimeter; of four feet, a tetrameter; of five feet, a pentameter; and of six feet, a hexameter.

Monometer.	$\_ \ \cup|$ Slowly.
Dimeter.	$\_ \ \cup \ \cup | \_ \ \cup \cup|$ Emblem of happiness.
Trimeter.	$\_ \ \cup|\_\cup| \_ \ \cup \ |$ Like a poet hidden.
Tetrameter.	$\_ \ \cup \ | \_ \ \cup| \ \_ \ \cup \ |\_ \ \ \cup \ |$ Tell me not in mournful numbers.
Pentameter.	$\cup \ \_ \ |\cup \ \_|\cup \ \_|\cup \ \ \_| \cup \ \ \ \_ \ |$ O, what a goodly outside falsehood hath.
Hexameter.	$\_ \ \cup \cup| \_\cup \ \ \cup| \_ \ \cup \ \ \cup \ | \_ \ \cup \cup| \_ \ \ \cup$ This is the forest primeval; the murmuring pines and $\cup \ | \ \_ \ \cup \ |$ the hemlocks.

When we say that a verse is of any particular kind, we do not mean that every foot in that line is necessarily of the same kind. Verse is named by stating first the prevailing foot which composes it, and second the number of feet in a line. A verse having four iambic feet is called iambic tetrameter. So we have dactylic hexameter, trochaic pentameter, iambic trimeter, anapestic dimeter, etc.

EXERCISES

A. Mark the accented and unaccented syllables in the following selections, and name the kind of verse : —

> 1. Build me straight, O worthy Master !
>   Stanch and strong, a goodly vessel
> That shall laugh at all disaster
> And with wave and whirlwind wrestle.
>
> — LONGFELLOW.

> 2. I know not where His islands lift
>   Their fronded palms in air,
> I only know I cannot drift
>   Beyond His love and care.
>
> — WHITTIER.

> 3. For tho' from out our bourne of Time and Place
>   The flood may bear me far,
> I hope to see my Pilot face to face
>   When I have crossed the bar.
>
> — TENNYSON.

4. Chanting of labor and craft, and of wealth in the pot and the garner ;
   Chanting of valor and fame, and the man who can fall with the foremost,
   Fighting for children and wife, and the field which his father bequeathed him,
   Sweetly and solemnly sang she, and planned new lessons for mortals.

> — KINGSLEY.

> 5. Have you read in the Talmud of old,
>   In the Legends the Rabbins have told,
>   Of the limitless realms of the air,
>   Have you read it, — the marvelous story
>   Of Sandalphon, the Angel of Glory,
>   Of Sandalphon, the Angel of Prayer ?
>
> — LONGFELLOW.

B. 1. Find three poems written in iambic verse, and three written in trochaic verse.

2. Write at least one stanza, using iambic verse.

3. Write at least one stanza, using the same kind of verse that you find in Tennyson's " Charge of the Light Brigade."

4. Write two anapestic lines.

111. Variation in Rhythm. — The name given to a verse is determined by the foot which prevails, but not every foot in the line needs to be of the same kind. Just as in music we may substitute a quarter for two eighth notes, so may we in poetry substitute one foot for another, provided it is given the same amount of time.

Notice in the following that the rhythm is perfect and the beat regular, although a three-syllable anapest has been substituted in the second line for a two-syllable iambus : —

$$\smile — | \cdot \smile \quad — | \smile \quad — | \smile \quad — | \smile \quad — |$$
Beneath those rugged elms, that yew tree's shade,
$$\smile \quad — \ | \smile \quad — | \smile —| \smile \smile —| \smile \quad — \ |$$
Where heaves the turf in many a moldring heap,
$$— \quad \smile | \smile \quad —| \smile \quad — | \smile \quad —| \smile —|$$
Each in his narrow cell for ever laid,
$$\smile \quad — | \smile \quad —| \smile \quad — \ |\smile —|$$
The rude forefathers of the hamlet sleep.

The following from *Evangeline* illustrates the substitution of trochees for dactyls : —

$$— \quad \smile \quad \smile | \ — \smile | \ — \quad \smile \quad \smile| — \quad \smile \quad \smile|—\smile \smile| — \smile|$$
Waste are those pleasant farms, and the farmers forever departed.
$$— \quad \smile \quad \smile | \ — \quad \smile | \ — \quad \smile \quad \smile | \ — \quad \smile| — \quad \smile \quad \smile|—\quad \smile$$
Scattered like dust and leaves, when the mighty blasts of October
$$— \quad \smile \quad \smile | \ — \quad \smile | \ — \quad \smile| — \quad \smile | \ — \quad \smile \quad \smile | —\smile| — \smile|$$
Seize them and whirl them aloft, and sprinkle them far o'er the ocean.
$$— \quad \smile \quad \smile|—\smile \quad \smile | \ — \quad \smile \quad \smile | \ — \quad \smile \smile|—\smile \quad \smile| \ — \quad \smile$$
Naught but tradition remains of the beautiful village of Grand-Pre.

It is evident that one foot can be substituted for another if the accent is not changed. Since both the iambus and the anapest are accented on the last syllable, they may be interchanged. The trochee and the dactyl are both accented on the first syllable and may, therefore, be interchanged.

There are some exceptions to the general rule just stated that in substituting one foot for another the accented syllable must be kept in the same part of the foot. Occasionally a poem in which the prevailing foot is iambic has a trochee for the first foot in order to start out with an accented syllable. At the beginning of a line the change of accent is scarcely noticeable.

$$\_\cup \mid \cup \_\mid \cup \_\mid \cup \_\mid$$
Over the rail my hand I trail.

$$\_\cup \mid \cup \_\mid \cup \_\mid \cup \_\mid$$
Silent the crumbling bridge we cross!

But if the reader has once fallen into the swing of iambic verse, the substitution of a trochee will bring the accent at an unexpected place, thus interrupting the smooth flow of the rhythm and producing a harsh and jarring effect. Such a change of accent is justified only when the sense of the verse leads the reader to expect the changed accent, or when the emphasis thus given to the sense of the poem more than compensates for the break in the rhythm produced by the change of accent.

Another form of metrical variation is that in which there are too few or too many syllables in a foot. This generally occurs at the end of a line, but may occur at the beginning. If the addition or omission of a syllable is skillfully done, the rhythm will be unbroken.

With the feet accented on the last syllable, the iambus

and the anapest, an extra syllable may be added at the
end of a line.

> ‿ — | ‿ ‿ — | ‿ — | ‿
> I stood on the bridge at midnight,
>   ‿ ‿ — | ‿ — | ‿ ‿ — |
>   As the clocks were striking the hour;
> ‿ ‿ — | ‿ — | ‿ — | ‿
> And the Moon rose o'er the city,
>   ‿ — | ‿ — | ‿   — |
>   Behind the dark church tower.

> —LONGFELLOW.

> ‿ — | ‿ — | ‿ — | ‿ — | ‿   — | ‿ — |
> Girt round with rugged moun[tains], the fair Lake Constance lies,
> ‿ — | ‿ — | ‿ — | ‿   — | ‿ — | ‿ — |
> In her blue heart reflect[ed] shine back the starry skies;
> ‿   — | ‿ — | ‿ — | ‿ — | ‿ — | ‿ — |
> And watching each white cloud[let] float silently and slow,
> ‿ — | ‿ — | ‿ — | ‿ — | ‿ — | ‿ — |
> You think a piece of heav[en] lies on our earth below.

> —ADELAIDE A. PROCTER.

In the second illustration the extra syllables have the
same relative position in the metrical scheme as in the
first, though they appear to be in the middle of the line.
The pauses fill in the time and preserve the rhythm
unbroken.

With the feet accented on the first syllable, the trochee
and the dactyl, a syllable may be omitted from the end of
a line as in the second and fourth below.

> — ‿ ‿ | — ‿ ‿ | — ‿ ‿ | — ‿ |
> Up with the lark in the first flush of morning,
> — ‿ ‿ | — ‿ ‿ | — ‿ ‿ | — |
> Ere the world wakes to its work or its play;
> — ‿ ‿ | — ‿ ‿ | — ‿ ‿ | — ‿ |
> Off for a spin to the wide-stretching country,
> — ‿ ‿ | — ‿ ‿ | — ‿ | — |
> Far from the close, stifling city away.

Sometimes we find it necessary to suppress a syllable
in order to make the rhythm more nearly perfect. Sylla-

bles may be suppressed in two ways : by suppressing a
vowel at the end of a word when the next word commences with a vowel ; by suppressing a vowel within a
word. The former method is termed elision, and the
latter, slurring.

Thou glorious mirror where the Almighty's form
Glasses itself in tempests.

— BYRON.

An accented syllable often takes the place of an entire
foot. This occurs most frequently at the end of a line,
but it is sometimes found at the beginning. Occasionally
whole lines are formed in this way. If a pause or rest is
made, the rhythm will be unbroken.

Break, break, break,
On thy cold gray stones, O sea !
And I would that my tongue could utter
The thoughts that arise in me.

— TENNYSON.

We frequently find verses in which a syllable is lacking
at the close of the line ; we also find many verses in
which an extra syllable is added. Verse that contains
the number of syllables required by its meter is said to be
acatalectic ; if it contains more than the required number
of syllables, it is said to be hypercatalectic ; and if it
lacks a syllable, it is termed catalectic. It is difficult to
tell whether a line has the required number of syllables
or not when it is taken by itself; but by comparing it
with the prevailing kind of lines in the rest of the stanza

we are enabled to tell whether it is complete or not.
Shakespeare's *Julius Cæsar* is written in iambic pentameter verse. Knowing this, we can detect the hypercatalectic and catalectic lines.

⌣ _| ⌣ _| ⌣ _| ⌣ _ |⌣_ |
You all did see that on the Lupercal

⌣ _ | ⌣ _| ⌣ _ |⌣_ |⌣ _ |
I thrice presented him a kingly crown

⌣ _| ⌣ _ |⌣_ | ⌣ _| ⌣_| ⌣
Which he did thrice refuse. Was this ambition?

⌣ _| ⌣ _| ⌣ _| ⌣ _|⌣
Yet Brutus says he was ambitious.

— SHAKESPEARE.

112. Cesura. — Besides the pauses caused by rests or
silences there is the cesural pause which needs to be considered in reading verse. A cesura is a pause determined
by the sense. It coincides with some break in the sense.
It is found in different parts of the verse and may be
entirely lacking. Its observance does not noticeably interfere with the rhythm. In the following selection it is
marked thus : ‖.

⌣ _| ⌣ _ | ⌣_| ⌣ _ |
The sun came up ‖ upon the left,

_ ⌣| ⌣ _ | ⌣ _|
Out of the sea ‖ came he ;

⌣ _| ⌣ _ | ⌣ _| ⌣ _ |
And he shone bright, ‖ and on the right

⌣ _ | ⌣_|⌣ _|
Went down ‖ into the sea.

— COLERIDGE.

Lives of great men ‖ all remind us
We can make our lives ‖ sublime,
And, departing, ‖ leave behind us,
Footprints ‖ on the sands of time.

— LONGFELLOW.

Read the selections on page 197 so as to indicate the
position of the cesural pauses.

113. **Scansion.** — Scansion is the separation of a line into the feet which compose it. In order to scan a line we must determine the rhythmic movement of it. This determines the accented syllables. Sometimes in scanning merely the accented syllables are marked. Usually the whole metrical scheme is indicated, as in the examples on page 199.

EXERCISE

Scan the following selections. Note substitutions and elisions.

1. The night has a thousand eyes,
   And the day but one;
   Yet the light of the bright world dies
   With the dying sun.
   The mind has a thousand eyes,
   And the heart but one;
   Yet the light of a whole life dies
   When love is gone.
   — FRANCIS W. BOURDILLON.

2. Laugh, and the world laughs with you,
   Weep, and you weep alone;
   For the sad old earth must borrow its mirth,
   But has trouble enough of its own.
   — ELLA WHEELER WILCOX.

3. Hear the robin in the rain,
   Not a note does he complain,
   But he fills the storm's refrain
   With music of his own.
   — CHARLES COKE WOODE.

4. The mistletoe hung in the castle hall,
   The holly branch shone on the old oak wall;
   And the baron's retainers are blithe and gay,
   And keeping their Christmas holiday.
   — THOMAS HAYNES BAGLEY.

114. Rhyme. — Rhyme is a regular recurrence of similar sounds. In a broad sense, it may include sounds either terminal or not, but as here used it refers to terminal sounds.

Just as we expect a recurrence of accent in a line, so may we expect a recurrence of similar sounds at the end of certain lines of poetry. The interval between the rhymes may be of different lengths in different poems, but when the interval is once established, it should be followed throughout the poem. A rhyme out of place jars upon the rhythmic perfection of a stanza just as an accent out of place interferes with the rhythm of the verse.

Not only should the rhymes occur at expected places, but they should be the expected rhymes; that is, real rhymes. If we are expecting a word which will rhyme with *blossom* and find *bosom*, or if we are expecting a rhyme for *breath* and find *beneath*, the effect is unpleasant. The rhymes named above are based on spelling, while a real rhyme is based on sound. A correct rhyme should have precisely the same vowel sounds and the final consonants should be the same, but the initial consonant should be different. For example : *death, breath; home, roam; tongue, young; debating, relating.*

Notice the arrangement of the rhymes in the following selections : —

<blockquote>

1. My soul to-day is far away,
     Sailing the Vesuvian Bay;
     My winged boat, a bird afloat,
     Swims round the purple peaks remote.
                    — T. Buchanan Read.

2. I come from haunts of coot and hern,
     I make a sudden sally,
     And sparkle out among the fern,
     To bicker down the valley.

</blockquote>

By thirty hills I hurry down,
  Or slip between the ridges,
By twenty thorps, a little town,
  And half a hundred bridges.

— TENNYSON.

3. I know it is a sin
    For me to sit and grin
      At him here;
    But the old three-cornered hat
    And the breeches, and all that,
      Are so queer!

— HOLMES.

4. The splendor falls on castle walls
    And snowy summits old in story;
  The long light shakes across the lakes
    And the wild cataract leaps in glory.
Blow, bugle, blow, set the wild echoes flying;
Blow, bugle; answer, echoes; dying, dying, dying.

— TENNYSON.

5. Breathes there a man with soul so dead
    Who never to himself hath said,
      This is my own, my native land!
    Whose heart hath ne'er within him burned
    As home his footsteps he hath turned
      From wandering in a foreign strand!
    If such there be, go mark him well:
    For him no minstrel raptures swell;
    High though his titles, proud his name,
    Boundless his wealth as wish can claim:
    Despite those titles, power, and pelf,
    The wretch concentered all in self,
    Living, shall forfeit fair renown
    And, doubly dying, shall go down
    To the vile dust from whence he sprung,
    Unwept, unhonored, and unsung.

— SCOTT.

115. Blank Verse. — When rhyme is omitted, we have blank verse. This is the most dignified of all kinds of verse, and is, therefore, appropriate for epic and dramatic poetry, where it is chiefly found. Most blank verse makes use of the iambic pentameter measure, but we find many exceptions. Read the following examples of blank verse so as to show the rhythm : —

> 1. So live, that when thy summons comes to join
>   The innumerable caravan that moves
>   To the pale realms of shade, where each shall take
>   His chamber in the silent halls of death,
>   Thou go not like the quarry slave at night
>   Scourged to his dungeon, but, sustained and soothed
>   By an unfaltering trust, approach the grave
>   Like one who wraps the drapery of his couch
>   About him, and lies down to pleasant dreams.
>
> — BRYANT.

> 2.   I stood upon the steps —
>   The last who left the door — and there I found
>   The lady and her friend.   The elder turned
>   And with a cordial greeting took my hand,
>   And rallied me on my forgetfulness.
>   Her eyes, her smile, her manner, and her voice
>   Touched the quick springs of memory, and I spoke
>   Her name.   She was my mother's early friend
>   Whose face I had not seen in all the years
>   That had flown over us, since, from her door,
>   I chased her lamb to where I found — myself.
>
> — HOLLAND.

116. The Stanza. — Some of our verse is continuous like Milton's *Paradise Lost* or Shakespeare's plays, but much of it is divided into groups called stanzas. The lines or verses composing a stanza are bound together by definite principles of rhythm and rhyme. Usually stanzas of the same poem have the same structure, but stanzas of different poems show a variety of structure.

Two of the most simple forms are the couplet and the triplet. They often form a part of a continuous poem, but they are occasionally found in divided poems.

1. The western waves of ebbing day
   Roll'd o'er the glen their level way.
   —SCOTT.

2. A chieftain's daughter seemed the maid;
   Her satin snood, her silken plaid,
   Her golden brooch such birth betray'd.
   —SCOTT.

A stanza of four lines is called a quatrain. The lines of quatrains show a variety in the arrangement of their rhymes. The first two lines may rhyme with each other and the last two with each other; the first and fourth may rhyme and the second and third; or the rhymes may alternate. Notice the example on page 208, and also the following: —

1. I ask not wealth, but power to take
   And use the things I have aright.
   Not years, but wisdom that shall make
   My life a profit and delight.
   —PHŒBE CARY.

2. I count this thing to be grandly true:
   That a noble deed is a step toward God, —
   Lifting the soul from the common sod
   To a purer air and a broader view.
   —HOLLAND.

A quatrain consisting of iambic pentameter verse with alternate rhymes is called an elegiac stanza.

Now fades the glimmering landscape on the sight,
  And all the air a solemn stillness holds,
Save where the beetle wheels his droning flight,
  And drowsy tinklings lull the distant folds.
—GRAY.

The Tennysonian stanza consists of four iambic tetrameter lines in which the first line rhymes with the fourth, and the second with the third.

> Let knowledge grow from more to more,
>   But more of reverence in us dwell;
>   That mind and soul, according well,
> May make one music as before.
>   — TENNYSON.

Five and six line stanzas are found in a great variety. The following are examples : —

> 1. We look before and after,
>   And pine for what is not;
>   Our sincerest laughter
>   With some pain is fraught;
>   Our sweetest songs are those that tell of saddest thought.
>   — SHELLEY.

> 2. And if I should live to be
>   The last leaf upon the tree
>   In the spring,
>   Let them smile as I do now,
>   At the old forsaken bough
>   Where I cling.
>
>   — HOLMES.

> 3. The upper air burst into life;
>   And a hundred fire flags sheen,
>   To and fro they were hurried about;
>   And to and fro, and in and out,
>   The wan stars danced between.
>   — COLERIDGE.

The Spenserian stanza consists of nine lines : the first eight are iambic pentameters, and the last line is an iambic hexameter or Alexandrine. Burns makes use of this stanza in *The Cotter's Saturday Night*. The following stanza from that poem shows the plan of the rhymes : —

> O Scotia! my dear, my native soil!
> For whom my warmest wish to Heaven is sent!

Long may thy hardy sons of rustic toil
 Be blest with health, and peace, and sweet content!
 And oh! may Heaven their simple lives prevent
From luxury's contagion, weak and vile!
 Then, howe'er crowns and coronets be rent,
 A virtuous populace may rise the while,
And stand a wall of fire around their much beloved isle.

EXERCISES

A. Scan the following : —

> Our birth is but a sleep and a forgetting:
> The soul that rises with us, our life's star,
> Hath had elsewhere its setting,
>   And cometh from afar :
> Not in entire forgetfulness,
> And not in utter nakedness,
> But trailing clouds of glory do we come
> From God, who is our home.
>
> — WORDSWORTH.

> Into the sunshine,
> Full of light,
> Leaping and flashing
> From morn to night!
>
> — LOWELL.

B. Name each verse in the following stanza : —

> Hear the sledges with the bells —
> Silver bells!
> What a world of merriment their melody foretells!
> How they tinkle, tinkle, tinkle,
> In the icy air of night!
> While the stars that oversprinkle
> All the heavens seem to twinkle
>   With a crystalline delight —
> Keeping time, time, time,
> In a sort of Runic rhyme
> To the tintinnabulation that so musically wells
> From the bells, bells, bells, bells,
>   Bells, bells, bells —
> From the jingling and the tinkling of the bells.   — POE.

117. Kinds of Poetry. — There are three general classes of poetry: narrative, lyric, and dramatic.

A. Narrative poetry, as may be inferred from its name, relates events which may be either real or imaginary. Its chief varieties are the epic, the metrical romance or lesser epic, the tale, and the ballad.

An epic poem is an extended narrative of an elevated character that deals with heroic exploits which are frequently under supernatural control. This kind of poetry is characterized by the intricacy of plot, by the delineation of noble types of character, by its descriptive effects, by its elevated language, and by its seriousness of tone. The epic is considered as the highest effort of man's poetic genius. It is so difficult to produce an epic that but few literatures contain more than one. Homer's *Iliad* and *Odyssey*, Virgil's *Æneid*, the German *Nibelungenlied*, the Spanish *Cid*, Dante's *Divine Comedy*, and Milton's *Paradise Lost* are important epics found in different literatures.

A *metrical romance* or lesser epic is a narrative poem, shorter and less dignified than the epic. Longfellow's *Evangeline* and Scott's *Marmion* and *Lady of the Lake* are examples of this kind of poetry.

A *metrical tale* is a narrative poem somewhat simpler and shorter than the metrical romance, but more complex than the ballad. Longfellow's *Tales of a Wayside Inn*, Tennyson's *Enoch Arden*, and Lowell's *Vision of Sir Launfal* are examples of the tale.

A *ballad* is the shortest and most simple of all narrative poems. It relates but a single incident and has a very simple structure. In this kind of poetry the interest centers upon the incident rather than on any beauty or elegance of language. Many of the Robin Hood Ballads are well known. Macaulay's *Lays of Ancient Rome* and Longfellow's *Wreck of the Hesperus* are other examples of the ballad. It may be well to note here that it is not always possible to draw definite lines between two different kinds of narrative poetry. In fact, there will sometimes be a difference of opinion as regards the classification.

B. Lyric poetry was the name originally applied to poetry that was to be sung to the accompaniment of the lyre, but now the name is often applied to poems that are not intended to be sung at all. Lyric poetry deals primarily with the feelings and emotions. Love, hate, jealousy, grief, hope, and praise are examples of what may be expressed in lyric poetry. Its chief varieties are the song, the ode, the elegy, and the sonnet.

A song is a short poem intended to be sung. Songs may be divided into sacred and secular. *Jerusalem, the Golden*, and *Lead, Kindly Light*, are examples of sacred songs. Secular songs may be patriotic, convivial, or sentimental.

An ode expresses exalted emotion and is more complex in structure than the song. Some of the best odes in our language are Dryden's *Ode to St. Cecelia*, Wordsworth's *Ode on Intimations of Immortality*, Keats's *Ode on a Grecian Urn*, Shelley's *Ode to a Skylark*, and Lowell's *Commemoration Ode*.

An elegy is a lyric pervaded by the feeling of grief or melancholy. Milton's *Lycidas*, Tennyson's *In Memoriam*, and Gray's *Elegy in a Country Churchyard* are all noted elegies.

A sonnet is a lyric poem of fourteen lines which deals with a single idea or sentiment. It is not a stanza taken from a poem, but is a complete poem itself. In the Italian sonnet and those modeled after it, the emotional feeling rises through the first two quatrains, reaching its climax at or near the end of the eighth line, and then subsides through the two tercets which make up the remaining six lines. If the sentiment expressed does not adjust itself to this ebb and flow, it is not suitable for a sonnet. Milton's sonnet on his blindness is one of the best. Notice the emotional transition in the middle of the eighth line. This sonnet will also illustrate the fixed rhyme scheme:—

> When I consider how my life is spent
> Ere half my days, in this dark world and wide,
> And that one talent, which is death to hide,
> Lodged with me useless, though my soul more bent
> To serve therewith my Maker, and present
> My true account, lest he, returning, chide;
> Doth God exact day labor, light denied?
> I fondly ask. But Patience, to prevent
> That murmur, soon replies, God doth not need,
> Either man's work or his own gifts. Who best
> Bear his mild yoke, they serve him best. His state
> Is kingly; thousands at his bidding speed,
> And post o'er land and ocean without rest;
> They also serve who only stand and wait.

There is a form of sonnet called the Shakespearean which differs in its arrangement from the Italian sonnet.

C. Dramatic poetry relates the occurrence of human events, and is designed to be spoken on the stage. If the drama has an unhappy ending, it is *a tragedy*. As is becoming in such a theme, the language is dignified and impressive, and the whole appeals to our deeper emotions. If the drama has a happy conclusion, it is *a comedy*. Here the movement is quicker, the language less dignified, and the effort is to make the whole light and amusing.

PART II

Description, Narration, Exposition, and Argument have been treated in an elementary way in Part I. A more extensive treatment of each is given in Part II. It has been deemed undesirable to repeat in Part II many things which have been previously treated. The treatment of any one of the forms of discourse as given in Part II is not complete. By reference to the index all the sections treating of any phase of any one subject may be found.

See page 224, *C*.

(218)

VIII. DESCRIPTION

118. Description Defined. — By means of our senses we gain a knowledge of the world. We see, hear, taste, smell, and feel; and the ideas so acquired are the fundamental elements of our knowledge, without which thinking would be impossible. It, therefore, happens that much of the language that we use has for its purpose the transmission to others of such ideas. Such writing is called description. We may, therefore, define description as that form of discourse which has for its purpose the formation of an image.

As here used, the term *image* applies to any idea presented by the senses. In a more limited sense it means the mental picture which is formed by aid of sight. It is for presenting images of this kind that description is most often employed. It is most frequently concerned with images of objects seen, less frequently with sounds, and seldom with ideas arising through touch, taste, and smell. In this chapter, therefore, we shall consider chiefly the methods of using language for the purpose of arousing images of objects seen.

119. Order of Observation. — In description we shall find it of advantage to use such language that the reader will form the image in the same way he would form an image from actual observation. There is a customary and natural order of observation, and if we present our material in that same order, the mind more easily forms the desired image.   Our first need in the study of description is to determine what this natural order of observation is.

Look at the building across the street.   Your *first* impression is that of size, shape, and color.   Almost instantly, but nevertheless *secondly*, you add certain details as to roof, door, windows, and surroundings.   Further observation adds to the number of details, such as the size of the window panes or the pattern of the lattice work.   Our first glance may assure us that we see a train, our second will tell us how many cars, our third will how us that each car is marked Michigan Central.   The oftener we look or the longer we look, the greater is the number of details of which we become conscious.   Any number of illustrations will show that we first see the general outline, and after that the details.   We do not observe the details one by one and then combine them into an object, but we first see the object as a whole, and our first impression becomes more vivid as we add detail after detail.

Following this natural order of observation a description should begin with a sentence that will give the reader a general impression of the whole.   Notice how this is done in the following selections.   After reading the italicized sentence in each, consider the image that it has caused you to form.

The door opened upon the main or living room. *It was a long apartment with low ceiling and walls of hewn logs chinked and plastered and all beautifully whitewashed and clean.*   The tables, chairs, and benches were all homemade.   On the floor were magnificent skins of wolf, bear, musk ox, and mountain goat.   The walls were decorated with heads and horns of deer and mountain sheep, eagle's wings, and a beautiful breast of a loon, which Gwen had shot and of which she was very proud.   At one end of the room a huge stone fireplace stood radiant in its summer decorations of ferns and grasses and wildflowers.   At the other end a door opened into another room, smaller, and richly furnished with relics of former grandeur.

— CONNOR: *The Sky Pilot.*

The stranger was of middle height, loosely knit and thin, with a cunning, brutal face. He had a bullet-shaped head, with fine, soft, reddish brown hair; a round, stubbly beard shot with gray; and small, beady eyes set close together.   He was clothed in an old, black, grotesquely fitting cutaway coat, with coarse trousers tucked into his boot tops.   A worn visored cloth cap was on his head.   In his right hand he carried an old muzzle-loading shotgun.

— GEORGE KIBBE TURNER : *Across the State* (" McClure's ").

120.   The Fundamental Image. — The first impression of the object as a whole is called the fundamental image. The beginning of a description should cause the reader to form a correct general outline, which will include the main characteristics of the object described.   While the fundamental image lacks definiteness and exactness, yet it must be such that it shall not need to be revised as we add the details.   If one should begin a description by saying, " Opposite the church there is a large two-story, brick house with a conservatory on the left," the reader would form at once a mental picture including the essential features of the house.   Further statements about the roof, the windows, the doors, the porch, the yard, and the fence, would each add something to the picture until it was complete.   The impression with which the reader started would be added to, but not otherwise changed.   But if we should conclude the description with the statement, " This house was distinguished from its neighbors by the fact that it was not of the usual rectangular form, but was octagonal in shape," the reader would find that the image which he had formed would need to be entirely changed. It is evident that if the word *octagonal* is to appear at all, it must be at the beginning.   Care must be taken to place all the words that affect the fundamental image in the sentence that gives the general characteristics of that which we are describing.

Hawthorne begins *The House of the Seven Gables* as follows : —

> Halfway down a by-street of one of our New England towns stands a rusty wooden house, with seven acutely peaked gables, facing towards various points of the compass, and a huge, clustered chimney in the midst. The street is Pyncheon street; the house is the old Pyncheon house ; and an elm tree, of wide circumference, rooted before the door, is familiar to every town-born child by the title of the Pyncheon elm. On my occasional visits to the town aforesaid, I seldom failed to turn down Pyncheon street, for the sake of passing through the shadow of these two antiquities, — the great elm tree and the weather-beaten edifice.

Later he gives a detailed description of the house on the morning of its completion as follows : —

> Maule's lane, or Pyncheon street, as it were now more decorous to call it, was thronged, at the appointed hour, as with a congregation on its way to church. All, as they approached, looked upward at the imposing edifice, which was henceforth to assume its rank among the habitations of mankind. There it rose, a little withdrawn from the line of the street, but in pride, not modesty. Its whole visible exterior was ornamented with quaint figures, conceived in the grotesqueness of a Gothic fancy, and drawn or stamped in the glittering plaster, composed of lime, pebbles, and bits of glass, with which the woodwork of the walls was overspread. On every side the seven gables pointed sharply towards the sky, and presented the aspect of a whole sisterhood of edifices, breathing through the spiracles of one great chimney. The many lattices, with their small, diamond-shaped panes, admitted the sunlight into hall and chamber, while, nevertheless, the second story, projecting far over the base, and itself retiring beneath the third, threw a shadowy and thoughtful gloom into the lower rooms. Carved globes of wood were affixed under the jutting stories. Little spiral rods of iron beautified each of the seven peaks. On the triangular portion of the gable, that fronted next the street,

was a dial, put up that very morning, and on which the sun was still marking the passage of the first bright hour in a history that was not destined to be all so bright. All around were scattered shavings, chips, shingles, and broken halves of bricks; these, together with the lately turned earth, on which the grass had not begun to grow, contributed to the impression of strangeness and novelty proper to a house that had yet its place to make among men's daily interests.

EXERCISES

A. Select the sentence or part of a sentence which gives the fundamental image in each of the following selections : —

1. It was a big, smooth-stone-faced house, product of the 'Seventies, frowning under an outrageously insistent Mansard, capped by a cupola, and staring out of long windows overtopped with "ornamental" slabs. Two cast-iron deer, painted death-gray, twins of the same mold, stood on opposite sides of the front walk, their backs toward it and each other, their bodies in profile to the street, their necks bent, however, so that they gazed upon the passer-by — yet gazed without emotion. Two large, calm dogs guarded the top of the steps leading to the front door; they also were twins and of the same interesting metal, though honored beyond the deer by coats of black paint and shellac.

— BOOTH TARKINGTON : *The Conquest of Canaan* ("Harper's").

2. At the first glance, Phœbe saw an elderly personage, in an old-fashioned dressing gown of faded damask, and wearing his gray or almost white hair of an unusual length. It quite overshadowed his forehead, except when he thrust it back, and stared vaguely about the room. After a very brief inspection of his face, it was easy to conceive that his footstep must necessarily be such an one as that which, slowly, and with as indefinite an aim as a child's first journey across a floor, had just brought him hitherward. Yet there were no tokens that his physical strength might not have sufficed for a free and determined gait. It was the spirit of a man that could not walk. The expression of his countenance — while, notwithstanding, it had the light of reason in it — seemed to waver, and glimmer, and nearly to die away, and feebly to recover itself again. It was like a flame which we see twinkling among half-extinguished embers ; we gaze at

it more intently than if it were a positive blaze, gushing vividly upward — more intently, but with a certain impatience, as if it ought either to kindle itself into satisfactory splendor, or be at once extinguished.

— HAWTHORNE : *The House of the Seven Gables.*

3. One of the best known of the flycatchers all over the country is the kingbird. He is a little smaller than a robin, and all in brownish black, with white breast. He has also white tips to his tail feathers, which look very fine when he spreads it out wide in flying. Among the head feathers of the kingbird is a small spot of orange color. This is called in the books a "concealed patch," because it is seldom seen, it is so hidden by the dark feathers.

— MARY ROGERS MILLER : *The Brook Book.*

(Copyright, 1902, by Doubleday, Page and Co.)

Notice the use of a comparison in establishing a correct fundamental image in example 3.

B. Select five buildings with which the members of the class are familiar. Write a single sentence for each, giving the fundamental image. Read these sentences to the class. Let them determine for which building each is written.

C. Notice the pictures on page 218. Write a single sentence for each, giving the fundamental image.

Theme LII. — *Write a paragraph, describing something with which you are familiar.*

Suggested subjects : —

    1. The county court house.

    2. The new church.

    3. My neighbor's house.

    4. Where we go fishing.

    5. A neighboring lake.

    6. A cozy nook.

(Underscore the sentence that gives the fundamental image. Will the reader get from it at once a correct

general outline of the object to be described ? Will he
need to change the fundamental image as your description
proceeds ?)

121. Point of View. — What we shall see first depends
upon the point of view.   Seen from one position, an
object or a landscape will present a different appearance
from that which it will present when viewed from another
position.   A careful writer will give that fundamental
image that would come from actual observation if the
reader were looking at the scene described from the point
of view chosen by the writer.   He will not include
details that cannot be seen from that position even
though he knows that they exist.

Notice that the following descriptions include only that
which can be seen from the place indicated in the italicized phrases : —

Forward from the bridge he beheld a landscape of wide valleys and
irregular heights, with groves and lakes and fanciful houses linked
together by white paths and shining streams.   The valleys were
spread below, that the river might be poured upon them for refresh-
ment in day of drought, and they were as green carpets figured with
beds and fields of flowers and flecked with flocks of sheep white as
balls of snow ; and the voices of shepherds following the flocks were
heard afar.   As if to tell him of the pious inscription of all he beheld,
the altars out under the open sky seemed countless, each with a
white-gowned figure attending it, while processions in white went
slowly hither and thither between them ; and the smoke of the altars
half risen hung collected in pale clouds over the devoted places.

                                 — WALLACE : *Ben-Hur.*
                              (Copyright, 1880.   Harper and Bros.)

The house stood unusually near the river, facing eastward, and
standing four-square, with an immense veranda about its sides, and
a flight of steps in front, spreading broadly downward, as we open
our arms to a child.   *From the veranda* nine miles of river were seen ;
and in their compass near at hand, the shady garden full of rare and

beautiful flowers; farther away broad fields of cane and rice, and the distant quarters of the slaves, and on the horizon everywhere a dark belt of cypress forest.

— CABLE : *Old Creole Days.*

122. Selection of Details Affected by Point of View. — A skillful writer will not ask his reader to perform impossible feats. We cannot see the leaves upon a tree a mile away, and so should not describe them. The finer effects and more minute details should be included only when our chosen point of view brings us near enough to appreciate them. In the selection below, Stevenson tells only as much about Swanston cottage as can be seen at a distance of six miles.

So saying she carried me around the battlements *towards the opposite or southern side of the fortress and indeed to a bastion* almost immediately overlooking the place of our projected flight. Thence we had a view of some foreshortened suburbs at our feet, and beyond of a green, open, and irregular country rising towards the Pentland Hills. The face of one of these summits (say two leagues from where we stood) is marked with a procession of white scars. And to this she directed my attention.

" You see those marks ? " she said. " We call them the Seven Sisters. Follow a little lower with your eye, and you will see a fold of the hill, the tops of some trees, and a tail of smoke out of the midst of them. That is Swanston cottage, where my brother and I are living."

— STEVENSON : *St. Ives.*
(Copyright, 1897. Charles Scribner's Sons.)

Notice in the selection below that for objects *near at hand* details so small as the lizard's eye are given, but that these details are not given, when we are asked to observe things far away.

Slow though their march had been, by this time *they had come to the end of the avenue, and were in the wide circular sweep before the castle.* They stopped here, and stood looking off over the garden, with its somber cypresses and bright beds of geranium, down upon the valley, dim and luminous in a mist of gold. Great, heavy, fantastic-shaped clouds, pearl-white with pearl-gray shadows, piled themselves up against the scintillant dark blue of the sky. In and out among the rose trees *near at hand*, where the sun was hottest, heavily flew, with a loud bourdonnement, the cockchafers promised by Annunziata, — big, blundering, clumsy, the scorn of their light-winged and business-like competitors, the bees. Lizards lay immobile as lizards cast in bronze, only their little glittering, watchful pin heads of eyes giving sign of life. And of course the blackcaps never for a moment left off singing.

—HENRY HARLAND : *My Friend Prospero* ("McClure's").

We round a corner of the valley, and beyond, far below us, looms the town of Sorata. From this distance the red tile roofs, the soft blue, green, and yellow of its stuccoed walls, look indescribably fresh and grateful. A closer inspection will probably dissipate this impression; it will be squalid and dirty, the river-stone paving of its street will be deep in the accumulation of filth, dirty Indian children will swarm in them with mangy dogs and bedraggled ducks, the gay frescoes of its walls will peel in ragged patches, revealing the 'dobe of their base, and the tile roofs will be cracked and broken. But from the heights at this distance and in the warm glow of the afternoon sun it looks like a dainty fairy village glistening in a magic splendor against the Titanic setting of the Andes.

—CHARLES JOHNSON POST: *Across the Highlands of the World*
("Harper's").

Come on, sir; here's the place. Stand still. How fearful
And dizzy 'tis to cast one's eyes so low!
The crows and choughs that wing the midway air
Show scarce so gross as beetles. Halfway down
Hangs one that gathers sampire, dreadful trade!
Methinks he seems no bigger than his head.
The fishermen that walk upon the beach
Appear like mice; and yond tall anchoring bark
Diminish'd to her cock; her cock, a buoy
Almost too small for sight. The murmuring surge,
That on the unnumber'd idle pebble chafes,
Cannot be heard so high. I'll look no more,
Lest my brain turn and the deficient sight
Topple down headlong.

—SHAKESPEARE : *King Lear.*

123. Implied Point of View. — Often the point of view is not specifically stated, but the language of the description shows where the observer is located. Often such an implied point of view gives a delicate touch to a description that could not be obtained by direct statements.

In which of the following selections is it merely implied?

1. Thus pondering and dreaming, he came by the road down a gentle hill with close woods on either hand; and so into the valley with a swift river flowing through it; and on the river a mill. So white it stood among the trees, and so merrily whirred the wheel as the water turned it, and so bright blossomed the flowers in the garden, that Martimor had joy of the sight, for it reminded him of his own country.

— HENRY VAN DYKE : *The Blue Flower.*
(Copyright, 1902. Charles Scribner's Sons.)

2. There is an island off a certain part of the coast of Maine, — a little rocky island, heaped and tumbled together as if Dame Nature had shaken down a heap of stones at random from her apron, when she had finished making the larger islands, which lie between it and the mainland. At one end, the shoreward end, there is a tiny cove, and a bit of silver sand beach, with a green meadow beyond it, and a single great pine; but all the rest is rocks, rocks. At the farther end the rocks are piled high, like a castle wall, making a brave barrier against the Atlantic waves; and on top of this cairn rises the lighthouse, rugged and sturdy as the rocks themselves, but painted white, and with its windows shining like great, smooth diamonds. This is Light Island.

— LAURA E. RICHARDS : *Captain January.*

124. Changing Point of View. — We cannot see the four sides of a house from the same place, though we may wish to have our reader know how each side looks. It is, therefore, necessary to change our point of view. It is immaterial whether the successive points of view are named or merely implied, providing the reader has due notice that we have changed from one to the other, and that for each we describe only what can be seen from that position. A description of a cottage that by its wording leads us to think ourselves inside of the building and then tells about the yard would be defective.

Notice the changing point of view in the following : —

At long distance, looking over the blue waters of the Gulf of St. Lawrence in clear weather, you might think that you saw a lonely sea gull, snow-white, perching motionless on a cobble of gray rock. Then, as your boat drifted in, following the languid tide and the soft southern breeze, you would perceive that the cobble of rock was a rugged hill with a few bushes and stunted trees growing in the crevices, and that the gleaming speck near the summit must be some kind of a building, — if you were on the coast of Italy or Spain you would say a villa or a farmhouse. Then as you floated still farther north and drew nearer to the coast, the desolate hill would detach itself from the mainland and become a little mountain isle, with a flock of smaller islets clustering around it as a brood of wild ducks keep close to their mother, and with deep water, nearly two miles wide, flowing between it and the shore ; while the shining speck on the seaward side stood clearly as a low, whitewashed dwelling with a sturdy, round tower at one end, crowned with a big eight-sided lantern — a solitary lighthouse.

— HENRY VAN DYKE : *The Keeper of the Light.*
(Copyright, 1905. Charles Scribner's Sons.)

125. Place of Point of View in Paragraph. — The point of view may be expressed or only implied or wholly omitted, but in any case the reader must assume one in order to form a clear and accurate image. Beginners will find that they can best cause their readers to form the desired images by stating a point of view. When so stated it must of necessity come early in the paragraph. We have already learned that the beginning of a description should present the fundamental image. For this reason the first sentence of a description frequently includes both the point of view and the fundamental image.

EXERCISES

A. Consider the following selections with reference to —
   (*a*) The point of view.
   (*b*) The fundamental image.
   (*c*) The completeness of the images which you have formed (see Sections 26, 27).

1. The Lunardi [balloon], mounting through a stagnant calm in a line almost vertical, had pierced the morning mists, and now swam emancipated in a heaven of exquisite blue. Below us by some trick of eyesight, the country had grown concave, its horizon curving up like the rim of a shallow bowl — a bowl heaped, in point of fact, with sea fog, but to our eyes with a froth delicate and dazzling as a whipped syllabub of snow. Upon it the traveling shadow of the balloon became no shadow, but a stain; an amethyst (you might call it) purged of all grosser properties than color and lucency. At times thrilled by no perceptible wind, rather by the pulse of the sun's rays, the froth shook and parted; and then behold, deep in the crevasses vignetted and shining, an acre or two of the earth of man's business and fret — tilled slopes of the Lothians, ships dotted on the Firth, the capital like a hive that some child had smoked — the ear of fancy could almost hear it buzzing.

— STEVENSON : *St. Ives.*
(Copyright, 1897. Charles Scribner's Sons.)

2. When Aswald and Corinne had gained the top of the Capitol, she showed him the Seven Hills and the city, bound first by Mount Palatinus, then by the walls of Servius Tullius, which inclose the hills, and by those of Aurelian, which still surround the greatest part of Rome. Mount Palatinus once contained all Rome, but soon did the imperial palace fill the space that had sufficed for a nation. The Seven Hills are far less lofty now than when they deserted the title of steep mountains, modern Rome being forty feet higher than its predecessor, and the valleys which separated them almost filled up by ruins; but what is still more strange, two heaps of shattered vases have formed new hills, Cestario and Testacio. Thus, in time, the very refuse of civilization levels the rock with the plain, effacing in the moral, as in the material world, all the pleasing inequalities of nature.

— MADAME DE STAËL : *Corinne : Italy.*

B. Select five descriptions from the following books and note whether each has a point of view expressed or implied : —

Cooper : Last of the Mohicans.

Scott : Ivanhoe.

Scott : Lady of the Lake.

Irving : Sketch Book.

Burroughs : Wake Robin.

Van Dyke : The Blue Flower.

Howells : The Rise of Silas Lapham.

Muir : Our National Parks.

Kate Douglas Wiggin : Rebecca of Sunnybrook Farm.

Theme LIII. — *Write a descriptive paragraph beginning with a point of view and a fundamental image.*

Suggested subjects : —

1. The crossroads inn.
2. A historical building.
3. The shoe factory.
4. The gristmill.
5. The largest store in town.
6. The union station.

(In your description underscore the sentence giving the point of view. Can you improve the description by using a different point of view? Will the reader form at once a correct general outline? Will the entire description enable the reader to form a clear and accurate image?)

126. Clear Seeing. — Clear statement depends upon clear seeing. Not only must we choose an advantageous point of view, but we must be able to reproduce what can be seen from that location. We may write a description while we are looking at the object, but it is frequently convenient to do the writing when the object is not visible. Oral descriptions are nearly always made without having the object at hand. When we attempt to describe we examine not the object itself, but our mental image of it. It is evident that at least the essential features of this mental picture must stand out clearly and definitely, or we shall be unable to make our description accurate.

The habit of accurate observation is a desirable acquisition, and our ability in this direction can be improved by effort. It is not the province of this book to provide a series of exercises which shall strengthen habits of accurate observation. Many of your studies, particularly the sciences, devote much attention to training the observing powers, and will furnish many suitable exercises. A few have been suggested below merely to emphasize the point that every successful effort in description must be preceded by a definite exercise in clear seeing.

EXERCISE

1. Walk rapidly past a building. Form a mental picture of it. Write down as many of the details as you can. Now look at the building again and determine what you have left out.

2. Call to mind some building with which you are familiar. Write a list of the details that you recall. Now visit the building and see what important ones you have omitted.

3. While looking at some scene make a note of the important details. Lay this list away for a day. Then recall the scene. After picturing the scene as vividly as you can, read your notes. Do they add anything to your picture?

4. Make a list of the things on some desk that you cannot see but with which you are familiar; for example, the teacher's desk. At the first opportunity notice how accurate your list is.

5. Look for some time at the stained glass windows of a church or at the wall paper of the room. What patterns do you notice that you did not see at first? What colors?

6. Make a list of the objects visible from your bedroom window. When you go home notice what you have omitted.

7. Practice observation contests similar to the following: Let two or more persons pass a store window. Each shall then make a list of what the window contains. Compare lists with one another.

Theme LIV. — *Write a description of some dwelling.*

(Select a house that you can see on the way home. Choose a point of view and notice carefully what can be seen from it. When you are ready to write, form as vivid a mental picture of the house as you can. Write the sentence that gives the fundamental image. Add such of the details as will enable the reader to form an accurate image.)

127. Selection of Essential Details. — After deciding upon a point of view and such general characteristics as are essential to the forming of a correct outline of the object to be described, we must next give our attention to the selection of the details. If our description has been properly begun, this general outline will not be changed, but each succeeding phrase or sentence will add to the clearness and distinctness of the picture.

Our first impression of a house may include windows, but the mention of them later will bring them out clearly on our mental picture much as the details appear when one is developing a negative in photography.

If the peculiarities of an object are such as to effect its general form, they need to be stated in the opening sentence; but when the peculiar or distinguishing characteristic does not affect the form, it may be introduced later. If we say, " On the corner across the street from the post office there is a large, two-story, red brick store," the reader can form at once a general picture of such a store. Only those things which give a general outline have been included. As yet nothing has been mentioned to distinguish the store from any other similar one. If some following sentence should be, " Though not wider, it yet presents a more imposing appearance than its neighbors, because the door has been placed at one side, thus providing a single wide display window instead of two stuffy, narrow ones," a detail has been added which, though not changing the general outline, makes the picture clearer and at the same time emphasizes the distinguishing feature of this particular store.

EXERCISES

1. Observe your neighbor's barn. What would you select as its characteristic feature?
2. Take a rapid glance at some stranger whom you meet. What did you notice most vividly?
3. In what respect does the Methodist church in your city differ from the other church buildings?
4. Does your pet dog differ from others of the same breed in appearance? In actions?

Theme LV. — *Write a descriptive paragraph, using one of the following subjects:* —

    1. A mountain view.
    2. An omnibus.
    3. A fort.
    4. A lighthouse.
    5. A Dutch windmill.
    6. A bend in the river.
    7. A peculiar structure.
    9. The picture on this page.

(Underscore the sentence that pictures the details most essential to the description. Consider the unity of your paragraph. Section 81.)

128. Selection and Subordination of Minor Details. — In many descriptions the minor details are wholly omitted, and in all descriptions many that might have been included have been omitted. A proper number of such details adds interest and clearness to the images; too many but serve to render the whole obscure. If properly selected and effectively presented, minor details add much to the beauty or usefulness of a description, but if strung together in short sentences, the effect may be both tiresome and confusing. A mere catalogue of facts is not a good description. They must be arranged so that those which are the more important shall have the greater prominence, while those of less importance shall be properly subordinated.

Often minor details may be stated in a word or phrase inserted in the sentence which gives the general view. Notice the italicized portion of the following : " Opposite the church, *and partly screened by the scraggly evergreens of a broad, unkempt lawn*, there is a large, octagonal, brick house, with a conservatory on the left." This arrangement adds to the general view and gives a better result than would be obtained by describing, the lawn in a separate sentence. Often a single adjective adds some element to a description more effectively than can be done with a whole sentence. Notice how much is added by the use of *scraggly* and *unkempt*.

EXERCISES

Make a careful study of the following selections with reference to the way in which the minor details are presented. Can any of them be improved by re-arranging them?

1. At night, as I look from my windows over Kassim Pasha, I never tire of that dull, soft coloring, green and brown, in which the brown of roofs and walls is hardly more than a shading of the green of the trees. There is the lonely curve of the hollow, with its small, square, flat houses of wood ; and above, a sharp line of blue-black cypresses on the spine of the hill; then the long desert plain, with its sandy road, shutting in the horizon. Mists thicken over the valley, and wipe out its colors before the lights begin to glimmer out of it. Below, under my windows, are the cypresses of the Little Field of the Dead,

vast, motionless, different every night. Last night each stood clear, tall, apart; to-night they huddle together in the mist, and seem to shudder. The sunset was brief, and the water has grown dull, like slate. Stamboul fades to a level mass of smoky purple, out of which a few minarets rise black against a gray sky with bands of orange fire. Last night, after a golden sunset, a fog of rusty iron came down, and hung poised over the jagged level of the hill. The whole mass of Stamboul was like black smoke; the water dim gray, a little flushed, and then like pure light, lucid, transparent, every ship and every boat sharply outlined in black on its surface; the boats seemed to crawl like flies on a lighted pane.

— ARTHUR SYMONS: *Constantinople : An Impression* ("Harper's").

2. The boy was advancing up the road, carrying a half-filled pail of milk. He was a child of perhaps ten years, exceedingly frail and thin, with a drawn, waxen face, and sick, colorless lips and ears. On his head he wore a thick plush cap, and coarse, heavy shoes upon his feet. A faded coat, too long in the arms, drooped from his shoulders, and long, loose overalls of gray jeans broke and wrinkled about his slender ankles.

— GEORGE KIBBE TURNER : *Across the State* ("McClure's").

3. They met few people abroad, even on passing from the retired neighborhood of the House of the Seven Gables into what was ordinarily the more thronged and busier portion of the town. Glistening sidewalks, with little pools of rain, here and there, along their unequal surface; umbrellas displayed ostentatiously in the shop windows, as if the life of trade had concentered itself in that one article ; wet leaves of the horse-chestnut or elm trees, torn off untimely by the blast, and scattered along the public way ; an unsightly accumulation of mud in the middle of the street, which perversely grew the more unclean for its long and laborious washing ; — these were the more definable points of a very somber picture. In the way of movement, and human life, there was the hasty rattle of a cab or coach, its driver protected by a water-proof cap over his head and shoulders; the forlorn figure of an old man, who seemed to have crept out of some subterranean sewer, and was stooping along the kennel, and poking the wet rubbish with a stick, in quest of rusty nails; a merchant or two, at the door of the post office, together with an editor, and a miscellaneous politician, awaiting a dilatory mail ; a few visages of

retired sea captains at the window of an insurance office, looking out vacantly at the vacant street, blaspheming at the weather, and fretting at the dearth as well of public news as local gossip. What a treasure trove to these venerable quidnuncs, could they have guessed the secret which Hepzibah and Clifford were carrying along with them!

— HAWTHORNE : *The House of the Seven Gables.*

Theme LVI. — *Write a description of one of the following : —*

1. A steamboat.
2. An orchard.
3. A colonial mansion.
4. A wharf.
5. A stone quarry.
6. A shop.

(Consider what you have written with reference to the point of view, fundamental image, and essential details. After these have been arranged to suit you, notice the way in which the minor details have been introduced. Have you given undue prominence to any? Can a single adjective or phrase be substituted for a whole sentence? Think of the image which your words will produce in the mind of the reader. Consider your theme with reference to unity. Section 81.)

129. Arrangement of Details. — The quality of a description depends as much upon the arrangement of the material as upon the selection. Under paragraph development we have discussed the necessity of arranging the details with reference to their natural position in space (see Sections 47 and 86). Such an arrangement is the most desirable one and should be departed from only with good reason. Such departures may, however, be made, as shown in the following selection : —

A pretty picture the lad made as he lay there dreaming over his earthly possessions — a pretty picture in the shade of the great elm, that sultry morning of August, three quarters of a century ago. The presence of the crutch showed there was something sad about it; and so there was; for if you had glanced at the little bare brown foot, set toes upward on the curbstone, you would have discovered that the fellow to it was missing — cut off about two inches above the ankle. And if this had caused you to throw a look of sympathy at his face, something yet sadder must long have held your attention. Set jauntily on the back of his head was a weather-beaten dark blue cloth cap, the patent leather frontlet of which was gone; and beneath the ragged edge of this there fell down over his forehead and temples and ears a tangled mass of soft yellow hair, slightly curling. His eyes were large and of a blue to match the depths of a calm sky above the tree-tops; the long lashes which curtained them were brown; his lips were red, his nose delicate and fine, and his cheek tanned to the color of ripe peaches. It was a singularly winning face, intelligent, frank, not describable. On it now rested a smile, half joyous, half sad, as though his mind was full of bright hopes, the realization of which was far away. From the neck fell the wide collar of a white cotton shirt, clean but frayed at the elbows, and open and buttonless down to his bosom. Over this he wore an old-fashioned satin waistcoat of a man, also frayed and buttonless. His dress was completed by a pair of baggy tow breeches, held up by a single tow suspender fastened to big brown horn buttons.

— James Lane Allen: Flute and Violin.
(Copyright, 1892, Harper and Brothers.)

The details are not stated with reference to their natural position in space, but they are given in the probable order of observation. If we were to look upon such a boy, the crutch would attract our attention. This would lead us to look at once for the reason why the boy needed it. That our sympathy would be aroused would be most expected, and so the writer skillfully uses it as a means of transition to the face. During the remainder of the description the natural position in space is closely followed.

Theme LVII. — *Write a description of one of the following :* —

1. The bayou.
2. Looking down the mountain.
3. Looking up the mountain.
4. The floorwalker.
5. An old-fashioned rig.
6. A house said to be haunted.
7. The deacon.

(Consider the arrangement of details with reference to their position in space. Consider your paragraphs with reference to coherence and emphasis. Sections 82 and 83.)

130. Effectiveness in Description. — Every part of a description should aid in rendering it effective, and this effectiveness is as much the purpose of the principles previously discussed as it is of those which follow. This paragraph is inserted here to separate more or less definitely those things which can be done under direction from those which cannot be determined by rule. Up to this point emphasis has been laid upon the clear presentation of a mental image as the object of description. But this does not go far enough. A point of view, a fundamental image, a judicious selection of essential and minor details and the relating of them with reference to their natural position in space, may set forth an image clearly and yet fail to be satisfactory as a description.

For the practical affairs of life it may be sufficient to limit ourselves to clear images set forth barely and sparely, but there is a pleasure and a profit in using the subtler arts of language, in placing a word here or a phrase there that shall give a touch of beauty or a flash of sugges-

tiveness and so save our descriptions from the commonplace. It is to these less easily demonstrated methods of
giving strength and beauty that we wish now to turn our
attention.

131. Word Selection. — The effectiveness of our description will depend largely upon our right choice of words.
If our range of vocabulary is limited, the possibility of
effective description is correspondingly limited. Only
when our working vocabulary contains many words may
we hope to choose with ease the one most suitable for the
effective expression of the idea we wish to convey. To
prepare a list of words that may apply and then attempt
to write a theme that shall make use of them is a mechanical process of little value. The idea we wish to
express should call up the word that exactly expresses
it. If our ideas are not clear or our vocabulary is limited,
we may be satisfied with the trite and commonplace; but
if our experience has been broad or our reading extended,
we may have at command the word which, because it is
just the right one, gives individuality and force to our
phrasing. Every one is familiar with dogs, and has in
his vocabulary many words which he applies to them, but
a reading of one or two good dog stories, such as *Bob,
Son of Battle*, or *The Call of the Wild*, will show how
wide is the range of such words and how much the description is enhanced by their careful use.

EXERCISE

Consider the following selections with reference to the
choice of words which add to the effectiveness of the
descriptions : —

1. She was a little, brown, thin, almost skinny woman with big,
rolling, violet-blue eyes and the sweetest manners in the world.

2. The sounds and the straits and the sea with its plump, sleepy islands lay north and east and south.

3. The mists of the Cuchullins are not fat, dull, and still, like lowland and inland mists, but haggard, and streaming from the black peaks, and full of gusty lines. We saw them first from the top of Beimna-Caillach, a red, round-headed mountain hard by Bradford, in the isle of Skye.

Shortly after noon the rain came up from the sea and drew long delicate gray lines against the cliffs. It came up licking and lisping over the surface of Cornisk, and drove us to the lee of rocks and the shelter of our ponchos, to watch the mists drifting, to listen to the swell and lull of the wind and the patter of the cold rain. There were glimpses now and then of the inner Cuchullins, a fragment of ragged sky line, the sudden jab of a black pinnacle through the mist, the open mouth of a gorge steaming with mist.

We climbed the great ridge, at length, of rock and wet heath that separates Cornisk from Glen Sligachan, slowly through the fitful rain and driving cloud, and saw Sgurr-nan-Gillian, sharp, black, and pitiless, the northernmost peak and sentinel of the Cuchullins. The yellow trail could be seen twisting along the flat, empty glen. Seven miles away was a white spot, the Sligachan Hotel.

I think it must be the dreariest glen in Scotland. The trail twists in a futile manner, and, after all, is mainly bog holes and rolling rocks. The Red Hills are on the right, rusty, reddish, of the color of dried blood, and gashed with sliding bowlders. Their heads seem beaten down, a Helot population, and the Cuchullins stand back like an army of iron conquerors. The Red Hills will be a vanished race one day, and the Cuchullins remain.

ARTHUR COLTON: The Mists o' Skye ("Harper's").

132. Additional Aids to Effectiveness. — Comparison and figures of speech not only aid in making our picture clear and vivid, but they may add a spice and flavor to our language, which counts for much in the effectiveness and beauty of our description. Notice the following descriptions: —

He was a mongoose, rather like a little cat in his fur and his tail, but quite like a weasel in his head and his habits. His eyes and the end of his restless nose were pink; he could scratch himself anywhere he pleased, with any leg, front or back, that he chose to use; he could fluff up his tail till it looked like a bottle brush, and his war cry as he scuttled through the long grass was Rikk-tikk-tikki-tikki-tikk.

— KIPLING: *Jungle Book.*

Ichabod was a suitable figure for such a steed. He rode with short stirrups, which brought his knees nearly up to the pommel of his saddle; his sharp elbows stuck out like grasshoppers' legs; he carried his whip perpendicularly in his hand, like a scepter, and, as his horse jogged on, the motion of his arms was not unlike the flapping of a pair of wings. A small wool hat rested on the top of his nose, for so his scanty strip of forehead might be called; and the skirts of his black coat fluttered out almost to the horse's tail. Such was the appearance of Ichabod and his steed, as they shambled out of the gate of Hans Van Ripper, and it was altogether such an apparition as is seldom to be met with in broad daylight.

— IRVING: *Legend of Sleepy Hollow.*

Theme LVIII. — *Write a description of one of the following:* —

1. My cat.
2. The pony at the farm.
3. The glen.
4. The prairie.
5. The milldam.
6. The motorman.
7. The picture on this page.

(Consider the effectiveness of your description. Can you improve your choice of words? Have you used comparisons or figures, and if so, do they improve your description? Consider your theme with reference to euphony. Section 16.)

133. **Classes of Objects Frequently Described.** — There is no limit to the things that we may wish to describe, but there are certain general classes of objects that are described more frequently than others. We have greater occasion to describe men or places than we have to describe pictures or trees. A person may be an accurate observer and have a large vocabulary applicable to one class of objects, thus enabling him to describe objects of that class clearly and effectively, though on account of limited experience and small vocabulary he cannot well describe objects belonging to some other class. The ability to observe accurately the classes of objects named below, and to appreciate descriptions of such objects when made by others, is a desirable acquisition. Every effort should be made to master as many as possible of the words applicable to each class of objects. A slight investigation will show how great is the number of such words with which we are unfamiliar.

1. *Descriptions of buildings or portions of buildings.*

In most buildings the basement story is heaviest, and each succeeding story increases in lightness; in the Ducal palace this is reversed, making it unique amongst buildings. The outer walls rest upon the pillars of open colonnades, which have a more stumpy appearance than was intended, owing to the raising of the pavement in the piazza. They had, however, no base, but were supported by a continuous stylobate. The chief decorations of the palace were employed upon the capitals of these thirty-six pillars, and it was felt that the peculiar prominence and importance given to its angles rendered it necessary that they should be enriched and softened by sculpture, which is interesting and often most beautiful. The throned figure of Venice above bears a scroll inscribed : *Fortis, justa, trono furias, mare sub pede, pono.* (Strong and just, I put the furies beneath my throne, and the sea beneath my foot.) One of the corners of the palace joined the irregular buildings connected with St. Mark's, and is not generally seen. There remained, therefore, only three angles to be decorated. The first main sculpture may be called the "Fig-tree angle," and its subject is the "Fall of Man." The second is "the Vine angle," and represents the "Drunkenness of Noah." The third sculpture is "the Judgment angle," and portrays the "Judgment of Solomon."

— HARE: *Venice.*

Theme LIX. — *Write a description of the exterior of some building.*

Theme LX. — *Write a description of some room.*

Theme LXI. — *Write a description of some portion of a building, such as an entrance, spire, window, or stairway.*

(Consider each description with reference to

a. Point of view.

b. Fundamental image.

c. Selection of essential details.

d. Selection and subordination of minor details.

e. Arrangement of details with reference to their natural positions in space.

f. Effective choice of words and comparisons.)

2. *Natural features: valleys, rivers, mountains, etc.*

Beyond the great prairies and in the shadow of the Rockies lie the Foothills. For nine hundred miles the prairies spread themselves out in vast level reaches, and then begin to climb over softly rounded mounds that ever grow higher and sharper, till here and there, they break into jagged points and at last rest upon the great bases of the mighty mountains. These rounded hills that join the prairies to the mountains form the Foothill Country. They extend for about a hundred miles only, but no other hundred miles of the great West are so full of interest and romance. The natural features of the country combine the beauties of prairie and of mountain scenery. There are valleys so wide that the farther side melts into the horizon, and uplands so vast as to suggest the unbroken prairie. Nearer the mountains the valleys dip deep and ever deeper till they narrow into canyons through which mountain torrents pour their blue-gray waters from glaciers that lie glistening between the white peaks far away.

— CONNOR: The Sky Pilot.

> Long lines of cliff breaking have left a chasm ;
> And in the chasm are foam and yellow sands ;
> Beyond, red roofs about a narrow wharf
> In cluster; then a molder'd church ; and higher
> A long street climbs to one tall tower'd mill ;
> And high in heaven behind it a gray down
> With Danish barrows, and a hazelwood,
> By autumn nutters haunted, flourishes
> Green in a cuplike hollow of the down.

— TENNYSON: Enoch Arden.

Theme LXII. — *Write a description of some valley, mountain, field, woods, or prairie.*

Theme LXIII. — *Write a description of some stream, pond, lake, dam, or waterfall.*

(Consider especially your choice of words.)

3. *Sounds or the use of sounds.*

And the noise of Niagara? Alarming things have been said about it, but they are not true. It is a great and mighty noise, but it is not, as Hennepin thought, an "outrageous noise." It is not a roar. It does not drown the voice or stun the ear. Even at the actual foot of the falls it is not oppressive. It is much less rough than the sound of heavy surf — steadier, more homogeneous, less metallic, very deep and strong, yet mellow and soft; soft, I mean, in its quality. As to the noise of the rapids, there is none more musical. It is neither rumbling nor sharp. It is clear, plangent, silvery. It is so like the voice of a steep brook — much magnified, but not made coarser or more harsh — that, after we have known it, each liquid call from a forest hillside will seem, like the odor of grapevines, a greeting from Niagara. It is an inspiriting, an exhilarating sound, like freshness, coolness, vitality itself made audible. And yet it is a lulling sound. When we have looked out upon the American rapids for many days, it is hard to remember contented life amid motionless surroundings; and so, when we have slept beside them for many nights, it is hard to think of happy sleep in an empty silence.

— Mrs. van Rensselaer: *Niagara* (" Century ").

> Yell'd on the view the opening pack ;
> Rock, glen, and cavern, paid them back ;
> To many a mingled sound at once
> The awaken'd mountain gave response.
> A hundred dogs bay'd deep and strong,
> Clatter'd a hundred steeds along,
> Their peal the merry horns rung out,
> A hundred voices join'd the shout ;
> With hark, and whoop, and wild halloo,
> No rest Benvoirlich's echoes knew.
> Far from the tumult fled the roe,
> Close in her covert cower'd the doe ;
> The falcon, from her cairn on high,
> Cast on the rout a wondering eye,
> Till far beyond her piercing ken
> The hurricane had swept the glen.
> Faint, and more faint, its failing din
> Return'd from cavern, cliff, and linn,
> And silence settled, wide and still,
> On the lone wood and mighty hill.
>
> — Scott : *Lady of the Lake.*

Theme LXIV. — *Describe some sound or combination of sounds, or write a description introducing sounds.*

Suggested subjects : —

1. Alone in the house.
2. In the woods at night.
3. Beside the brook.
4. In the factory.
5. A day at the beach.
6. Before the Fourth.
7. On the seashore.

(Notice especially the words that indicate sound.)

4. *Color or the use of color.*

A gray day! soft gray sky, like the breast of a dove; sheeny gray sea with gleams of steel running across; trailing skirts of mist shutting off the mainland, leaving Light Island alone with the ocean; the white tower gleaming spectral among the folding mists; the dark pine tree pointing a somber finger to heaven; the wet, black rocks, from which the tide had gone down, huddling together in fantastic groups as if to hide their nakedness.

—LAURA E. RICHARDS: *Captain January.*

The large branch of the Po we crossed came down from the mountains which we were approaching. As we reached the post road again they were glowing in the last rays of the sun, and the evening vapors that settled over the plain concealed the distant Alps, although the snowy top of the Jungfrau and her companions the Wetterhorn and Schreckhorn rose above it like the hills of another world. A castle or church of brilliant white marble glittered on the summit of one of the mountains near us, and, as the sun went down without a cloud, the distant summits changed in hue to a glowing purple, mounting almost to crimson, which afterwards darkened into a deep violet. The western half of the sky was of a pale orange and the eastern a dark red, which blended together in the blue of the zenith, that deepened as twilight came on.

—TAYLOR: *Views Afoot.*

Theme LXV. — *Write a description in which the color element enters largely.*

5. *Animals, birds, fishes, etc.*

The Tailless Tyke had now grown into an immense dog, heavy of muscle and huge of bone. A great bull head; undershot jaw, square and lengthy and terrible; vicious yellow gleaming eyes; cropped ears; and an expression incomparably savage. His coat was a tawny lionlike yellow, short, harsh, dense; and his back running up from shoulder to loins ended abruptly in a knoblike tail. He looked like the devil of a dog's hell, and his reputation was as bad as his looks. He never attacked unprovoked; but a challenge was never ignored and he was greedy of insults.

—ALFRED OLLIVANT: *Bob, Son of Battle.*
(Copyright, Doubleday and McClure.)

Read the description of the kingbird (page 224), and of the mongoose (page 242).

Theme LXVI. — *Write a description of some animal, bird, or fish.*

(What questions should you ask yourself about each description you write?)

6. *Trees and plants.*

How shall kinnikinnick be told to them who know it not? To a New Englander it might be said that a whortleberry bush changed its mind one day and decided to be a vine, with leaves as glossy as laurel, bells pink-striped and sweet like the arbutus, and berries in clusters and of scarlet instead of black. The Indians call it kinnikinnick, and smoke it in their pipes. White men call it bearberry, I believe; and there is a Latin name for it, no doubt, in the books. But kinnikinnick is the best, — dainty, sturdy, indefatigable kinnikinnick, green and glossy all the year round, lovely at Christmas and lovely among flowers at midsummer, as content and thrifty on bare, rocky hillsides as in grassy nooks, growing in long, trailing wreaths, five feet long, or in tangled mats, five feet across, as the rock or the valley may need, and living bravely many weeks without water, to make a house beautiful. I doubt if there be in the world a vine I should hold so precious, indoors and out.

— HELEN HUNT JACKSON: *Bits of Travel at Home.*

A mango tree is beautiful and attractive. It grows as large as the oak, and has a rich and glossy foliage. The fruit is shaped something like a short, thick cucumber, and is as large as a large pear. It has a thick, tough skin, and a delicious, juicy pulp. When ripe it is a golden color. A tree often bears a hundred bushels of mangoes.

— MARIAN M. GEORGE.

Theme LXVII. — *Write a description of some tree that you have seen.*

(Consider your theme with reference to the general principles of composition treated in Chapter V.)

134. Description of Persons: Character Sketches. — The general principles of description are applicable to the description of a person, and should be followed for the purpose of presenting a clear and vivid image. Our interest, however, so naturally runs beyond the appearance and is concerned with the character, that most descriptions of persons become character sketches. Even the commonest terms of description, such as *keen gray eyes, square chin, rugged countenance*, are interpreted as showing character, thus departing somewhat from pure description. Often the sole purpose of description is to show character, and only those details are introduced which accomplish this purpose.

In life we judge a man's character by his actions, and so in the character sketch we are led to infer his character from what he does. The character indicated by his appearance is corroborated by a statement of his actions and especially by showing how he acts. (See Section 10.) Sometimes no descriptive matter is given, but we are left to make our own picture to fit the character indicated by the actions. In many books the descriptive elements which would enable us to form an image of some person are distributed over several pages, each being introduced where it supplements and emphasizes the character shown by the actions.

Notice the following examples: —

The Rev. Daniel True stood beside the holy table. For such a scene, perhaps for any scene, he was a memorable figure. He had the dignity of early middle life, but none of its signs of advancing age. His hair was quite black, and curled on his temples boyishly; his mustache, not without a worldly cut, was as dark as his hair, and concealed a mouth so clean and fine that it was an ethical mistake to cover it. He had sturdy shoulders, although not quite straight; they had the scholar's stoop; his hands were thin, with long fingers; his gestures were sparing and significant; his expression was so sincere that its evident devoutness commanded respect; so did his voice, which was authoritative enough to be a little priestly and lacking somewhat in elocutionary finish as the voices of ministers are apt to be, but genuine, musical, persuasive, at moments vibrant with oratorical power. He had a warm eye and a lovable smile. He was every inch a minister, but he was every nerve a man.

— ELIZABETH STUART PHELPS: *A Sacrament* ("Harper's").

She was not more than fifteen. Her form, voice, and manner belonged to the period of transition from girlhood. Her face was perfectly oval, her complexion more pale than fair. The nose was faultless; the lips, slightly parted, were full and ripe, giving to the lines of the mouth warmth, tenderness, and trust; the eyes were blue and large, and shaded by drooping lids and long lashes; and, in harmony with all, a flood of golden hair, in the style permitted to Jewish brides, fell unconfined down her back to the pillion on which she sat. The throat and neck had the downy softness sometimes seen which leaves the artist in doubt whether it is an effect of contour or color. To these charms of feature and person were added others more indefinable — an air of purity which only the soul can impart, and of abstraction natural to such as think much of things impalpable. Often, with trembling lips, she raised her eyes to heaven, itself not more deeply blue; often she crossed her hands upon her breast, as in adoration and prayer; often she raised her head like one listening eagerly for a calling voice. Now and then midst his slow utterance, Joseph turned to look at her, and, catching the expression kindling her face as with light, forgot his theme, and with bowed head, wondering, plodded on.

— LEW WALLACE: *Ben-Hur.*
(Copyright, 1880, Harper and Bros.)

When Washington was elected general of the army he was forty-three years of age. In stature he a little exceeded six feet; his limbs were sinewy and well proportioned; his chest broad, his figure stately, blending dignity of presence with ease of manner. His robust constitution had been tried and invigorated by his early life in the wilderness, his habit of occupation out of doors, and his rigid temperance, so that few equalled him in strength of arm or power of endurance. His complexion was florid, his hair dark brown, his head in shape perfectly round. His broad nostrils seemed formed to give expres-

sion and escape to scornful anger. His dark blue eyes, which were
deeply set, had an expression of resignation and an earnestness that
was almost sad.

— BANCROFT.

There were many Englishmen of great distinction there, and Tennyson was the most conspicuous among the guests. Tennyson's appearance was very striking and his figure might have been taken as a
living illustration of romantic poetry. He was tall and stately, wore
a great mass of thick, long hair — long hair was then still worn even
by men who did not affect originality; his frame was slightly stooping, his shoulders were bent as if with the weight of thought; there
was something entirely out of the common and very commanding in
his whole presence, and a stranger meeting him in whatever crowd
would probably have assumed at once that he must be a literary king.
— JUSTIN MCCARTHY: *Literary Portraits from the Sixties* ("Harper's").

The door opened and there appeared to these two a visitor. He
was a young man, and tall, — so tall that, even with his hat off, his
head barely cleared the ceiling of the low-studded room. He was
slim and fair-haired and round-shouldered. He had the pink and
white complexion of a girl; soft, fair hair; dark, serious eyes; the
high, white brow of a thinker; the nose of an aristocrat; and he was
in clerical garb.

— SEWALL FORD : *The Renunciation of Petruo* ("Harper's").

EXERCISE

Notice the pictures on page 253. Can you determine
from the picture anything about the character of the
person? Just what feature in each helps you in this?

Theme LXVIII. — *Describe some person known to most
of the class.*

(Do not name the person, but combine description and
character sketching so that the class may be able to tell
whom you mean.)

135. Impression of a Description. — Often the effectiveness of a description is determined more by the impression
which it makes upon our feelings than by the vividness of

the picture which it presents.   Read the following description of the Battery in New York by Howells.   Notice
how the details which have been selected emphasize the
" impression of forlornness."   The sickly trees, the decrepit shade, the mangy grass plots, hungry-eyed and
hollow children, the jaded women, silent and hopeless, the
shameless houses, the hard-looking men, unite to give
the one impression.   Even the fresh blue water of the
bay, which laughs and dances beyond, by its very contrast
gives greater emphasis to the melancholy and forlorn
appearance of the Battery.

All places that fashion has once loved and abandoned are very melancholy ; but of all such places, I think the Battery is the most forlorn.   Are there some sickly locust trees there that cast a tremulous
and decrepit shade upon the mangy grass plots ?   I believe so, but I
do not make sure ; I am certain only of the mangy grass plots, or
rather the spaces between the paths, thinly overgrown with some
kind of refuse and opprobrious weed, a stunted and pauper vegetation
proper solely to the New York Battery.   At that hour of the summer
morning when our friends, with the aimlessness of strangers who are
waiting to do something else, saw the ancient promenade, a few scant
and hungry-eyed little boys and girls were wandering over this weedy
growth, not playing, but moving listlessly to and fro, fantastic in the
wild inaptness of their costumes.   One of these little creatures wore,
with an odd, involuntary jauntiness, the cast-off best dress of some
happier child, a gay little garment cut low in the neck and short in
the sleeves, which gave her the grotesque effect of having been at a
party the night before.   Presently came two jaded women, a mother
and a grandmother, that appeared, when they crawled out of their
beds, to have put on only so much clothing as the law compelled.
They abandoned themselves upon the green stuff, whatever it was,
and, with their lean hands clasped outside their knees, sat and stared,
silent and hopeless, at the eastern sky, at the heart of the terrible
furnace, into which in those days the world seemed cast to be burnt
up, while the child which the younger woman had brought with her
feebly wailed unheeded at her side.   On one side of the women were
the shameless houses out of which they might have crept, and which

somehow suggested riotous maritime dissipation; on the other side were those houses in which had once dwelt rich and famous folk, but which were now dropping down to the boarding-house scale through various unhomelike occupations to final dishonor and despair. Down nearer the water, and not far from the castle that was once a play-house and is now the depot of emigration, stood certain express wagons, and about these lounged a few hard-looking men. Beyond laughed and danced the fresh blue water of the bay, dotted with sails and smokestacks.

— HOWELLS : *Their Wedding Journey.*

The successive images of the preceding selection are clear enough, but they are bound together by a common purpose, which is the creation of a single impression. Often, however, a description may present, not a single impression, but a series of such impressions, to which a unity is given by the fact that they are all connected with one event, or occur at the same time, or in the same place. This is illustrated in the following : —

It is a phenomenon whose commonness alone prevents it from being most impressive, that departure of the night-express. The two hundred miles it is to travel stretch before it, traced by those slender clews, to lose which is ruin, and about which hang so many dangers. The drawbridges that gape upon the way, the trains that stand smoking and steaming on the track, the rail that has borne the wear so long that it must soon snap under it, the deep cut where the over-hanging mass of rocks trembles to its fall, the obstruction that a piti-less malice may have placed in your path, you think of these after the journey is done, but they seldom haunt your fancy while it lasts. The knowledge of your helplessness in any circumstances is so perfect that it begets a sense of irresponsibility, almost of security ; and as you drowse upon the pallet of the sleeping car and feel yourself hurled forward through the obscurity, you are almost thankful that you can do nothing, for it is upon this condition only that you can endure it; and some such condition as this, I suppose, accounts for many heroic acts in the world. To the fantastic mood which possesses you equally, sleeping or waking, the stoppages of the train have a weird character, and Worcester, Springfield, New Haven, and Stamford are rather

points in dreamland than well-known towns of New England. As
the train stops you drowse if you have been waking, and wake if you
have been in a doze; but in any case you are aware of the locomotive
hissing and coughing beyond the station, of flaring gas-jets, of clatter-
ing feet of passengers getting on and off; then of some one, conductor
or station master, walking the whole length of the train; and then
you are aware of an insane satisfaction in renewed flight through the
darkness. You think hazily of the folk in their beds in the town
left behind, who stir uneasily at the sound of your train's departing
whistle; and so all is blank vigil or a blank slumber.

— HOWELLS: *Their Wedding Journey.*

136. Impression as the Purpose of Description. — The
impression that it gives may become the central purpose
of a description. It is evident in Howells's description of
the Battery that the purpose was the creating of an impression of forlornness, and that the author kept this purpose in mind when choosing the details. If his aim had
been to enable us to form a clear picture of the Battery in
its physical outlines, he would have chosen different
details and would have presented them in different
language.

The same scene or object may present a different appearance to two different observers because each may discover a different set of likenesses or resemblances and so
select different essential characteristics. An artist will
paint a picture that centers around some one feature.
Each added detail seems but to set forth and increase the
effect of this central element of the picture. Similarly
the observer will in his description lay emphasis on the
central point and will select details that bear a helpful
relation to it. If he wished to present the picture of a
valley, he would lay emphasis on its fundamental image
and essential details with reference to its appearance; but
if his desire was to present the impression of fertility or of

rural simplicity and quiet, the elements that were important for the producing of the desired impression might not be at all the ones essential to his former picture.

When the presentation of a picture is our central purpose, we attempt to present it as it appears to us, and select details that will enable others to form the desired image; but if we desire to set forth how a scene affected us, we must choose details that will make our reader feel as we felt.

137. Necessity of Observing our Impressions. — In order to write a description which shall give our impression of an object or scene, we must know definitely what that impression is. Just as clear seeing is necessary for the reproduction of definite images, so is the clear perception of our impressions necessary to their reproduction. Furthermore, we may know what our impressions are without being able to select those elements in a scene that have produced them ; but in order to write a description that shall affect others as the scene itself affected us, we must know what these elements are and emphasize them in the description. Thus it becomes necessary to pay attention both to our impression and to the selection of those details which create that impression. One glance at a room may cause us to believe that the housekeeper is untidy. If we wish to convey this impression to our reader, our description must include the details that give that impression of untidiness to us.

Nor are we limited to sight alone, for our impressions may be made stronger by the aid of the other senses. Sound and smell and taste may supplement the sight, and though they add little to the clearness, yet they add much to the impression which we get.

Within the cabin, through which Basil and Isabel now slowly moved, there were numbers of people lounging about on the sofas, in various attitudes of talk or vacancy; and at the tables there were others reading *Lothair*, a new book in the remote epoch of which I write, and a very fashionable book indeed. There was in the air that odor of paint and carpet which prevails on steamboats; the glass drops of the chandeliers ticked softly against each other, as the vessel shook with her respiration, like a comfortable sleeper, and imparted a delicious feeling of coziness and security to our travelers.

— HOWELLS : *Their Wedding Journey.*

138. Impression Limited to Experience. — If we attempt to write a description for the sake of giving an impression, it must be an impression that we have ourselves experienced. If the sight of the gorge of Niagara has filled us with a feeling of sublimity and awe, we shall find it hard to write a humorous account of it. If we see the humorous elements of a situation, we cannot easily make our description give the impression of grief. Neither can we successfully imitate the impressions of others. No two persons are affected in the same way by the same thing. Our age, our temperament, our emotional attitude, and all of our past experiences affect our way of looking at things and modify the impressions which we get. The successful presentation of our impression will depend largely upon the definite perception of our feelings.

139. Impression Affected by Mood. — Not only is our impression affected by details in the scene observed, but it is even more largely influenced by our mood at the time of the observation. The same landscape may cheer at one time and dishearten at another. To-day we see the ridiculous; to-morrow, the sad and sorrowful. A thousand things may change our mood, but under certain general conditions, certain impressions are likely to arise. There is something in the air of spring, or the heat of summer, which affects us all. The weather, too, has its effect. Sunshine and shadow find answering attitudes in our feelings, and the skillful writer takes advantage of these emotional tendencies.

> Not far we fared —
> The river left behind — when, looking back,
> I saw the mountain in the searching light
> Of the low sun. Surcharged with youthful pride
> In my adventure, I can ne'er forget
> The disappointment and chagrin which fell
> Upon me; for a change had passed. The steep
> Which in the morning sprang to kiss the sun,
> Had left the scene; and in its place I saw
> A shrunken pile, whose paths my steps had climbed,
> Whose proudest height my humble feet had trod.
> Its grand impossibilities and all
> Its store of marvels and of mysteries
> Were flown away, and would not be recalled.
> — HOLLAND: *Katrina.*

140. **Union of Image and Impression.** — Because we have discussed image making and impression giving separately, it must not be judged that they necessarily occur separately. They are in fact always united. No image, however clear, can fail to make some impression, and no description, however strong the impression it gives, fails to create some image. It is rather the placing of the emphasis that counts. Some descriptions have for their purpose the giving of an image, and the impression is of little moment. Other descriptions aim at producing impressions, and the images are of less importance. In the description of the Battery (page 254) the images are clear enough, but they are subordinate to the impression. This subordination may even go farther. Often the impression is made prominent and we are led by suggestion to form images which fit it, while in reality few definite images have been set. Notice in the following selection that the impression of desolation is given without attempting to picture exactly what was seen : —

The country at the foot of Vesuvius is the most fertile and best cultivated of the kingdom, most favored by Heaven in all Europe. The celebrated *Lacrymæ Christi* vine flourishes beside land totally devastated by lava, as if nature here made a last effort, and resolved to perish in her richest array. As you ascend, you turn to gaze on Naples, and on the fair land around it — the sea sparkles in the sun as if strewn with jewels; but all the splendors of creation are extinguished by degrees, as you enter the region of ashes and smoke, that announces your approach to the volcano. The iron waves of other years have traced their large black furrows in the soil. At a certain height birds are no longer seen; further on, plants become very scarce; then even insects find no nourishment. At last all life disappears. You enter the realm of death and the slain earth's dust alone sleeps beneath your unassured feet.

— MADAME DE STAËL: *Corinne: Italy.*

EXERCISES

Discuss the following selections with reference to the impression given by each : —

The third of the flower vines is Wood-Magic. It bears neither flowers nor fruit. Its leaves are hardly to be distinguished from the leaves of the other vines. Perhaps they are a little rounder than the Snowberry's, a little more pointed than the Partridge-berry's; sometimes you might mistake them for the one, sometimes for the other. No marks of warning have been written upon them. If you find them, it is your fortune; if you taste them, it is your fate. For as you browse your way through the forest, nipping here and there a rosy leaf of young wintergreen, a fragrant emerald tip of balsam fir, a twig of spicy birch, if by chance you pluck the leaves of Wood-Magic and eat them, you will not know what you have done, but the enchantment of the treeland will enter your heart and the charm of the wildwood will flow through your veins. You will never get away from it. The sighing of the wind through the pine trees and the laughter of the stream in its rapids will sound through all your dreams. On beds of silken softness you will long for the sleep-song of whispering leaves above your head, and the smell of a couch of balsam boughs. At tables spread with dainty fare you will be hungry for the joy of the hunt, and for the angler's sylvan feast. In proud cities you will weary for the sight of a mountain trail; in great cathedrals you will think of the long, arching aisles of the woodland : and in the noisy solitude of crowded streets you will hone after the friendly forest.

— HENRY VAN DYKE: *The Blue Flower*.

Running your eye across the map of the State, you see two slowly converging lines of railroad writhing out between the hills to the seacoast. Three other lines come down from north to south by the river valleys and the jagged shore. Along these, huddled in the corners of the hills and the sea line, lie the cities and the larger towns. A great majority of mankind, swarming in these little spots, or scuttling to and fro along the valleys on those slender lines, fondly dream they are acquainted with the land in which they live. But beyond and around all this rises the wide, bare face of the country, which they will never know — the great patches of second-growth woods, the mountain pastures sown thick with stones, the barren acres of the hillside farmer — a desolate land, latticed with gray New England roads, dotted with commonplace or neglected houses, and pitted with the staring cellars of the abandoned homes of disheartened and defeated men.

Out here in this semi-obscurity, where the regulating forces of society grow tardy and weak, strange and dangerous beings move to and fro, avoiding the apprehension of the law. Occasionally we hear of them — of some shrewd and desperate city fugitives brought to bay in a corner of the woods, or some brutal farmhouse murderer still lurking uncaptured among the hills. Often they pass through the country and out beyond, where they are never seen again.

In the extreme southwestern corner of the State the railroads do not come; the vacant spaces grow between the country roads, and the cities dwindle down to half-deserted crossroads hamlets. Here the surface of the map is covered up with the tortuous wrinkles of the hills. It is a beautiful but useless place. As far as you can see, low, unformed lumps of mountains lie jumbled aimlessly together between the ragged sky lines, or little silent cups of valleys stare up between them at their solitary patch of sky.   It seems a sort of waste yard of creation, flung full of the remnants of the making of the earth.

— GEORGE KIBBE TURNER: *Across the State*

("McClure's").

When once the shrinking dizzy spell was gone,
I saw below me, like a jeweled cup,
The valley hollowed to its heaven-kissed lip —
The serrate green against the serrate blue —
Brimming with beauty's essence; palpitant
With a divine elixir — lucent floods
Poured from the golden chalice of the sun,
At which my spirit drank with conscious growth,
And drank again with still expanding scope
Of comprehension and of faculty.

I felt the bud of being in me burst
With full, unfolding petals to a rose,
And fragrant breath that flooded all the scene.
By sudden insight of myself I knew
That I was greater than the scene, — that deep
Within my nature was a wondrous world,
Broader than that I gazed on, and informed
With a diviner beauty, — that the things
I saw were but the types of those I held,
And that above them both, High Priest and King,
I stood supreme, to choose and to combine,
And build from that within me and without
New forms of life, with meaning of my own,
And then alone upon the mountain top,
Kneeling beside the lamb, I bowed my head
Beneath the chrismal light and felt my soul
Baptized and set apart for poetry.

— HOLLAND: *Katrina.*

Theme LXIX. — *Write a description the purpose of which is to give an impression that you have experienced.*

SUMMARY

1. Description is that form of discourse which has for its purpose the creation of an image.

2. The essential characteristics of a description are : —

    a. A point of view.

        (1) It may be fixed or changing.

        (2) It may be expressed or implied.

        (3) Only those details should be included that can be seen from the point of view chosen.

    b. A correct fundamental image.

    c. A few characteristic and essential details

        (1) Close observation on the part of the writer is necessary in order to select the essential details.

    d. A proper selection and subordination of minor details.

    e. A suitable arrangement of details with reference to their natural position in space.

    f. That additional effectiveness which comes from

        (1) Proper choice of words.

        (2) Suitable comparisons and figures.

        (3) Variety of sentence structures.

3. The foregoing principles of description apply in the describing of many classes of objects. A description of a person usually gives some indication of his character and so becomes to some extent a character sketch.

4. A description may also have for its purpose the giving of an impression.

    a. The writer must select details which will aid in conveying the impression he desires his readers to receive.

b. The writer must observe his own impressions accurately, because he cannot convey to others that which he has not himself experienced.

c. The impression received is affected by the mood of the person.

d. Impression and image are never entirely separated.

IX. NARRATION

141. Kinds of Narration. — Narration consists of an account of happenings, and, for this reason, it is, without doubt, the most interesting of all forms of discourse. It is natural for us all to be interested in life, movement, action ; hence we enjoy reading and talking about them. To be convinced that this is true we need only to listen to conversations, notice what constitutes the subject-matter of letters of friendship, read newspapers and magazines, and observe what classes of books are most frequently drawn from our libraries.

Narration assumes a variety of forms. Since it relates happenings, it must include anecdotes, incidents, short stories, letters, novels, dramas, histories, biographies, and stories of travel and exploration. It also includes many newspaper articles such as those that give accounts of accidents and games and reports of various kinds of meetings. Evidently the field of narration is a broad one, for wherever life or action may be found or imagined, a subject for a narrative exists.

EXERCISES

1. Name four different events that have actually taken place in your school in which you think your classmates are interested.
2. Name three events that have taken place in other schools that may be of interest to members of your school.

3. Name four events of general interest that have occurred in your city during the last two or three years.
4. From a daily paper, pick out a narrative that is interesting to you.
5. Select one that you think ought to interest the most of your classmates.
6. Name three national events of recent occurrence.
7. Name three or four strange or mysterious events of which you have heard.
8. Name an actual occurrence that interested you because you wanted to see how it turned out.
9. Would an ordinary account of a bicycle or automobile trip be interesting ?   If not, why not ?

Theme LXX. — *Write a letter to a pupil in a neighboring high school, telling about something interesting that has happened in your own school.*

(Review forms of letter writing.   Consider your use of paragraphs.)

142. Plot. — By plot we mean the outline of the story told in a few words.   All narratives consist of accounts of connected happenings, and this naturally implies action on the part of the characters.   The principal action briefly told constitutes the plot.   The simple plot of Tennyson's *Princess* is as follows : —

A prince of the North, after being affianced as a child to a princess of the South, has fallen in love with her portrait and a lock of her hair.   When, however, the embassy appears to fetch home the bride, she sends back the message that she is not disposed to be married. Upon receipt of this word the Prince and two friends, Florian and Cyril, steal away to seek the Princess, and learn on reaching her father's court that she has established a Woman's College on a distant estate.   Having got letters authorizing them to visit the Princess, they ride into her domain, where they determine to go dressed like girls and apply for admission as students in the College. They arrive in disguise, and are admitted. On the first day the young men enroll themselves as students of Lady Psyche, who recognizes Florian as her brother and agrees not to expose them, since — by a law of the College inscribed above the gates, which darkness has kept them from seeing — the penalty of their discovery would be death. Melissa, a student, overhears them, and is bound over to keep the secret. Lady Blanche, mother of Melissa and rival to Lady Psyche, also learns of the alarming invasion, and remains silent for sinister reasons of her own. On the second day the principal personages picnic in a wood. At dinner Cyril sings a song that is better fit for the smoking room than for the ears of ladies; the Prince, in his anger, betrays his sex by a too masculine reproof; and dire confusion is the result. The Princess in her flight falls into the river, from which she is rescued by the Prince. Cyril and Lady Psyche escape together, but the Prince and Florian are brought before the Princess. At this important moment despatches are brought from her father saying that the Prince's father has surrounded her palace with soldiers, taken him prisoner, and holds him as a hostage. The Prince, after pleading to deaf ears, is sent away at dawn with Florian, and goes with him to the camp. Meantime during the night, the Princess's three brothers have come to her aid with an army. An agreement is reached to decide the case and end the war by a tournament between the brothers, with fifty men, on one side; the Prince and his two friends, with fifty men, on the other. This happens on the third day. The Prince and his men are vanquished, and he himself is badly wounded.

But the Princess is now gradually to discover that she has "overthrown more than her enemy," — that she has defeated yet saved herself. She has said of Lady Psyche's little child: —

> "I took it for an hour in mine own bed
> This morning: there the tender orphan hands
> Felt at my heart, and seem'd to charm from thence
> The wrath I nursed against the world."

When Cyril pleads with her to give the child back to its mother, she kisses it and feels that "her heart is barren." When she passes near the wounded Prince, and is shown by his father — his beard wet with his son's blood — her hair and picture on her lover's heart,

> Her iron will was broken in her mind,
> Her noble heart was broken in her breast.

From the Princess's cry then, "Grant me your son to nurse," it is but a natural result that she should bring the Prince's wounded men with him into the College, now a hospital. Through ministering to her lover, she comes to love him; and theories yield to "the lord of all."

— COPELAND-RIDEOUT : *Introduction to Tennyson's Princess.*

Theme LXXI. — *Write the plot of one of the following :* —

1. *Lochinvar*, Scott.
2. *Rip Van Winkle*, Irving.
3. One story from *A Tale of Two Cities*, Dickens.
4. *Silas Marner*, George Eliot.
5. The last magazine story you have read.
6. Some story assigned by the teacher.

Theme LXXII. — *Write three brief plots. Have the class choose the one that will make the most interesting story.*

Theme LXXIII. — *Write a story, using the plot selected by the class in the preceding theme.*

(Are the events related in your story probable or improbable ?)

143. The Introduction. — Our pleasure in a story depends upon our clear understanding of the various situations, and this understanding may often be best given by an introduction that states something of the time, place, characters, and circumstances as shown in Section 6. The purpose of the introduction is to make the story more effective, and what it shall contain is determined by the needs of the story itself. The last half of a well-written story will not be interesting to one who has not read the first half, because the first half will contain much that is essential to the complete understanding of the main point of the story. A story begun with conversation at once arouses interest, but care must be taken to see that the reader gets sufficient descriptive and explanatory matter to enable him to understand the story as the plot develops, or the interest will begin to lag.

Theme LXXIV. — *Write a narrative.*

Suggested subjects : —

1. The Christmas surprise.
2. How the mortgage was paid.
3. The race between the steam roller and the traction engine.
4. The new girl in the boarding school.
5. The Boss, and how he won his title.

(Be sure that your introduction is such that the entire situation is understood. Name different points in the story that led you to say what you have in the introduction. Have you mentioned any unnecessary points?)

144. The Incentive Moment. — It is the business of a story-teller to arouse the interest of his readers, and the sooner it is done, the better. Usually he tries to do this from the very beginning of his story. He therefore places in the introduction or near it a statement designed to stimulate the curiosity of his readers. The point at which interest begins has been termed the incentive moment. In the following selection notice that the first sentence tells who, when, where, and why. (Section 6.) The second sentence causes us to ask, what was it? and by the time that is answered we are curious to know what happened and how the adventure ended.

On a mellow moonlight evening a cyclist was riding along a lonely road in the northern part of Mashonaland. As he rode, enjoying the somber beauty of the African evening, he suddenly became conscious of a soft, stealthy, heavy tread on the road behind him. It seemed like the jog trot of some heavy, cushion-footed animal following him.

Turning round, he was scared very badly to find himself looking into the glaring eyes of a large lion. The puzzled animal acted very strangely, now raising his head, now lowering it, and all the time sniffling the air in a most perplexed manner. Here was a surprise for the lion. He could not make out what kind of animal it was that could roll, walk, and sit still all at the same time; an animal with a red eye on each side, and a brighter one in front. He hesitated to pounce upon such an outlandish being — a being whose blood smelled so oily.

I believe no cyclist ever "scorched" with more honesty and single-mindedness of purpose. But although he pedaled and pedaled, although he perspired and panted, his effort to get away did not seem to place any more space between him and the lion; the animal kept up his annoyingly calm jog trot, and never seemed to tire.

The poor rider was finally so exhausted from terror and exertion that he decided to have the matter settled right away. Suddenly slowing down, he jumped from his wheel, and, facing abruptly about, thrust the brilliant headlight full into the face of the lion. This was too much for the beast. The sudden glare destroyed the lion's nerve, for at this fresh evidence of mystery on the part of the strange rider-animal, who broke himself into halves and then cast his big eye in any direction he pleased, the monarch of the forest turned tail, and with a wild rush retreated in a very hyena-like manner into the jungle, evidently thanking his stars for his miraculous escape from that awful being. Thereupon the bicyclist, with new strength returning and devoutly blessing his acetylene lamp, pedaled his way back to civilization.

— P. L. WESSELS.

Theme LXXV. — *Write a short imaginative story.*

Suggested subjects : —

1. A bicycle race with an unfriendly dog.
2. An unpleasant experience.
3. A story told by the school clock.

4. Disturbing a hornet's nest.
5. The fate of an Easter bonnet.
6. Chased by a wolf.

(Where is the incentive moment? Is it introduced naturally?)

145. Climax. — You have already noticed in your reading that usually somewhere near the close of the story, there is a turning point. That turning point is called the climax. At this point, the supense of mind is greatest, for the fate of the principal character is being decided. If the story is well written as regards the plot, our interest will continually increase from the incentive moment to the climax.

In the novel and the drama, both of which may have a complicated plot, several minor climaxes or crises may be found. There may be a crisis to each single event or episode, yet they should all be a part of and lead up to the principal or final climax. Instead of detracting from, they add to the interest of a carefully woven plot. For example, in the *Merchant of Venice*, we have a crisis in both the casket story and the Lorenzo and Jessica episode; but so skillfully are the stories interwoven that the minor climaxes do not lessen our interest in the principal one.

In short stories, the turning point should come near the close. There should be but little said after that point is reached. In novels, and especially in dramas, we find that the climax is not right at the close, and considerable action sometimes takes place after the climax has been reached.

EXERCISES

A. Point out the climax in each of five stories that you have read.

B. Where is the climax in the following selection?

He spoke, and Sohrab kindled at his taunts,
And he too drew his sword; at once they rushed
Together, as two eagles on one prey
Come rushing down together from the clouds,
One from the east, one from the west; their shields
Dashed with a clang together, and a din
Rose, such as that the sinewy woodcutters
Make often in the forest's heart at morn,
Of hewing axes, crashing trees — such blows
Rustum and Sohrab on each other hailed.
And you would say that sun and stars took part
In that unnatural conflict; for a cloud
Grew suddenly in heaven, and darked the sun
Over the fighters' heads; and a wind rose
Under their feet, and moaning swept the plain,
And in a sandy whirlwind wrapped the pair.
In gloom they twain were wrapped, and they alone;
For both the onlooking hosts on either hand
Stood in broad daylight, and the sky was pure,
And the sun sparkled on the Oxus stream.
But in the gloom they fought, with bloodshot eyes
And laboring breath; first Rustum struck the shield
Which Sohrab held stiff out; the steel-spiked spear
Rent the tough plates, but failed to reach the skin,
And Rustum plucked it back with angry groan.
Then Sohrab with his sword smote Rustum's helm,
Nor clove its steel quite through; but all the crest
He shore away, and that proud horsehair plume,
Never till now defiled, sank to the dust;
And Rustum bowed his head; but then the gloom
Grew blacker, thunder rumbled in the air,
And lightnings rent the cloud; and Ruksh, the horse,
Who stood at hand, uttered a dreadful cry; —
No horse's cry was that, most like the roar
Of some pained desert lion, who all day
Hath trailed the hunter's javelin in his side,
And comes at night to die upon the sand.
The two hosts heard that cry, and quaked for fear,
And Oxus curdled as it crossed his stream.
But Sohrab heard, and quailed not, but rushed on,

And struck again; and again Rustum bowed
His head; but this time all the blade, like glass,
Sprang in a thousand shivers on the helm,
And in the hand the hilt remained alone.
Then Rustum raised his head; his dreadful eyes
Glared, and he shook on high his menacing spear,
And shouted: "Rustum!" — Sohrab heard that shout,
And shrank amazed: back he recoiled one step,
And scanned with blinking eyes the advancing form;
And then he stood bewildered; and he dropped
His covering shield, and the spear pierced his side.
He reeled, and, staggering back, sank to the ground,
And then the gloom dispersed, and the wind fell,
And the bright sun broke forth, and melted all
The cloud; and the two armies saw the pair —
Saw Rustum standing, safe upon his feet,
And Sohrab wounded, on the bloody sand.

— MATTHEW ARNOLD: *Sohrab and Rustum.*

Theme LXXVI. — *Write a story and give special attention to the climax.*

Suggested subjects: —

1. The immigrant's error.
2. A critical moment.
3. An intelligent dog.
4. The lost key.
5. Catching a burglar.
6. A hard test.
7. Won by the last hit.
8. A story suggested by a picture you have seen.

(Name the incidents leading up to the climax. Is the mind held in suspense until the climax is reached? Are any unnecessary details introduced?)

146. Conversation in Narration. — When introduced into narration, a conversation is briefer than when actually spoken. It is necessary to have the conversation move quickly, for we read with less patience than we listen. The sentences must be for the most part short, and the changes from one speaker to another frequent, or the dialogue will have a "made to order" effect. Notice the conversation in as many different stories as possible. Observe how variation is secured in indicating the speaker. How many substitutes for " He said " can you name? In relating conversation orally, we are less likely to secure such variety. Notice in your own speech and that of others how often "I said " and " He said " occur.

EXERCISES

A. Notice the indentation and sentence length in the following selection : —

Louden looked up calmly at the big figure towering above him.

"It won't do, Judge," he said ; that was all, but there was a significance in his manner and a certainty in his voice which caused the uplifted hand to drop limply.

"Have you any business to set foot upon my property ? " he demanded.

"Yes," answered Joe. "That's why I came."

"What business have you got with me ? "

"Enough to satisfy you, I think. But there's one thing I don't want to do " — Joe glanced at the open door — "and that is to talk about it here — for your own sake and because I think Miss Tabor should be present. I called to ask you to come to her house at eight o'clock to-night."

"You did ! " Martin Pike spoke angrily, but not in the bull bass of yore. "My accounts with her estate are closed," he said harshly. "If she wants anything let her come here."

Joe shook his head. "No. You must be there at eight o'clock."
— BOOTH TARKINGTON : *The Conquest of Canaan* (" Harper's ").

B. Notice the conversation in the following narrative. Consider also the incentive moment and the climax. Suggest improvements.

When Widow Perkins saw Widower Parsons coming down the road she looked as mad as a hornet and stepped to the back door.

"William Henry," she called to the lank youth chopping wood, "you've worked hard enough for one day. Come in and rest."

"Guess that's the first time you ever thought I needed a rest since I was born. I'll keep right on chopping till you get through acceptin' old Hull," he replied, whereupon the widow slammed the door and looked twice as mad as before.

"Mornin', widdy," remarked the widower, stalking into the room, taking a chair without an invitation, and hanging his hat on his knee. "Cold day," he added cheerfully.

The widow nodded shortly, at the same time inwardly prophesying a still colder day for him before he struck the weather again.

"Been buyin' a new cow," resumed the caller, impressively.

"Have, eh?" returned the widow, with a jerk, bringing out the ironing board and slamming it down on the table.

"An' two hogs," went on the widower, wishing the widow would glance at him just once and see how affectionate he looked. "They'll make pork enough for all next winter and spring."

"Will, eh?" responded the widow, with a bang of the iron that nearly wrecked the table.

"An' a — a — lot o' odd things 'round the house; an' the fact is, widdy, you see — that is, you know — was going to say if you'll agree" — the widower lost his words, and in his desperation hung his hat on the other knee and hitched a trifle nearer the ironing board.

"No, Hull Parsons, I don't see a single mite, nor I don't know a particle, an' I ain't agreein' the least bit," snapped the widow, pounding the creases out of the tablecloth.

"But say, widdy, don't get riled so soon," again ventured Parsons. "I was jest goin' to tell you that I've been proposing to Carpenter Brown to build a new — "

By this time the widow was glancing at him in a way he wished she wouldn't.

"Is that all the proposin' you've done in the last five months, Hull Parsons?" she demanded stormily. "You ain't asked every old maid for miles around to marry you, have you, Hull Parsons? An' you didn't tell the last one you proposed to that if she didn't take you there would be only one more chance left — that old pepper-box of a

Widow Perkins? You didn't say that, now, did you, Hull Parsons?"
and the widow's eyes and voice snapped fire all at once.

The caller turned several different shades of red and realized that
he had struck the biggest snag he'd ever struck in any courting
career, past or present. He laughed violently for a second or two,
tried to hang his hat on both knees at the same time, and finally sank
his voice to a confidential undertone: —

"Now, widdy, that's the woman's way o' puttin' it. They've been
jealous o' you all 'long, fur they knew where my mind was sot. I
wouldn't married one o' them women for nothing," added the widower,
with another hitch toward the ironing board.

"Huh!" responded the widow, losing a trifle of her warlike cast
of countenance. "S'pose all them women hadn't refused you, Hull
Parsons, what then?"

"They didn't refuse me, widdy," returned the widower, trying to
look sheepish, and dropping his voice an octave lower. "S'pose I
hadn't oughter tell on 'em, but — er — can you keep a secret,
widdy?"

"I ain't like the woman who can't," remarked the widow, shortly.

"Well, then, I was the one who did the refusin' — the hull gang
went fer me right heavy, guess 'cause 'twas leap year, or they was
tryin' on some o' them new women's ways, or somethin' like that. But
my mind was sot all along, d'ye see, widdy?"

And the Widow Perkins invited Widower Parsons to stay to
dinner, because she thought she saw.

Theme LXXVII. — *Complete the story on pages 79–80,
or one of the following:* —

THE AUDACIOUS REPORTER

Soon after Fenimore Dayton became a reporter his city editor sent
him to interview James Mountain. That famous financier was then
approaching the zenith of his power over Wall Street and Lombard
Street. It had just been announced that he had "absorbed" the Great
Eastern and Western Railway System — of course, by the methods
which have made some men and some newspapers habitually speak of
him as "the Royal Bandit." The city editor had two reasons for
sending Dayton — first because he did not like him; second, because
any other man on the staff would walk about for an hour and come

back with the report that Mountain had refused to receive him, while Dayton would make an honest effort.

Seeing Dayton saunter down Nassau Street — tall, slender, calm, and cheerful — you would never have thought that he was on his way to interview one of the worst-tempered men in New York, for a newspaper which that man peculiarly detested, and on a subject which he did not care to discuss with the public. Dayton turned in at the Equitable Building and went up to the floor occupied by Mountain, Ranger, & Blakehill. He nodded to the attendant at the door of Mountain's own suite of offices, strolled tranquilly down the aisle between the several rows of desks at which sat Mountain's personal clerks, and knocked at the glass door on which was printed "Mr. Mountain" in small gilt letters.

"Come!" It was an angry voice — Mountain's at its worst.

Dayton opened the door. Mountain glanced up from a mass of papers before him. His red forehead became a network of wrinkles and his scant white eyebrows bristled. "And who are you?" he snarled.

"My name is Dayton — Fenimore Dayton," replied the reporter, with a gracefully polite bow. "Mr. Mountain, I believe?"

It was impossible for Mr. Mountain altogether to resist the impulse to bow in return. Dayton's manner was compelling.

"And what the dev — what can I do for you?"

"I'm a reporter from the — "

"What!" roared Mountain, leaping to his feet in a purple, swollen veined fury. . . .

—DAVID GRAHAM PHILIPS ("McClure's").

CAUGHT MASQUERADING

When I took my aunt and sister to the Pequot hotel, the night before the Yale-Harvard boat race, I found a gang of Harvard boys there. They celebrated a good deal that night, in the usual Harvard way.

Some of the Harvard men had a room next to mine. About three A.M. things quieted down. When I woke up next morning, it was broad daylight, and I was utterly alone. The race was to be at eleven o'clock. I jumped out of bed and looked at my watch — it was nearly ten! I looked for my clothes. My valise was gone! I rang the bell, but in the excitement downstairs, I suppose, no one answered it.

What was I to do? Those Harvard friends of mine thought it a good joke on me to steal my clothes and take themselves off to the race without waking me up. I don't know what I should have done in my anguish, when, thank goodness, I heard a tap at my door, and went to it.

"Well, do hurry!" (It was my sister's voice.) "Aunt won't go to the race; we'll have to go without her."

"They've stolen my clothes, Mollie — those Harvard fellows."

"Haven't you anything?" she asked through the keyhole.

"Not a thing, dear."

"Oh, well! it's a just punishment to you after last night! That — noise was dreadful!"

"Perhaps it is," I said, "but don't preach now, sister dear — get me something to put on. I want to see the race."

"I haven't anything except some dresses and one of aunt's."

"Get me Aunt Sarah's black silk," I cried. "I will wear anything rather than not see the race, and it's half-past ten nearly now."

(Correct your theme with reference to the points mentioned in Section 146.)

147. Number and Choice of Details — Unity. — In relating experiences the choice of details will be determined by the purpose of the narrative and by the person or persons for whom we are writing. If we are writing a brief account of an accident for a newspaper, we shall need to select only a few important facts and state them clearly and concisely. If we are relating a traveling experience, we shall make it more interesting and vivid if we select several facts and treat each quite fully. This is especially true if the experience took place in a country or part of a country not familiar to our readers. If we are writing for those with whom we are acquainted, we can easily decide what will interest them. If we write to different persons an account of the same event, we find that these accounts differ from each other. We know what each will enjoy, and we try to adapt our writing to each individual taste. Our narrative will be improved by adapting it to an imaginary audience in case we do not know exactly who our readers will be. In your high school work you know your readers and can select your facts accordingly.

To summarize : a narration should possess unity, that is, it should say all that should be said about the subject and not more than needs to be said. The length of the theme, the character of the audience to which it is addressed, and the purpose for which it is written, determine what facts are necessary and how many to choose in order to give unity. (See Section 81.)

148. Arrangement of Details — Coherence. — An arrangement of our facts that gives coherence to our theme should be used. In a coherent theme each sentence or paragraph is naturally suggested by the preceding one. It has been pointed out in Sections 82–85 that in narration we gain coherence by relating our facts in the order of their occurrence. When a single series of events is set forth, we can follow the real time-order, omitting such details as are not essential to the unity of the story.

If, however, more than one series of events are given, we cannot follow the exact time-order, for, though two events occur at the same time, one must be told before the other. Here, the actual time relations must be carefully indicated by the use of expressions ; as, *at the same time*, *meanwhile*, *already*, etc. (See Section 12.) Two or more series of events belong in the same story only if they finally come together at some time, usually at the point of the story. They should be carried along together so that all that is necessary for the understanding of the point when reached shall be in the minds of the reader. In short stories the changes from one series to another

are close together.   In a long book one or more chapters
may give one series of incidents, while the following
chapters may be concerned with a parallel series of incidents.   Notice the introductory paragraph of each chapter
in Scott's *Ivanhoe* or Cooper's *The Last of the Mohicans*.   Many of these indicate that a new series of events
is to be related.

It will be of advantage in writing a narrative to construct an outline as indicated in Section 84.   Such an
outline will assist us in making our narrative clear by
giving it unity, coherence, and emphasis.

EXERCISES

1. Name events that have occurred in your school or
   city which could be related in their exact time-order.
   Relate one of them orally.
2. Name two accidents that could not be related in their
   exact time-order.   Relate one of them orally.
3. Name subjects for real narratives that would need to
   be written in the first person; in the third person.
4. In telling about a runaway accident, what points would
   you mention if you were writing a short account for
   a newspaper?
5. What points would you add if you were writing to
   some one who was acquainted with the persons in
   the accident?
6. Consider the choice and arrangement of details in the
   next magazine story that you read.

Theme LXXVIII. — *Write a personal narrative in which
the time-order can be carefully followed.*

Suggested subjects : —

1. The irate conductor.
2. A personal adventure with a window.
3. An interrupted nap.
4. Lost in the woods.
5. In a runaway.
6. An amusing adventure.
7. A day at grandfather's.

(Consider the unity and coherence of the theme.)

Theme LXXIX. — *Write in the third person a true narrative in which different events are going on at the same time.*

Suggested subjects : —

1. A skating accident.
2. The hunters hunted.
3. Capsized on the river.
4. How he won the race.
5. An experience with a balky horse.
6. The search for a lost child.
7. How they missed each other.
8. A strange adventure.
9. A tip over in a bobsleigh.

(How many series of events have you in your narrative? Are they well connected? What words have you used to show the time-order of the different events?)

149. Interrelation of Plot and Character. — Though in narration the interest centers primarily in the action, yet in the higher types of narration interest in character is closely interwoven with interest in plot. In reading, our attention is held by the plot; we follow its development, noticing the addition of incidents, their relation to one another and to the larger elements of action in the story, and their union in the final disentanglement of the plot; but our complete appreciation of the story runs far beyond the plot and depends to a large extent upon our interpretation of the character of the individuals concerned. The mere story may be exciting and interesting, but its effect will be of little permanent value if it does not stir within us some appreciation of character, which we shall find reflected in our own lives or in the lives of those about us. We may read the *Merchant of Venice* for its story, but a deeper study of the play sets forth and reënforces the character of Portia, Shylock, and the others. With many of the celebrated characters of literature this interest has grown quite apart from interest in the plot, and they stand to-day as the embodiment of phases of human nature. Thus by means of action does the skillful author portray his conception of human life and human character.

On the other hand, when we write we shall need to distinguish action that indicates character from that which is merely incidental to the plot. In order to develop a story to its climax we may need to have the persons concerned perform certain actions. If by skillful wording we can show not only what was done but also to some extent the way in which it was done, we may give our readers some notion of the character of the individuals in our story. (See Section 10.) This portrayal of character may be aided by the use of description. (See Section 134.)

Notice that the purpose of the following selection is to indicate the character of Pitkin rather than to relate the incident. If the author were to relate other doings of Pitkin, he would need to make the actions of Pitkin in each case consistent with the character indicated by this sketch.

It was the day of our great football game with Harvard, and when I heard my friend Pitkin returning to the room we shared in common, I knew that he was mad. And when I say mad I mean it, — not angry, nor exasperated, nor aggravated, nor provoked, but mad : not mad according to the dictionary, that is, crazy, but mad as we common folk use the term. So I say my friend Pitkin was mad. I thought so when I heard the angry click-clack of his heels on the cement walk, and I carefully put all the chairs against the wall; I was sure of it when the door slammed, and I set the coal scuttle in the corner behind the stove. There was no doubt of it when he mounted the stairs three steps at a time, and I hastily cleared his side of the desk. You may wonder why I did all these things, but you have never seen Pitkin mad.

Why was Pitkin mad? I did not then know. I had not seen him yet, for I was so busy — so very, very busy — that I did not look up when he slammed his books on the desk with a resounding whack which caused the ink bottle to tremble and the lampshade to clatter as though chattering its teeth with fear, while the pens and pencils, tumbling from the holder, scurried away to hide themselves under the desk.

I was still busily engaged with my books while he threw his wet overcoat and dripping hat on the white bedspread and kicked his rubbers under the stove, the smell of which soon warned me to rescue them before they melted. Pitkin must be very mad this time. He was taking off his collar and even his shoes. Pitkin always took off his collar when very mad, and if especially so, put on his slippers, even if he had to change them again in fifteen minutes.

"What are you doing? Why don't you say something? You are a pretty fellow not to speak or even look up." Such was Pitkin's first remark. Sometimes he was talkative and would insist on giving his opinion of things in general. At other times he preferred to be left alone to bury himself and his wrath in his books. Since he had failed to poke the fire, though the room was very warm, I had decided that he would dive into his books and be heard no more until a half hour past his suppertime, but I had made a mistake. To-day he was in a talkative mood, and knowing that work was impossible, I devoted the next half hour to listening to a dissertation on the general perverseness of human nature, and to an elaborate description of my friend Pitkin's scheme for endowing a rival institution with a hundred million, and making things so cheap and attractive that our university would have to go out of business. When Pitkin reached this point, I knew that I could safely ask the special reason of his anger and that, having answered, he would settle down to his regular work. I gently insinuated that I was still ignorant of the matter, and received the reply quite in keeping with Pitkin's nature, "I bet on Harvard and won."

EXERCISES

1. Read one of Dickens's books and bring to class selections that will show how Dickens portrays character by use of action.

2. What kind of man is Silas Marner? What leads you to think so?

3. Select three persons from *Ivanhoe* and state your opinion of their character.

4. Notice the relative importance of plot and character in three magazine stories.

5. Select some person from a magazine story. Tell the class what makes you form the estimate of his character that you do. To what extent does the descriptive matter help you determine his character?

Theme LXXX. — *Write a character sketch or a story which shows character by means of action.*

Suggested subjects : —

1. The girl from Texas.
2. The Chinese cook.
3. Taking care of the baby.
4. Nathan's temptation.
5. The small boy's triumph.
6. A village character.
7. The meanest man I ever knew.

(Consider the development of the plot. To what extent have you shown character by action? Can you make the impression of character stronger by adding some description?)

150. History and Biography. — Historical and biographical narratives may be highly entertaining and at the same time furnish us with much valuable information. Such writings often contain much that is not pure narration. A historian may set forth merely the program of events, but most histories contain besides a large amount of description and explanation. Frequently, too, all of this is but the basis of either a direct or an implied argument. Likewise a biographer may be chiefly concerned with the acts of a man, but he usually finds that the introduction of description and explanation aids him in making clear the life purpose of the man about whom he writes. In shorter histories and biographies, the expository and descriptive matter often displaces the narrative matter to such an extent that the story ceases to be interesting.

The actual time-order of events need not be followed. It will often make our account clearer to discuss the literary works of a man at one time, his education at another, and his practical achievements at a third. Certain portions of his life may need to be emphasized while others are neglected. What we include in a biography and what we emphasize will be determined by the purpose for which it is written. As a matter of pure information, a short account is desirable, but a long account is of greater interest. If a man is really great, the most insignificant events may be read with interest, but a good biographer will select such events with good taste and then present them so that they have a bearing upon the more important phases of the man's life and character. Hundreds of the stories told about Lincoln would be trivial but for the fact that they help us better to understand the real character of the man.

EXERCISE

1. Select some topic briefly mentioned in the history text you study. Look up a more extended account of it and come to the class prepared to recite the topic orally. Make your report clear, concise, and interesting. Decide beforehand just what facts you will relate and in what order. (See Sections 39, 52, 53.)

Theme LXXXI. — *Come to class prepared to write upon some topic assigned by the teacher, or upon one of the following:* —

> 1. Pontiac's conspiracy.
> 2. The battle of Marathon.
> 3. The Boston tea party.
> 4. The battle of Bannockburn.
> 5. Sherman's march to the sea.
> 6. Passage of the Alps by Napoleon.

(Is your narrative told in an interesting way? Are any facts necessary to the clear understanding of it omitted?)

EXERCISES

1. Name an English orator, an English statesman, and an English writer about each of whom an interesting biography might be written.
2. With the same purpose in view name two American orators, two American writers, and two American statesmen.

Theme LXXXII. — *Write a short biography of some prominent person. Include only well-known and important facts, but do not give his name. Read it before the class and have them tell who it is.*

151. Description in Narration. — The descriptive elements of narration should always have for their purpose something more than the mere creating of images. If a house is described, the description should enable us to bring to mind more vividly the events that take place within or around it. If the description aids us in understanding how or why the events occur, it is helpful; but if it fails to do this, it has no place in the narrative. Description when thus used serves as a background for the actions told in the story, and has for its purpose the explanation of how or why they occur.

Sometimes the descriptions are given before the incident and sometimes the two are intermixed. In the following incident from the *Legend of Sleepy Hollow*, notice how the description prepares the mind for the action that follows. We are told that the brook which Ichabod must cross runs into a marshy and thickly wooded glen ; that the oaks and chestnuts matted with grapevines throw a gloom over the place, and already we feel that it is a dreadful spot after dark. The fact that André was captured here adds to the feeling. We are prepared to have some exciting action take place, and had Ichabod ridden quietly across the bridge, we should have been disappointed.

About two hundred yards from the tree a small brook crossed the road, and ran into a marshy and thickly wooded glen, known by the name of Wiley's swamp. A few rough logs, laid side by side, served for a bridge over this stream. On that side of the road where the brook entered the woods, a group of oaks and chestnuts, matted thick

with wild grapevines, threw a cavernous gloom over it.   To pass this
bridge was the severest trial.   It was at this identical spot that the
unfortunate André was captured, and under covert of those vines were
the sturdy yeomen concealed who surprised him.   This has ever
since been considered a haunted stream, and fearful are the feelings
of the schoolboy who has to pass it alone after dark.

As he approached the stream his heart began to thump; he summoned up, however, all his resolution, gave his horse half a score of
kicks in the ribs, and attempted to dash briskly across the bridge;
but instead of starting forward, the perverse old animal made a lateral
movement, and ran broadside against the fence.   Ichabod, whose fears
increased with the delay, jerked the reins on the other side, and kicked
lustily with the contrary foot.   It was all in vain; his steed started,
it is true, but it was only to plunge to the opposite side of the road
into a thicket of brambles and alder bushes.   The schoolmaster now
bestowed both whip and heel upon the starveling ribs of old Gun-
powder, who dashed forward, snuffling and snorting, but came to a
stand just by the bridge, with a suddenness that had nearly sent his
rider sprawling over his head.   Just at this moment a plashy tramp
by the side of the bridge caught the sensitive ear of Ichabod.   In the
dark shadow of the grove, on the margin of the brook, he beheld
something huge, misshapen, black, and towering.   It stirred not, but
seemed gathered up in the gloom like some gigantic monster ready to
spring upon the traveler.

— IRVING : *Legend of Sleepy Hollow*.

The most important use of description in connection
with narration is that of portraying character.   Though
it is by their actions that the character of persons is most
strongly brought out, yet the descriptive matter may do
much to strengthen the impression of character which we
form.   (Section 134.)   Much of the description found in
literature is of this nature.   Stripped of its context such
a description may fail to satisfy our ideals as judged by
the principles of description discussed in Chapter VIII.
Nevertheless, in its place it may be perfectly adapted to
its purpose and give just the impression the author wished
to give.   Such descriptions must be judged in their

settings, and the sole standard of judgment is not their beauty or completeness as descriptions, but how well they give the desired impressions.

Theme LXXXIII. — *Write a short personal narrative containing some description which explains how or why events occur.*

(Is there anything in the descriptive part that does not bear on the narration?)

Theme LXXXIV. — *Write a narrative containing description that aids in giving an impression of character.*

Suggested subjects : —

1. Holding the fort.
2. A steamer trip.
3. How I played truant.
4. Kidnaped.
5. The misfortunes of our circus.
6. Account for the situation shown in a picture that you have seen.

(Will the reader get the impression of character which you wish him to have? Consider your theme with reference to its introduction, incentive moment, selection and arrangement of details, and climax.)

SUMMARY

1. Narration assumes a variety of forms, — incidents, anecdotes, stories, letters, novels, histories, biographies, etc., — all concerned with the relation of events.
2. The essential characteristics of a narration are, —
   a. An introduction which tells the characters, the time, the place, and enough of the attendant circumstances to make clear the point of the narrative.

b. The early introduction of an incentive moment.

c. A climax presented in such a way as to maintain the interest of the reader.

d. The selection of details essential to the climax in accordance with the principle of unity.

e. The arrangement of these details in a coherent order.

f. The skillful introduction of minor details which will assist in the appreciation of the point.

g. The introduction of all necessary description and explanation.

h. That additional effectiveness which comes from

    (1) Proper choice of words.

    (2) Suitable comparisons and figures.

    (3) Variety of sentence structure.

i. A brief conclusion.

X. EXPOSITION

152. Purpose of Exposition. — It is the purpose of exposition to make clear to others that which we ourselves understand. Its primary object is to give information. Herein lies one of the chief differences between the two forms of discourse just studied and the one that we are about to study. The primary object of most description and narration is to please, while that of exposition is to inform. Exposition answers such questions as how? why? what does it mean? what is it used for? and so attempts to satisfy demands for knowledge.

In the following selections notice that the first tells us *how* to burnish a photograph; the second, *how* to split a sheet of paper : —

1. When the prints are almost dry they can be burnished. The burnishing iron should be heated and kept hot during the burnishing, about the same heat as a flatiron in ironing clothes. Care must be taken to keep the polished surface of the burnisher bright and clean. When the iron is hot enough the prints should be rubbed with a glacé polish, which is sold for this purpose, and is applied with a small wad of flannel. Then the prints should be passed through the burnisher two or three times, the burnisher being so adjusted that the pressure on the prints is rather light; the degree of pressure will be quickly learned by experience, more pressure being required if the prints have been allowed to become dry before being polished. White castile soap will do very well as a lubricator for the prints before burnishing, and is applied in the same manner as above.

— *The Amateur Photographer's Handbook.*

2. Paper can be split into two or even three parts, however thin the sheet. It may be convenient to know how to do this sometimes ; as, for instance, when one wishes to paste in a scrapbook an article printed on both sides of the paper.

Get a piece of plate glass and place it on a sheet of paper. Then let the paper be thoroughly soaked. With care and a little skill the sheet can be split by the top surface being removed.

The best plan, however, is to paste a piece of cloth or strong paper to each side of the sheet to be split. When dry, quickly, and without hesitation, pull the two pieces asunder, when one part of the sheet will be found to have adhered to one, and part to the other. Soften the paste in water, and the two pieces can easily be removed from the cloth.

EXERCISES

A. Explain orally any two of the following : —

      1. How to fly a kite.

      2. How a robin builds her nest.

      3. How oats are harvested.

      4. How tacks are made.

      5. How to make a popgun.

      6. How fishes breathe.

      7. How to swim.

      8. How to hemstitch a handkerchief.

      9. How to play golf.

    10. How salt is obtained.

B. Name several subjects with whose explanation you are unfamiliar.

Theme LXXXV. — *Select for a subject something that you know how to do. Write a theme on the subject chosen.*

(Have you made use of either general description or general narration ? See Sections 67 and 68.)

Very frequently explanations of *how* and *why* anything is done are combined, as in the following : —

In cases of sunstroke, place the person attacked in a cool, airy place. Do not allow a crowd to collect closely about him. Remove his clothing, and lay him flat upon his back. Dash him all over with cold water — ice-water, if it can be obtained — and rub the entire body with pieces of ice. This treatment is used to reduce the heat of the body, for in all cases of sunstroke the temperature of the body is greatly increased. When the body has become cooler, wipe it dry and remove the person to a dry locality. If respiration ceases, or becomes exceedingly slow, practice artificial respiration. After the patient has apparently recovered, he should be kept quiet in bed for some time.

— BALDWIN : *Essential Lessons in Human Physiology and Hygiene.*

Notice that the following selection answers neither the question *how?* nor *why?* but explains what journalism is : —

JOURNALISM

What is a journal? What is a journalist? What is journalism ? Is it a trade, a commercial business, or a profession? Our word *journal* comes from the French. It has different forms in the several Romantic languages, and all go back to the Latin *diurnalis*, daily, from *dies*, a day. Diurnal and diary are derived from the same source. The first journals were in fact diaries, daily records of happenings, compiled often for the pleasure and use of the compiler alone, sometimes for monarchs or statesmen or friends ; later to be circulated for the information of a circle of readers, or distributed in copies to subscribers among the public at large. These were the first newspapers. While we still in a specific sense speak of daily newspapers as journals, the term is often enlarged to comprise nearly all publications that are issued periodically and distributed to subscribers.

A journalist is one whose business is publishing a journal (or more than one), or editing a journal, or writing for journals, especially a person who is regularly employed in some responsible directing or creative work on a journal, as a publisher, editor, writer, reporter, critic, etc. This use of the word is comparatively modern, and it is commonly restricted to persons connected with daily or weekly newspapers. Many older newspaper men scout it, preferring to be known as publishers, editors, writers, or contributors. Journalism, however, is a word that is needed for its comprehensiveness. It includes the theory, the business, and the art of producing newspapers in all departments of the work. Hence, any school of professional journalism must be presumed to comprise in its scope and detail of instruction the knowledge that is essential to the making and conduct of newspapers. It must have for its aim the ideal newspaper which is ideally perfect in every department.

Journalism, so far as it is more than mere reporting and mere money making, so far as it undertakes to frame and guide opinion, to educate the thought and instruct the conscience of the community, by editorial comment, interpretation and homily, based on the news, is under obligation to the community to be truthful, sincere, and uncorrupted; to enlighten the understanding, not to darken counsel; to uphold justice and honor with unfailing resolution, to champion morality and the public welfare with intelligent zeal, to expose wrong and antagonize it with unflinching courage. If journalism has any mission in the world besides and beyond the dissemination of news, it is a mission of maintaining a high standard of thought and life in the community it serves, strengthening all its forces that make for righteousness and beauty and fair growth.

This is not solely, nor peculiarly, the office of what is called the editorial page. To be most influential, it must be a consistent expression in all departments, giving the newspaper a totality of power in such aim. This is the right ideal of journalism whenever it is considered as more than a form of commercialism. No newspaper attains its ideal in completeness. If it steadfastly works toward attainment, it gives proof of its right to be. The advancing newspaper, going on from good to better in the substance of its character and the ability of its endeavor, is the type of journalism which affords hope for the future. And one strong encouragement to fidelity in a high motive is public appreciation.

— *The Boston Herald.*

EXERCISES

Give as complete an answer as possible to any two of the following questions : —

1. Why do fish bite better on a cloudy day than on a bright one ?

2. Why should we study history ?

3. Why does a baseball curve?
4. Why did the American colonies revolt against England?
5. Why did the early settlers of New England persecute the Quakers?
6. Why should trees be planted either in early spring or late autumn?
7. Why do we lose a day in going from America to China?
8. In laying a railroad track, why is there a space left between the ends of the rails?

Theme LXXXVI. — *Choose one of the above or a similar question as a subject for a theme. Write out as complete and exact an explanation as possible.*

EXERCISE

Write out a list of subjects the explanation of which would not answer the questions *why?* or *how?* How many of them can you explain?

Theme LXXXVII. — *Write out the explanation of one of the subjects in the above list.*

(Read what you have written and consider it with reference to clearness, unity, and coherence.)

153. Importance of Exposition. — This form of discourse is important because it deals so extensively with important subjects, such as questions of government, facts in science, points in history, methods in education, and processes of manufacture. It enters vitally into our lives, no matter what our occupation may be. Business men make constant use of this kind of discourse. In fact, it would be impossible for business to be transacted with any degree of success without explanations. Loans of money would not be made if men did not understand how they could have security for the sums loaned. A manufacturer cannot expect to have good articles produced if he is unable to give needful explanations concerning their manufacture. In order that a merchant be successful he must be able to explain the relative merits of his goods to his customers.

Very much of the work done in our schools is of an expository nature. The text-books used are expositions. When they of themselves are not sufficient for the clear understanding of the subject, it is necessary to consult reference books. Then, if the subject is still lacking in clearness, the teacher is called upon for additional explanation. On the other hand, the greater part of the pupil's recitations consists simply in explaining the subjects under discussion. Much of the class-room work in our schools consists of either receiving or giving explanations.

EXERCISES

1. Name anything outside of school work that you have been called upon to explain during the last week or two.
2. Name anything outside of school work that you have recently learned through explanation.
3. Name three topics in each of your studies for to-day that call for explanation.
4. Name some topic in which the text-book did not seem to make the explanation clear.

Theme LXXXVIII. — *Write out one of the topics mentioned in number three of the preceding exercise.*

(Have you included everything that is necessary to make your explanation clear? Can anything be omitted without affecting the clearness?)

154. Clear Understanding. — The first requisite of a good explanation is a clear understanding on the part of the one who is giving the explanation. It is evident that if we do not understand a subject ourselves we cannot make our explanations clear to others. If the ideas in our mind are in a confused state, our explanation will be equally confused. If you do not understand a problem in algebra, your attempt to explain it to others will prove a failure. If you attempt to explain how a canal boat is taken through a lock without thoroughly understanding it yourself, you will give your listeners only a confused idea of how it is done.

The principal reason why pupils fail in their recitations and examinations is that in preparing their lessons, they do not make themselves thoroughly acquainted with the topics that they are studying. They often go over them hurriedly and carelessly. They come to class with confused ideas, and when they attempt to recite, there is, if anything, an additional confusion of ideas, and the recitation proves a failure. Failure to prepare daily recitations, failure to ask for additional explanations, and failure to listen to explanations given, cause inevitable failure when tests or examinations are called for.

EXERCISES

1. Name five subjects about which you know so little that it would be useless to attempt an explanation.
2. Name five about which you know something, but not enough to give clear explanations of them.
3. Name four about which you know but little, but concerning which you feel sure that you can obtain information.

4. Name six that you think you clearly understand. Report orally on one of them.

Theme LXXXIV. — *Write out an explanation of one of the subjects named in number four of the preceding exercise.*

(Read your theme and criticise as to clearness. In listening to the themes read by other members of the class consider them as to clearness. Call for further explanation of any part not perfectly clear to you.)

155. Selection of Facts — Unity. — After we have been given a subject for explanation or have chosen one for ourselves, we must decide concerning the facts to be presented. In some kinds of exposition this selection is rather difficult. Since the purpose is to make our meaning clear to the person addressed, we secure unity by including all that is necessary to that purpose and by omitting all that is not necessary. It is evident that selection of facts to secure unity depends to some extent upon the audience. If a child asks us to explain what a trust is, our explanation will differ very much from that which we would give if we were addressing a body of men who were familiar with the term *trusts*, but do not understand the advantages and disadvantages arising from their existence.

Examine the following as to selection of facts. For what class of people do you think it was written? What seems to be the purpose of it?

THE FEUDAL SYSTEM

This connection of king as sovereign, with his princes and great men as vassals, must be attended to and understood, in order that you may comprehend the history which follows. A great king, or sovereign prince, gave large provinces, or grants of land, to his dukes, earls, and noblemen ; and each of these possessed nearly as much power, within his own district, as the king did in the rest of his dominions. But then the vassal, whether duke, earl, or lord, or whatever he was, was obliged to come with a certain number of men to assist the sovereign, when he was engaged in war; and in time of peace, he was bound to attend on his court when summoned, and do homage to him, that is, acknowledge that he was his master and liege lord. In like manner, the vassals of the crown, as they were called, divided the lands which the king had given them into estates, which they bestowed on knights, and gentlemen, whom they thought fitted to follow them in war, and to attend them in peace; for they, too, held courts, and administered justice, each in his own province. Then the knights and gentlemen, who had these estates from the great nobles, distributed the property among an inferior class of proprietors, some of whom cultivated the land themselves, and others by means of husbandmen and peasants, who were treated as a sort of slaves, being bought and sold like brute beasts, along with the farms which they labored.

Thus, when a great king, like that of France or England, went to war, he summoned all his crown vassals to attend him, with the number of armed men corresponding to his fief, as it was called, that is, territory which had been granted to each of them. The prince, duke, or earl, in order to obey the summons, called upon all the gentlemen to whom he had given estates, to attend his standard with their followers in arms. The gentlemen, in their turn, called on the franklins, a lower order of gentry, and upon the peasants; and thus the whole force of the kingdom was assembled in one array. This system of holding lands for military service, that is, for fighting for the sovereign when called upon, was called the *feudal system*. It was general throughout all Europe for a great many ages.

— SCOTT: *Tales of a Grandfather.*

Theme LXXXV. — *Write a theme on one of the following:* —

1. Tell your younger brother how to make a whistle.
2. Explain some game to a friend of your own age.
3. Give an explanation of the heating system of your school to a member of the school board of an adjoining city.

4. Explain to a city girl how butter is made.

5. Explain to a city boy how hay is cured.

6. Explain to a friend how to run an automobile.

(Consider the selection of facts as determined by the person addressed.)

156. Arrangement — Coherence. — Some expositions are of such a nature that there is but little question concerning the proper arrangement of the topics composing them. In order to be coherent, all we do is to follow the natural order of occurrence in time and place. This is especially true of general narrations and of some general descriptions. In explaining the circulation of the blood, for instance, it is most natural for us to follow the course which the blood takes in circulating through the body. In explaining the manufacture of articles we naturally commence with the material as it first comes to the factory, and trace it through its successive stages.

In other kinds of exposition a coherent arrangement is somewhat difficult. We should not, however, fail to pay attention to it. A clear understanding of the subject, on the part of the listener, depends largely upon the proper arrangement of topics. As you study examples of expositions of some length, you will notice that there are topics which naturally belong together. These topics form groups, and the groups are treated separately. If the expositions are good ones, the related facts will not only be united into groups, but the groups will also be so arranged and the transition from one group to another be so naturally made that there will be no confusion in the mind concerning it.

In brief explanations of but one paragraph there should be but one group of facts. Even these need to be so arranged as to make the whole clear. The writer may understand the whole, but in order to make it clear to the reader, he must present certain facts before he does others. The clearness of an explanation depends on arranging the facts so that those which are necessary to the understanding of others shall come first.

Examine the following expositions as to the grouping of related facts and ideas and the arrangement of those groups : —

Fresh, pure air at all times is essential to bodily comfort and good health. Air may become impure from many causes. Poisonous gases may be mixed with it; sewer gas is especially to be guarded against; coal gas which is used for illuminating purposes is very poisonous and dangerous if inhaled; the air arising from decaying substances, foul cellars, or stagnant pools, is impure and unhealthy, and breeds diseases ; the foul and poisonous air which has been expelled from the lungs, if breathed again, will cause many distressing symptoms. Ventilation has for its object the removal of impure air and the supplying of fresh, wholesome air in its place. Proper ventilation should be secured in all rooms and buildings, and its importance cannot be overestimated.

In the summer time and in climates which permit of it with comfort, ventilation may be secured by having the doors and windows open, thus allowing the fresh air to circulate freely through the house. In stormy and cold weather, however, some other means of ventilation must be supplied. If open fires or grates are used for heating purposes, good ventilation exists, for under such circumstances, the foul and impure air is drawn out of the rooms through the chimneys, and the fresh air enters through the cracks of the doors and windows.

Where open fireplaces are not used, several plans of ventilation may be used, as they all operate on the same principle. Two openings should be in the room, one of them near the floor, through which the fresh air may enter, the other higher up, and connected with a shaft or chimney, which producing a draft, may serve to free the room from impure air. The size of these openings may be regulated according to the size of the room.

— BALDWIN : *Essential Lessons in Human Physiology.*

THE QUEEN BEE

It is a singular fact, also, that the queen is made, not born. If the entire population of Spain or Great Britain were the offspring of one mother, it might be found necessary to hit upon some device by which a royal baby could be manufactured out of an ordinary one, or else give up the fashion of royalty. All the bees in the hive have a common parentage, and the queen and the worker are the same in the egg and in the chick; the patent of royalty is in the cell and in the food; the cell being much larger, and the food a peculiar stimulating kind of jelly. In certain contingencies, such as the loss of the queen with no eggs in the royal cells, the workers take the larva of an ordinary bee, enlarge the cell by taking in the two adjoining ones, and nurse it and stuff it and coddle it, till at the end of sixteen days it comes out a queen. But ordinarily, in the natural course of events, the young queen is kept a prisoner in her cell till the old queen has left with the swarm. Not only kept, but guarded against the mother queen, who only wants an opportunity to murder every royal scion in the hive. Both the queens, the one a prisoner and the other at large, pipe defiance at each other at this time, a shrill, fine, trumpetlike note that any ear will at once recognize. This challenge, not being allowed to be accepted by either party, is followed, in a day or two, by the abdication of the old queen; she leads out the swarm, and her successor is liberated by her keepers, who, in her turn, abdicates in favor of the next younger. When the bees have decided that no more swarms can issue, the reigning queen is allowed to use her stiletto upon her unhatched sisters. Cases have been known where two queens issued at the same time, when a mortal combat ensued, encouraged by the workers, who formed a ring about them, but showed no preference, and recognized the victor as the lawful sovereign. For these and many other curious facts we are indebted to the blind Huber.

It is worthy of note that the position of the queen cells is always vertical, while that of the drones and workers is horizontal; majesty stands on its head, which fact may be a part of the secret.

The notion has always very generally prevailed that the queen of the bees is an absolute ruler, and issues her royal orders to willing subjects. Hence Napoleon the First sprinkled the symbolic bees over the imperial mantle that bore the arms of his dynasty; and in the country of the Pharaohs the bee was used as the emblem of a people sweetly submissive to the orders of its king. But the fact is, a swarm of bees is an absolute democracy, and kings and despots can find no warrant in their example. The power and authority are entirely vested in the great mass, the workers. They furnish all the brains and foresight of the colony, and administer its affairs. Their word is law, and both king and queen must obey. They regulate the swarming, and give the signal for the swarm to issue from the hive; they select and make ready the tree in the woods and conduct the queen to it.

The peculiar office and sacredness of the queen consists in the fact that she is the mother of the swarm, and the bees love and cherish her as a mother and not as a sovereign. She is the sole female bee in the hive, and the swarm clings to her because she is their life. Deprived of their queen, and of all brood from which to rear one, the swarm loses all heart and soon dies, though there be an abundance of honey.

The common bees will never use their sting upon the queen, — if she is to be disposed of they starve her to death; and the queen herself will sting nothing but royalty — nothing but a rival queen.

— John Burroughs : Birds and Bees.

Theme LXXXVI. — *Write an expository theme.*

Suggested subjects : —

1. Duties of the sheriff.
2. How a motor works.
3. How wheat is harvested.
4. Why the tide exists.
5. How our schoolhouse is ventilated.
6. What is meant by the theory of evolution.
7. The manufacture of ——.
8. How to make a ——.

(Consider the arrangement of your statements.)

157. Use of an Outline. — Before beginning to write an explanation we need to consider what we know about the subject and what our purpose is; we need to select facts that will make our explanations clear to our readers;

and we need to decide what arrangement of these facts will best show their relation to each other. We shall find it of advantage, especially in lengthy explanations, to express our thoughts in the form of an outline. An outline helps us to see clearly whether our facts are well chosen, and it also helps us to see whether the arrangement is orderly or not. Clearness is above all the essential of exposition, and outlines aid clearness by giving unity and coherence.

EXERCISES

Select three of the following subjects and make lists of facts that you know about them. From these select those which would be necessary in making a clear explanation of each. After making out these lists of facts, arrange them in what seems to you the best possible order for making the explanation clear to your classmates.

1. The value of a school library.
2. Sponges.
3. The manufacture of clocks.
4. Drawing.
5. Athletics in the high school.
6. Examinations.
7. Debating societies.

Theme LXXXVII. — *Following the outline, write an exposition on one of the subjects chosen.*

(Notice the transition from one paragraph to another. See Section 87.)

158. Exposition of Terms — Definition. — Explanation of the meaning of general terms is one form of exposition (Section 63). The first step in the exposition of a term is the giving of a definition. This may be accomplished by the use of a synonym (Section 64). We make a term intelligible to the reader by the use of a synonym with which he is familiar ; and though such a definition is inexact, it gives a rough idea of the meaning of the term in question, and so serves a useful purpose. If, however, we wish exactness, we shall need to make use of the logical definition.

159. The Logical Definition. — The logical definition sets exact limits to the meaning of a term. An exact definition must include all the members of a class indicated by the term defined, and it must exclude everything that does not belong to that class. A logical definition is composed of two parts. It first names the class to which the term to be defined belongs, and then it names the characteristic that distinguishes that term from all other members of the same class. The class is termed the *genus*, and the distinguishing characteristics of the different members of the class are termed the *differentia*. Notice the following division into genus and differentia.

Term to be Defined	Class (*Genus*)	Distinguishing Character-istic (*Differentia*)
A parallelogram	is a quadrilateral	whose opposite sides are parallel.
Exposition	is that form of discourse	which seeks to explain the meaning of a term.

Each definition includes three elements : the term to be defined, the genus, and the differentia ; but these are not necessarily arranged in the order named.

EXERCISE

Select the three elements (the term to be defined, the genus, and the differentia) in each of the following : —

1. A polygon of three sides is called a triangle.
2. A square is an equilateral rectangle.
3. A rectangle whose sides are equal is a square.
4. Description is that form of discourse which aims to present a picture.
5. The characters composing written words are called letters.
6. The olfactory nerves are the first pair of cranial nerves.
7. Person is that modification of a noun or pronoun which denotes the speaker, the person spoken to, or the person or things spoken of.
8. The diptera, or true flies, are readily distinguishable from other insects by their having a single pair of wings instead of two pairs, the hind wings being transformed into small knob-headed pedicles called balancers or halters.

160. Difficulty of Framing Exact Definitions. — In order to frame a logical definition, exactness of thought is essential. Even when the thought is exact, it will be found difficult and often impossible to frame a satisfactory definition. Usually there is little difficulty in selecting the genus, still care should be taken to select one that includes the term to be defined. We might begin the definition of iron by saying, "Iron is a metal," since all iron is metal, but it would be incorrect to begin the definition of rodent by saying, "A rodent is a beaver," because the term beaver does not include all rodents. We must also take care to choose for the genus some term familiar to the reader, because the object of the definition is to make the meaning clear to him.

The chief difficulty of framing logical definitions arises in the selection of differentia. In many cases it is not easy to decide just what characteristics distinguish one member of a class from all other members of that class. We all know that iron is a metal, but most of us would find it difficult to add to the definition just those things which distinguish iron from other metals. We may say, " A flute is a musical instrument " ; so much of the definition is easily given. The difficulty lies in distinguishing it from all other musical instruments.

EXERCISES

A. Select proper differentia for the following : —

TERM TO BE DEFINED	CLASS (*Genus*)	DISTINGUISHING CHARACTERISTIC (*Differentia*)
1. Narration	is that form of discourse	?
2. A circle	is a portion of a plane	?
3. A dog	is an animal	?
4. A hawk	is a bird	?
5. Physiography	is the science	?
6. A sneak	is a person	?
7. A quadrilateral	is a plane figure	?
8. A barn	is a building	?
9. A bicycle	is a machine	?
10. A lady	is a woman	?

B. Give logical definitions for at least four words in the list below.

1. Telephone.	4. Novel.	7. Camera.
2. Square.	5. Curiosity.	8. Brick.
3. Hammer.	6. Door.	9. Microscope.

161. Inexact Definitions. — If the distinguishing characteristics are not properly selected, the definition though logical in form may be inexact, because the differentia do not exclude all but the term to be defined. If we say, " Exposition is that form of discourse which gives information," the definition is inexact because there are other forms of discourse that give information. Many definitions given in text-books are inexact. Care should be taken to distinguish them from those which are logically exact.

EXERCISE

Which of the following are exact ?

1. A sheep is a gregarious animal that produces wool.
2. A squash is a garden plant much liked by striped bugs.
3. A pronoun is a word used for a noun.
4. The diaphragm is a sheet of muscle and tendon, convex on its upper side, and attached by bands of striped muscle to the lower ribs at the side, to the sternum, and to the cartilage of the ribs which join it in front, and at the back by very strong bands to the lumbar vertebræ.
5. A man is a two-legged animal without feathers.
6. Argument is that form of discourse which has for its object the proof of the truth or falsity of a proposition.
7. The base of an isosceles triangle is that side which is equal to no other.
8. Zinc is a metal used under stoves.
9. The epidermis of a leaf is a delicate, transparent skin which covers the whole leaf.

Theme LXXXVIII. — *Write an expository paragraph about one of the following :* —

Suggested subjects : —

1. Household science and arts.
2. Architecture.
3. Æsthetics.
4. Poetry.
5. Fiction.

6. Half tones.
7. Steam fitting.
8. Swimming.

(Consider the definitions you have used.)

162. Division. — The second step in the exposition of a term is division. Definition establishes the limits of the term. Division separates into its parts that which is included by the term. By definition we distinguish triangles from squares, circles, and other plane figures. By division we may separate them into scalene, isosceles, and equilateral, or if we divide them according to a different principle into right and oblique triangles. In either case the division is complete and exact. By completeness is meant that every object denoted by the term explained is included in the division given, thus making the sum of these divisions equal to the whole. By exactness is meant that but a single principle has been used, and so no object denoted by the term explained will be included in more than one of the divisions made. There are no triangles which are neither right nor oblique, so the division is complete; and no triangle can be both right and oblique, so the division is exact. Such a complete and exact division is called *classification*.

Nearly every term may be divided according to more than one principle. We may divide the term *books* into ancient and modern, or into religious and secular, or in any one of a dozen other ways. Which principle of division we shall choose will depend upon our purpose. If we wish to discuss *sponges* with reference to their shapes, our division will be different from what it would be if we were to discuss them with reference to their uses. When a principle of division has once been chosen it is essential that it be followed throughout. The use of two principles causes an overlapping of divisions, thus producing what is called cross division. Using the principle of use, a tailor may sort his bolts of cloth into cloth for overcoats, cloth for suits, and cloth for trousers ; using the principle of weight, into heavy weight and light weight ; or he may sort them with reference to color or price. In any case but a single principle is used. It would not do to divide them into cloth for suits, light weight goods, and brown cloth. Such a division would be neither complete nor exact ; for some of the cloth would belong to none of the classes while other pieces might properly be placed in all three.

In the exact sciences complete exposition is the aim, and classification is necessary ; but in other writing the purpose in hand is often better accomplished by omitting minor divisions. A writer of history might consider the political growth, the wars, and the religion of a nation and omit its domestic life and educational progress, especially if these did not greatly influence the result that he wishes to make plain. If we wished to explain the plan of the organization of a high school, it would be satisfactory to divide the pupils into freshmen, sophomores, juniors, and seniors, even though, in any particular school, there might be a few special and irregular pupils who belonged to none of these classes. An exposition of the use of hammers would omit many occasional and unimportant uses. Such a classification though exact is incomplete and is called *partition*.

EXERCISES

A. Can you tell which of the following are classifications ? Which are partitions ? Which are defective ?

1. The inhabitants of the United States are Americans, Indians, and negroes.
2. Lines are straight, curved, and crooked.
3. Literature is composed of prose, poetry, and fiction.
4. The political parties in the last campaign were Republican and Democrat.
5. The United States Government has control of states and territories.
6. Plants are divided into two groups: (1) the phanerogams, or flowering plants, and (2) cryptogams, or flowerless plants.
7. All phanerogamous plants consist of (1) root and (2) shoot; the shoot consisting of (*a*) stem and (*b*) leaf. It is true that some exceptional plants, in maturity, lack leaves, or lack root. These exceptions are few.
8. We may divide the activities of the government into: keeping order, making law, protecting individual rights, providing public schools, providing and mending roads, caring for the destitute, carrying the mail, managing foreign relations, making war, and collecting taxes.

B. Notice the following paragraphs. State briefly the divisions made.

1. **Plan of the Book.** — What is government? Who is the government? We shall begin by considering the American answers to these questions.

What does The Government do? That will be our next inquiry. And with regard to the ordinary practical work of government, we shall see that government in the United States is not very different from government in the other civilized countries of the world.

Then we shall inquire how government officials are chosen in the United States, and how the work of government is parceled out among them. This part of the book will show what is meant by self-government and local self-government, and will show that our system differs from European systems chiefly in these very matters of self-government and local self-government.

Coming then to the details of our subject, we shall consider the names and duties of the principal officials in the United States; first, those of the township, county, and city, then those of the state, and then those of the federal government.

Finally, we shall examine certain operations in the American system, such as a trial in court, and nominations for office, and conclude with an outline of international relations, and a summary of the commonest laws of business and property.

— CLARK : *The Government.*

2. Zoölogy and its Divisions. — What things we do know about the dog, however, and about its relatives, and what things others know can be classified into several groups; namely, things or facts about what a dog does or its behavior, things about the make-up of its body, things about its growth and development, things about the kind of dog it is and the kinds of relatives it has, and things about its relations to the outer world and its special fitness for life.

All that is known of these different kinds of facts about the dog constitutes our knowledge of the dog and its life. All that is known by scientific men and others of these different kinds of facts about all the 500,000 or more kinds of living animals, constitutes our knowledge of animals and is the science *zoölogy.* Names have been given to these different groups of facts about animals. The facts about the bodily make-up or structure of animals constitute that part of zoölogy called animal *anatomy* or *morphology;* the facts about the things animals do, or the functions of animals, compose animal *physiology;* the facts about the development of animals from young to adult condition are the facts of animal *development;* the knowledge of the different kinds of animals and their relationships to each other is called *systematic* zoölogy or animal *classification;* and finally the knowledge of the relations of animals to their external surroundings, including the inorganic world, plants and other animals, is called animal *ecology.*

Any study of animals and their life, that is, of zoölogy, may include all or any of these parts of zoölogy.

— KELLOGG : *Elementary Zoölogy.*

3. Are not these outlines of American destiny in the near-by future rational ? In these papers an attempt has been made : —

First, to picture the physical situation and equipment of the American in the modern world.

Second, to outline the large and fundamental elements of American character, which are : —

(*a*) Conservatism — moderation, thoughtfulness, and poise.

(*b*) Thoroughness — conscientious performance, to the minutest detail, of any work which we as individuals or people may have in hand.

(*c*) Justice — that spirit which weighs with the scales of righteousness our conduct toward each other and our conduct as a nation toward the world.

(*d*) Religion — the sense of dependence upon and responsibility to the Higher Power ; the profound American belief that our destiny is in His hands.

(*e*) The minor elements of American character — such as the tendency to organize, the element of humor, impatience with frauds, and the movement in American life toward the simple and sincere.

— BEVERIDGE: *Americans of To-day and To-morrow.*

C. Consult the table of contents or opening chapters of any text-book and notice the main divisions.

D. Find in text-books five examples of classification or division.

E. Make one and if possible more divisions of each of the following : —

1. The pupils in your school.
2. Your neighbors.
3. The books in the school library.
4. The buildings you see on the way to school.
5. The games you know how to play.
6. Dogs.
7. Results of competition.

Theme LXXXIX. — *Write an introductory paragraph showing what divisions you would make if called upon to write about one of the following topics :* —

1. Mathematics.
2. The school system of our city.
3. The churches of our town.
4. Methods of transportation.
5. Our manufacturing interests.

6. Games that girls like.

7. The inhabitants of the United States.

(Have you mentioned all important divisions of your subject? · Have you included any minor and unimportant divisions? Consider other possible principles of division of your subject. Have you chosen the one best suited to your purpose?)

163. Exposition of a Proposition. — Two terms united into a sentence so that one is affirmed of the other become a proposition. Propositions, like terms, may be either specific or general. " Napoleon was ambitious " is a specific proposition ; " Politicians are ambitious " is a general one.

When a proposition is presented to the mind, its meaning may not at once be clear. This may arise from the fact that some of the terms in the proposition are unfamiliar, or are obscure, or misleading. In this case the first step, and often the only step necessary, is the explanation of the terms in the proposition. The following taken from Dewey's *Psychology* illustrates the exposition of a proposition by explaining its terms : —

The habitual act thus occurs automatically and mechanically. When we say that it occurs automatically, we mean that it takes place, as it were, of itself, spontaneously, without the intervention of the will. By saying that it is mechanical, we mean that there exists no consciousness of the process involved, nor of the relation of the means, the various muscular adjustments, to the end, locomotion.

It is possible for our listeners or readers to understand each term in a proposition and yet not be able to understand the meaning of the proposition as a whole. When this is the case, we shall find it necessary to make use of methods of exposition discussed later.

EXERCISES

Explain orally the following propositions by explaining any of the terms liable to be unfamiliar or misunderstood :

1. The purpose of muscular contraction is the production of motion.
2. Ping-pong is lawn tennis in miniature, with a few modifications.
3. An inevitable dualism bisects nature.
4. Never inflict corporal chastisement for intellectual faults.
5. Children should be led to make their own investigations and to draw their own inferences.
6. The black willow is an excellent tonic as well as a powerful antiseptic.
7. Give the Anglo-Saxon equivalent for " nocturnal."
8. A negative exponent signifies the reciprocal of what the expression would be if the exponent were positive.

Theme XC. — *Write an explanation of one of the following :* —

1. Birds of a feather flock together.
2. Truths and roses have thorns about them.
3. Where there's a will, there's a way.
4. Who keeps company with a wolf will learn to howl.
5. He gives nothing but worthless gold, who gives from a sense of duty.
6.   All things that are,
Are with more spirit chased than enjoyed.
7. Be not simply good — be good for something.
8. He that hath light within his own clear breast,
May sit i' the center, and enjoy bright day ;
But he that hides a dark soul and foul thoughts

Benighted walks under the midday sun;
Himself is his own dungeon.

(Select the one that seems most difficult to you, determine what it means, and then attempt to make an explanation that will show that you thoroughly understand its meaning.)

164. Exposition by Repetition. — In discussing paragraph development (Section 50) we have already learned that the meaning of a proposition may be made clearer by the repetition of the topic statement. This repetition may be used to supplement the definition of terms, or it may by itself make clear both the meaning of the terms and of the proposition. Each repetition of the proposition presents it to the reader in a new light or in a stronger light. Each time the idea is presented it seems more definite, more familiar, more clear. Such statements of a proposition take advantage of the fact that the reader is thinking, and we merely attempt to direct his thought in such a way that he will turn the proposition over and over in his mind until it is understood.

Notice how the following propositions are explained largely by means of repetitions, each of which adds a little to the original statement.

How to live? — that is the essential question for us. Not how to live in the mere material sense only, but in the widest sense. The general problem, which comprehends every special problem, is the right ruling of conduct in all directions under all circumstances. In what way to treat the body; in what way to treat the mind; in what way to manage our affairs; in what way to bring up a family; in what way to behave as a citizen; in what way to utilize all those sources of happiness which nature supplies — how to use all our faculties to the greatest advantage of ourselves and others — how to live completely? And this being the great thing needful for us to learn, is, by consequence, the great thing which education has to teach. To prepare us for complete living is the function which education has to discharge : and the only radical mode of judging of any educational course, is, to judge in what degree it discharges such functions.

— HERBERT SPENCER: *Education.*

The gray squirrel is remarkably graceful in all his movements. It seems as though some subtle curve was always produced by the line of the back and tail at every light bound of the athletic little creature. He never moves abruptly or jerks himself impatiently, as the red squirrel is continually doing. On the contrary, all his movements are measured and deliberate, but swift and sure. He never makes a bungling leap, and his course is marked by a number of sinuous curves almost equal to those of a snake. He is here one minute, and the next he has slipped away almost beyond the ability of our eyes to follow.

— F. SCHUYLER MATTHEWS: *American Nut Gatherers.*

Theme XCI. — *Write a paragraph explaining one of the propositions below by means of repetition.*

1. Physical training should be made compulsory in the high school.
2. Some people who seem to be selfish are not really so.
3. The dangers of athletic contests are overestimated.
4. The Monroe Doctrine is a warning to European powers to keep their hands off territory in North and South America.
5. By the " treadmill of life " we mean the daily routine of duties.
6. The thirst for novelty is one of the most powerful incentives that takes a man to distant countries.
7. There are unquestionably increasing opportunities for an honorable and useful career in the civil service of the United States.

(Have you used any method besides that of repetition ? Does your paragraph really explain the proposition ?)

165. Exposition by Use of Examples. — Exposition treats of general subjects, and the topic statement of a paragraph is, therefore, a general statement. In order to understand what it means, the reader may need to think of a concrete case. The writer may develop his paragraph by furnishing concrete cases. (See Section 44.) In many cases no further explanation is necessary.

The following paragraph illustrates this method of explanation : —

The lower portions of stream valleys which have sunk below sea level are called *drowned valleys*. The lower St. Lawrence is perhaps the greatest example of a drowned valley in the world, but many other rivers are in the same condition. The old channel of the Hudson River may be traced upon the sea bottom about 125 miles beyond its present mouth, and its valley is drowned as far up as Troy, 150 miles. The sea extends up the Delaware River to Trenton, and Chesapeake Bay with its many arms is the drowned valleys of the Susquehanna and its former tributaries. Many of the most famous harbors in the world, as San Francisco Bay, Puget Sound, the estuaries of the Thames and the Mersey, and the Scottish firths, are drowned valleys.
— DRYER: *Lessons in Physical Geography.*

Theme XCII. — *Develop one of the following topic statements into an expository paragraph by use of examples :* —

1. Weather depends to a great extent upon winds.
2. Progress in civilization has been materially aided by the use of nails.
3. Habit is formed by the repetition of the same act.
4. Men become criminals by a gradual process.
5. Men's lives are affected by small things.
6. Defeat often proves to be real success.

(Have you made your meaning clear ? Does your example really illustrate the topic statement ? Can you think of other illustrations ?)

166. Exposition by Comparison or Contrast. — We can frequently make our explanations clear by comparing the subject under discussion with something that is already familiar to the reader. In this case we shall need to show in what respect it is similar to that with which it is compared or in what way it differs from it. (Section 48.) It is customary in our explanations to compare the term under discussion with some well-known term, but this is not always necessary. In the example below the term *socialism* is probably no more familiar than the term *anarchism*. Both are here explained, and the explanations are made clearer by contrasting the one with the other.

Socialism, which is curiously confounded by the indiscriminating with Anarchism, is its exact opposite. Anarchy is the doctrine that there should be no government control; Socialism — that is, State Socialism — is the doctrine that government should control everything. State Socialism affirms that the state — that is, the government — should own all the tools and implements of industry, should direct all occupations, and should give to every man according to his need and require from every man according to his ability. State Socialism points to the evils of overproduction in some fields and insufficient production in others, under our competitive system, and proposes to remedy these evils by assigning to government the duty of determining what shall be produced and what each worker shall produce. If there are too many preachers and too few shoemakers, the preacher will be taken from the pulpit and assigned to the bench; if there are too many shoemakers and too few preachers, the shoemaker will be taken from the bench and assigned to the pulpit. Anarchy says, no government; Socialism says, all government; Anarchy leaves the will of the individual absolutely unfettered, Socialism leaves nothing to the individual will; Anarchism would have no social organism which is not dependent on the entirely voluntary assent of each individual member of the organism at every instant of its history; Socialism would have every individual of the social organism wholly subordinate in all his lifework to the authority of the whole body expressed through its properly constituted officers. It is true that there are some writers who endeavor to unite these two antagonistic doctrines by teaching that society should be organized wholly for industry, not at all for government. But how a coöperative industry can be carried on without a government which controls as well as counsels, no writer, so far as I have been able to discover, has ever even suggested.

— LYMAN ABBOTT: *Anarchism: Its Cause and Cure.*

Theme XCIII. — *Write an exposition that makes use of comparison:* —

Suggested subjects : —

1. A bad habit is a tyrant.
2. Typewritten letters.
3. The muskrat's house.
4. Compare Shylock with Barabas in Marlowe's *Jew of Malta.*
5. Methods of reading.
6. All the world's a stage.
7. Compare life to a flower.

(Can you suggest any other comparisons which you might have used? Have you been careful in your selection of facts and arrangement ?)

167. Exposition by Obverse Statements. — In explaining an idea it is necessary to distinguish it from any related or similar idea with which it may be confused in the minds of our readers. Clearness is added by the statement that one is *not* the other. To say that socialism is not anarchy is a good preparation for the explanation of what socialism really is. A similar result is obtained in the following selection from Burke, by excluding different kinds of peace and so emphasizing the kind which he has in mind.

The proposition is peace. Not peace through the medium of war; not peace to be hunted through the labyrinth of intricate and endless negotiations; not peace to arise out of universal discord, fomented from principle, in all parts of the empire; not peace to depend on the juridical determination of perplexing questions, or the precise marking the shadowy boundaries of a complex government. It is simple peace; sought in its natural course, and in its ordinary haunts. — It is peace sought in the spirit of peace; and laid in principles purely pacific. I propose, by removing the ground of the difference, and by restoring the *former unsuspecting confidence of the colonies in the Mother Country*, to give permanent satisfaction to your people; and (far from a scheme of ruling by discord) to reconcile them to each other in the same act, and by the bond of the very same interest which reconciles them to British government.

168. Exposition by Giving Particulars or Details. — One of the most natural methods of explaining is to give particulars or details. After a general statement has been made, our minds naturally look for details to make the meaning of that statement clearer. (See Sections 45–47.) This method is used very largely in generalized descriptions and narrations.

Notice the use of particulars or details in the following examples : —

Happy the boy who knows the secret of making a willow whistle ! He must know the best kind of willow for the purpose, and the exact time of year when the bark will slip. The country boy seems to know these things by instinct. When the day for whistles arrives he puts away marbles and hunts the whetstone. His jackknife must be in good shape, for the making of a whistle is a delicate piece of handicraft. The knife has seen service in mumblepeg and as nut pick since whistle-making time last year. Surrounded by a crowd of spectators, some admiring, some skeptical, the boy selects his branch. There is an air of mystery about the proceeding. With a patient indulgent smile he rejects all offers of assistance. He does not attempt to explain why this or that branch will not do. When finally he raises his shining knife and cuts the branch on which his choice has fallen, all crowd round and watch. From the large end between two twigs he takes a section about six inches long. Its bark is light green and smooth. He trims one end neatly and passes his thumb thoughtfully over it to be sure it is finished to his taste. He then cuts the other end of the stick at an angle of about 45°, making a clean single cut. The sharp edge of this is now cut off to make a mouthpiece. This is a delicate operation, for the bark is apt to crush or split if the knife is dull, or the hand is unskillful. The boy holds it up, inspecting his own work critically. Sometimes he is dissatisfied and cuts again. If he makes a third cut and is still unsuccessful he tosses the spoiled piece away. It is too short now. A half dozen eager hands reach for the discarded stick, and the one who gets it fondles it lovingly. I once had such a treasure and cherished it until I learned the secret of the whistle-maker's art. He next places the knife edge about half an inch back from the end of the mouthpiece and cuts straight towards the center of the branch about one-fourth the way through. A three-cornered piece is now cut out, and the chip falls to the ground unheeded.

When this is finished the boy's eye runs along the stick with a calculating squint. The knife edge is placed at the middle, then moved a short distance towards the mouthpiece. With skillful hand he cuts through the bark in a perfect circle round the stick. While we watch in fascinated silence, he takes the knife by the blade and resting the unfinished whistle on his knees he strikes firmly but gently the part of the stick between the ring and the mouthpiece. Only the wooden part of the handle touches the bark. He goes over and over it until every spot on its surface has felt his light blow. Now he lays the knife aside, and grasping the stick with a firm hand below the ring in the bark, with the right hand he holds the pounded end. He tries it with a careful twist. It sticks. Back to his knees it goes and the tap, tap, begins again. When he twists it again it slips, and the bark comes off smoothly in one piece, while we breathe a sigh of relief. How white the stick is under the bark! It shines and looks slippery. Now the boy takes his knife again. He cuts towards the straight jog where the chip was taken out, paring the wood away, sloping up to within an inch of the end of the bark. Now he cuts a thin slice of the wood between the edge of the vertical cut and the mouthpiece.

The whistle is nearly finished. We have all seen him make them before and know what comes next. Our tongues seek over moist lips sympathetically, for we know the taste of peeled willow. He puts the end of the stick into his mouth and draws it in and out until it is thoroughly wet. Then he lifts the carefully guarded section of bark and slips it back into place, fitting the parts nicely together.

The willow whistle is finished. There remains but to try it. Will it go? Does he dare blow into it and risk our jeers if it is dumb?

With all the fine certainty of the Pied Piper the boy lifts the humble instrument to his lips. His eyes have a far-off look, his face changes; while we strain eyes and ears, he takes his own time. The silence is broken by a note, so soft, so tender, yet so weird and unlike other sounds! Our hands quiver, our hearts beat faster. It is as if the spirit of the willow tree had joined with the spirit of childhood in the natural song of earth.

It goes!

—MARY ROGERS MILLER: *The Brook Book.*
(Copyright, 1902, Doubleday, Page and Co.)

Theme XCIV. — *Write an exposition on one of the following subjects, making use of particulars or details:* —

1. How ice cream is made.
2. The cultivation of rice.
3. Greek architecture.
4. How paper is made.
5. A tornado.
6. Description of a steam engine.
7. The circulatory system of a frog.
8. A western ranch.
9. Street furniture.
10. A street fair.

(Have you used particulars sufficient to make your meaning clear? Have you used any unnecessary ones? Why is the arrangement of your topics easy in this theme?)

169. Exposition by Cause and Effect. — When our general statement is in the form of a cause or causes, the question naturally arises in our mind as to the effects resulting from those causes. In like manner, when the general statement takes the form of an effect, we want to know what the causes are that produce such an effect. From the very nature of exposition we may expect to find much of this kind of discourse relating to causes and effects. (See Section 49.)

Notice the following example : —

The effect of the polar whirls may be seen in the rapid rotation of water in a pan or bowl. The centrifugal force throws the water away from the center, where the surface becomes depressed, and piles it up around the sides, where the surface becomes elevated. The water being deeper at the sides than at the center, its pressure upon the bottom is proportionately greater. A similar effect is produced by the whirl of the air around the polar regions. It is thrown away from the polar regions and piled up around the circumference of the whirl. There is less air above the polar regions than above latitude 30°–40°, and the atmospheric pressure is correspondingly low at one place and high at the other. Thus the centrifugal force of the polar whirl makes the pressure low in spite of the low temperature. The position of the tropical belts of high pressure is a resultant of the high temperature of the equatorial regions on one side and the polar whirls on the other.

— DRYER: *Lessons in Physical Geography.*

Theme XCV. — *Write an expository theme using cause or effect.*

Suggested subjects : —

1. The causes of the French Revolution.
2. How ravines are formed.
3. Irrigation.
4. Effects of smoking.
5. Lack of exercise.
6. Volcanic eruptions.

(Did you find it necessary to make use of any other method of explanation ? Did you make use of description in any place?)

SUMMARY

1. Exposition is that form of discourse the purpose of which is to explain.
2. The essential characteristics of an exposition are —
     a. That it possess unity because it contains only those facts essential to its purpose.
     b. That the facts used be arranged in a coherent order.
3. Exposition is concerned with (*a*) general terms or (*b*) general propositions.
4. The steps in the exposition of a term are —
     a. Definition. This may be —
          (1) By synonym (inexact).
          (2) By use of the logical definition (exact).
     b. Division. This may be —
          (1) Complete (classification).
          (2) Incomplete (partition).
     The same principle of division should be followed throughout.
5. Exposition of a proposition may use any one of the following methods —
     a. By repetition.
     b. By giving examples.
     c. By stating comparisons and contrasts.
     d. By making obverse statements.
     e. By relating particulars or details.
     f. By stating cause or effect.
     g. By any suitable combination of these methods.

XI. ARGUMENT

170. Difference between Argument and Exposition. —
Argument differs from exposition in its purpose. By
exposition we endeavor to make clear the meaning of a
proposition ; by argument we attempt to prove its truth.
If a person does not understand what we mean, we explain;
if, after he does understand, he does not believe, we argue.

Often a simple explanation is sufficient to convince.
As soon as the reader understands the real meaning of a
proposition, he accepts our view of the case. A heated
discussion may end with the statement, " Oh, if that is
what you mean, I agree with you." In Section 70, we
have learned that the first step in argument is explanation,
by which we make clear the meaning of the proposition
whose truth we wish to establish. This may include both
the expounding of the terms in the proposition and the
explanation of the proposition as a whole.

This suggests another difference between exposition
and argument, for we cannot argue about single terms,
though we may explain them. We may explain what is
meant by the term *elective studies*, or *civil service ;* but
an argument requires a proposition such as, Pupils should
be allowed to choose their own studies, or, Civil Service
should be established. Even with such a topic as Expansion or Restricted Immigration, which seems to be a
subject of argument, there is really an implied proposition
under discussion ; as, The United States should acquire

control of territory outside of its present boundaries ; or, It should be the policy of our government to restrict immigration. We may explain the meaning of single terms or of propositions, but in order to argue, we must have a proposition either expressed or implied.

171. Proposition of Fact and Proposition of Theory. — Some propositions state facts and some propositions state theories. Every argument therefore aims either to prove the occurrence of a fact or the truth of a theory. The first would attempt to show the actual or probable truth of a specific proposition ; for example : —

> Nero was guilty of burning Rome.
>
> Joan of Arc was burned at the stake.
>
> Barbara Frietchie actually existed.
>
> Sheridan never made the ride from Winchester.
>
> Homer was born at Chios.

The second would try to establish the probable truth of a general theory ; for example : —

> A college education is a profitable investment.
>
> Light is caused by a wave motion of ether.

172. Statement of the Proposition. — The subject about which we argue may be stated in any one of the three forms discussed in Section 74 ; that is, as a declarative sentence, a resolution, or a question. The statement does not necessarily appear first in the argument, but it must be clearly formulated in the mind of the writer before he attempts to argue. Before trying to convince others he must know exactly what he himself believes, and the attempt to state his belief in the form of a proposition will assist in making his own thought clear and definite.

If we are going to argue concerning elective studies, we should first of all be sure that we understand the meaning of the term ourselves. Then we must consider carefully what we believe about it, and state our proposition so that it shall express exactly this belief. On first thought we may believe the proposition that pupils should be allowed to choose their own studies. But is this true of all pupils in the grades as well as in the high schools ? Or is it true only of the upper classes in the high school or only for college students ? Can you state this proposition so that it will express your own belief on the subject ?

EXERCISES

A. Use the following terms in expressed propositions : —

1. Immigration.
2. Elevated railways.
3. American history.
4. Military training.
5. Single session.
6. Athletics.

B. Explain the following propositions : —

1. The United States should adopt a free-trade policy.
2. Is vivisection justifiable ?
3. The author has greater influence than the orator.
4. The civil service system should be abolished.
5. The best is always cheapest.

C. Can you restate the following propositions so that the meaning of each will be made more definite ?

1. Athletics should be abolished. (Should *all* athletic exercises be abolished ?)
2. Latin is better than algebra. (*Better* for what purpose ? *Better* for whom ?)
3. Training in domestic arts and sciences should be provided for high school pupils. (Define domestic arts and sciences. Should they be taught to *all* high school pupils ?)
4. Punctuality is more important than efficiency.

5. The commercial course is better than the classical course.

6. A city should control the transportation facilities within its limits.

Theme XCVI. — *Write out an argument favoring one of the propositions as restated in Exercise C above.*

(Before writing, make a brief as indicated in Section 77. Consider the arrangement of your argument.)

173. Clear Thinking Essential to Argument. — Having clearly in mind the proposition which we wish to prove, we next proceed to give arguments in its support. The very fact that we argue at all assumes that there are two sides to the question. If we hope to have another accept our view we must present good reasons. We cannot convince another that a proposition is true unless we can tell him why it is true ; and certainly we cannot tell him why until we know definitely our own reasons for believing the statement. In order to present a good argument we must be clear logical thinkers ourselves ; that is, we must be able to state definite reasons for our beliefs and to draw the correct conclusions.

174. Inductive Reasoning. — One of the best preparations for trying to convince others is for us to consider carefully our own reasons for believing as we do. Minds act in a similar manner, and what leads you and me to believe certain truths will be likely to cause others to believe them also. A brief consideration of how our belief in the truth of a proposition has been established will indicate the way in which we should present our material in order to cause others to believe the same proposition. If you ask yourself the question, What leads me to believe as I do ? the answer will undoubtedly be effective in convincing others.

Are the following propositions true or false ? Why do you believe or refuse to believe each ?

1. Maple trees shed their leaves in winter.
2. Dogs bark.
3. Kettles are made of iron.
4. Grasshoppers jump.
5. Giraffes have long necks.
6. Raccoons sleep in the daytime.
7. The sun will rise to-morrow.
8. Examinations are not fair tests of a pupil's knowledge.
9. Honest people are respected.
10. Water freezes at 32° Fahrenheit.
11. Boys get higher standings in mathematics than girls do.

It is at once evident that we believe a proposition such as one of these, because we have known of many examples. If we reject any of the propositions it is because we know of exceptions (we have seen kettles not made of iron), or because we do not know of instances (we may never have seen a raccoon, and so do not know what he does in the daytime). The greater the number of cases which have occurred without presenting an exception, the stronger our belief in the truth of the proposition (we expect the sun to rise because it has never failed).

The process by which, from many individual cases, we establish the truth of a proposition is called **inductive reasoning**.

175. Establishing a General Theory. — A general theory is established by showing that for all known particular cases it will offer an acceptable explanation. By investigation or experiment we note that a certain fact is true in one particular instance, and, after a large number of individual cases have been noted, and the same fact found to be true in each, we assume that such is true of all like cases, and a general law is established. This is the natural scientific method and is constantly being made use of in pursuing scientific studies. By experiment, it was found that one particular kind of acid turned blue litmus red. This, of course, was not sufficient proof to establish a general law, but when, upon further investigation, it was found to be true of all known acids, scientists felt justified in stating the general law that acids turn blue litmus red.

In establishing a new theory in science it is necessary to bring forward many facts which seem to establish it, and the argument will consist in pointing out these facts. Frequently the general principle is assumed to be true, and the argument then consists in showing that it will apply to and account for all the facts of a given kind. Theories which have been for a time believed have, as the world progressed in learning, been found unable to account for all of a given class of conditions, and so they have been replaced by other theories, just as the Copernican theory of astronomy has displaced the Ptolemaic theory.

Our belief may be based upon the absence of facts proving the contrary as well as upon the presence of facts proving the proposition. If A has never told an untruth, that fact is an argument in favor of his truthfulness on the present occasion. A man who has never been dishonest may point to this as an argument in favor of placing him in a position of trust. Often the strongest evidence that we can offer in favor of a proposition is the absence of any fact that would support the negative conclusion.

The point of the whole matter is that from the observation of a large number of cases, we may establish the *probable* truth of a proposition, but emphasis needs to be laid upon the probability. We cannot be sure. Not all crows are black, though you may never have seen a white one. The sun may not rise to-morrow, though it has never failed up to this time. Still it is by this observation of many individual cases that the truth of the propositions that men do believe has been established. We realize that our inductions are often imperfect, but the general truths so established will be found to underlie every process of reasoning, and will be either directly or indirectly the basis upon which we build up all argument.

We may then redefine inductive reasoning as the process by which from many individual cases we establish the *probable* truth of a general proposition.

EXERCISES

Notice in the following selections that the truth of the conclusion is shown by giving particular examples: —

1. It is curious enough that *we always remember people by their worst points*, and still more curious that *we always suppose that we ourselves are remembered by our best*. I once knew a hunchback who had a well-shaped hand, and was continually showing it. He never believed that anybody noticed his hump, but lived and died in the conviction that the whole town spoke of him no otherwise than as the man with the beautiful hand, whereas, in fact, they only looked at his hump, and never so much as noticed whether he had a hand at all. This young lady, so pretty and so clever, is simply the girl who had that awkward history with So-and-so; that man, who has some of the very greatest qualities, is nothing more than the one who behaved so badly on such an occasion. It is a terrible thing to think that we are all always at

watch one upon the other, to catch the false step in order that we may have the grateful satisfaction of holding our neighbor for one who cannot walk straight. No regard is paid to the better qualities and acts, however numerous; all the attention is fixed upon the worst, however slight. If St. Peter were alive he would be known as the man who denied his Master; St. Paul would be the man who stoned Stephen; and St. Thomas would never be mentioned in any decent society without allusions to that unfortunate request for further evidence. Probably this may be the reason why we all have so much greater a contempt for and distrust of each other than would be warranted by a correct balance between the good and the evil that are in each.

— THOMAS GIBSON BOWLES: *Flotsam and Jetsam.*

2. In the first place, 227 withered leaves of various kinds, mostly of English plants, were pulled out of worm burrows in several places. Of these, 181 had been drawn into the burrows by or near their tips, so that the footstalk projected nearly upright from the mouth of the burrow; 20 had been drawn in by their bases, and in this case the tips projected from the burrows; and 26 had been seized near the middle, so that these had been drawn in transversely and were much crumpled. Therefore 80 per cent (always using the nearest whole number) had been drawn in by the tip, 9 per cent by the base or footstalk, and 11 per cent transversely or by the middle. This alone is almost sufficient to show that *chance does not determine the manner in which leaves are dragged into the burrows.*

— DARWIN: *Vegetable Mold and Earthworms.*

3. *The catastrophe of every play is caused always by the folly or fault of a man; the redemption, if there be any, is by the wisdom and virtue of a woman, and, failing that, there is none.* The catastrophe of King Lear is owing to his own want of judgment, his impatient vanity, his misunderstanding of his children; the virtue of his one true daughter would have saved him from all the injuries of the others, unless he had cast her away from him; as it is, she all but saves him. Of Othello, I need not trace the tale; nor the one weakness of his so mighty love; nor the inferiority of his perceptive intellect to that even of the second woman character in the play, the Emilia who dies in wild testimony against his error: —

" Oh, murderous coxcomb! what should such a fool
    Do with so good a wife?"

In *Romeo and Juliet*, the wise and brave stratagem of the wife is brought to ruinous issue by the reckless impatience of her husband. In *The Winter's Tale*, and in *Cymbeline*, the happiness and existence of two princely households, lost through long years, and imperiled to the death by the folly and obstinacy of the husbands, are redeemed at last by the queenly patience and wisdom of the wives. In *Measure for Measure*, the foul injustice of the judge, and the foul cowardice of the brother, are opposed to the victorious truth and adamantine purity of a woman. In *Coriolanus*, the mother's counsel, acted upon in time, would have saved her son from all evil; his momentary forgetfulness of it is his ruin; her prayer, at last, granted, saves him — not, indeed, from death, but from the curse of living as the destroyer of his country.

— RUSKIN: Sesame and Lilies.

4. *Bas.* So may the outward shows be least themselves;
The world is still deceived with ornament.
In law, what plea so tainted and corrupt
But, being season'd with a gracious voice,
Obscures the show of evil? In religion,
What damned error, but some sober brow
Will bless it and approve it with a text,
Hiding the grossness with fair ornament?
There is no vice so simple but assumes
Some mark of virtue on his outward parts:
How many cowards, whose hearts are all as false
As stairs of sand, wear yet upon their chins
The beards of Hercules and frowning Mars,
Who, inward search'd, have livers white as milk;
And these assume but valor's excrement
To render them redoubted! Look on beauty,
And you shall see 'tis purchased by the weight;
Which therein works a miracle in nature,
Making them lightest that wear most of it:
So are those crisped snaky golden locks
Which make such wanton gambols with the wind,
Upon supposed fairness, often known
To be the dowry of a second head,
The skull that bred them in the sepulcher.
Thus ornament is but the guiled shore

To a most dangerous sea; the beauteous scarf
Veiling an Indian beauty; in a word,
The seeming truth which cunning times put on
To entrap the wisest.   Therefore, thou gaudy gold,
Hard food for Midas, I will none of thee;
Nor none of thee, thou pale and common drudge
'Tween man and man: but thou, though meager lead,
Which rather threatenest than dost promise aught,
Thy paleness moves me more than eloquence;
And here choose I: joy be the consequence!
                        — SHAKESPEARE: *Merchant of Venice.*

Theme XCVII. —*Write a paragraph proving the truth of one of the following statements:* —

1. It is a distinct advantage to a large town to be con-
     nected with the smaller towns by electric car lines.
2. Vertical penmanship should be taught in all elemen-
     tary schools.
3. Examinations develop dishonesty.
4. Novel reading is a waste of time.
5. Tramps ought not to be fed.

(Make a brief.   Consider the arrangement of your arguments.   Read Section 72.)

176. Errors of Induction. — A common error is that of too hasty generalization.   We conclude that something is always so because it happened to be so in the few cases that have come under our observation.   A broader expe-rience frequently shows that the hastily made generaliza-tion will not hold.

Some people are led to lose faith in all humanity because one or two of their acquaintances have shown themselves unworthy of their trust.   Others are ready to pronounce a merchant dishonest because some article purchased at his store has not proved to be so good as it was expected to be. There are those who are superstitious concerning the wearing of opals, claiming that they bring the wearer ill luck, and they cite several instances where misfortune seemed to follow the wearing of that particular stone. What may seem to be causes and effects at first may, upon further investigation or inquiry, prove to be merely chance coincidences. In your work in argument, whether for the class room or outside, be careful about this point. Remember that your induction will be weak or even worthless if you draw conclusions from too few examples.

Often one example seems sufficient to cause belief. We might believe that all giraffes have long necks, even though we had seen but one ; but such a belief would exist because, by many examples of other animals, we have learned that a single specimen will fairly represent all other specimens of the same class. On the other hand, if this one giraffe should possess one brown eye and one white eye, we would not expect all other giraffes to have such eyes, for our observation of many hundreds of animals teaches us that the eyes of an animal are usually alike in color. In order to establish a true generalization, the *essential* characteristics must be selected, and these cannot be determined by rule, but rather by common sense.

177. Deductive Reasoning. — When once a general principle has been established, we may demonstrate the truth of a specific proposition by showing that the general principle applies to it. We see a gold ring and say, "This ring is valuable," because we believe the general proposition, "All articles made of gold are valuable." Expressed in full, the process of reasoning would be --

A. All articles made of gold are valuable.

B. This ring is made of gold.

C. Therefore this ring is valuable.

A series of statements such as the above is called a syllogism. It consists of a major premise (*A*), a minor premise (*B*), and a conclusion (*C*).

Of course we shall not be called upon to prove so simple a proposition as the one given, but with more difficult ones the method of reasoning is the same. The process which applies a general proposition (*A*) to a specific instance (*C*), is called **deductive reasoning**.

178. Relation between Inductive and Deductive Reasoning. — Deductive reasoning is shorter and seems more convincing than inductive reasoning, for if the premises are true and the statement is made in correct form, the conclusions are irresistible. Each conclusion carries with it, however, the weakness of the premises on which it is based, and as these premises are general principles that have been themselves established by inductive reasoning, the conclusions of deductive reasoning can be no more *sure* than those of inductive reasoning. Each may prove only that the proposition is probably true rather than that it is surely true, though in many cases this probability becomes almost a certainty.

179. The Enthymeme. — We seldom need to state our argument in the syllogistic form. One of the premises is usually omitted, and we pass directly from one premise to the conclusion. If we say, " Henry will not succeed as an engineer," and when asked why he will not, we reply, " Because he is not good in mathematics," we have omitted the premise, " A knowledge of mathematics is necessary for success in engineering." A shortened syllogism, that is, a syllogism with one premise omitted, is called an enthymeme.

Thus in ordinary matters our thought turns at once to the conclusion in connection with but one premise. We make a thousand statements which a moment's thought will show that we believe because we believe some unexpressed general principle. If I should say of my dog, "Fido will die sometime," no sensible person would doubt the truth of the statement. If asked to prove it, I would say, "Because he is a dog, and all dogs die sometime." Thus I apply to a specific proposition, Fido will die, the general one, All dogs die, a proposition about which there is no doubt.

Frequently the suppressed premise is not so well established as in this case, and the belief or nonbelief of the proposition will be determined by the individuals addressed, each in accordance with his experience. Suppose that in reading we find the statement, "A boy of fourteen ought not to be allowed to choose his own subjects of study, because he will choose all the easy ones and avoid the more difficult though more valuable ones." The omitted premise that all boys will choose easy studies, needs to be established by induction. If a high school principal had noticed that out of five hundred boys, four hundred elected the easy studies, he would admit the truth of the omitted premise, and so of the conclusion. But if only one hundred had chosen the easy subjects, he would reject the major premise and likewise the conclusion.

It is evident that in order to be sure of the truth of a proposition we must determine the truth of the premises upon which it is based. An argument therefore is frequently given over wholly to establishing the premises. If their truth can be demonstrated, the conclusion inevitably follows.

EXERCISES

A. Supply the missing premise for the following : —
1. John will succeed because he has a college education.
2. Henry is happy because he has plenty of money.
3. Candy is nutritious because it is made of sugar.
4. These biscuits will make me ill because they are heavy.
5. This dog must be angry because he is growling.
6. This fish can swim.
7. The plural of the German noun *der Garten* is *die Gärten.*
8. It will hurt to have this tooth filled.

B. Supply the reasons and complete the syllogism for each of the following : —
1. This book should not be read.
2. This hammer is useful.
3. That dog will bite.
4. This greyhound can run rapidly.
5. The leaves have fallen from the trees.
6. That boy ought to be punished.
7. It is too early to go nutting.
8. This boy should not study.
9. You ought not to vote for this man for mayor.

Theme XCVIII. —*Write a paragraph proving the truth of one of the following propositions:* —
1. Labor-saving machinery is of permanent advantage to mankind.
2. New Orleans will some day be a greater shipping port than New York.

3. **Poetry** has a greater influence on the morals of a nation than prose writing.
4. Boycotting injures innocent persons and should never be employed.
5. Ireland should have Home Rule.
6. The President of the United States should be elected by the direct vote of the people.

(Consider your argument with reference to the suppressed premises.)

180. Errors of Deduction. — The deductive method of reasoning, if properly used, is effective, but much care needs to be taken to avoid false conclusions. A complete exposition of the variations of the syllogism is not necessary here, but it will be of value to consider briefly three chief errors.

If the terms are not used with the same meaning throughout, the conclusion is valueless. A person might agree with you that domestic arts should be taught to girls in school, but if you continued by saying that scrubbing the floor is a form of domestic art, therefore the girls should be taught to scrub the floor, he would reject your conclusion because the meaning of the term *domestic art*, as he understood it in the first statement, is not that used in the second.

It will be noticed that each syllogism includes three terms. For example, the syllogism, —

> All hawks eat flesh ;
> This bird is a hawk ;
> Therefore this bird eats flesh, —

contains the three terms, *hawk*, *eats flesh*, *this bird;* of these but two appear in the conclusion. The one which does not (in this case *hawk*) is called the middle term. If the major premise does not make a statement about every member of the class denoted by the middle term, the conclusion may not be valid even though the premises are true. For example : —

> All hawks are birds ;
> This chicken is a bird ;
> Therefore this chicken is a hawk.

In this case the middle term is *birds*, and the major premise, *All hawks are birds*, does not make a statement which applies to all birds. The conclusion is therefore untrue. Such an argument is a fallacy.

The validity of the conclusion is impaired if either premise is false. In the enthymeme, " Henry is a coward ; he dare not run away from school," the suppressed premise, " All persons who will not run away from school are cowards," is not true, and so invalidates the conclusion. It is well to test the validity of your own argument and that of your opponent by seeking for the suppressed premise and stating it, for this may reveal a fatal weakness in the thought.

EXERCISES

Which of the following are incorrect ?

1. The government should pay for the education of its people ;
   Travel is a form of education ;
   Therefore the government should pay the traveling expenses of the people.
2. All horses are useful ;
   This animal is useful ;
   Therefore this animal is a horse.

3. I ought not to study algebra because it is a very difficult subject.
4. Pupils ought not to write notes because note writing
interferes with the rights of others.
5. All fish can swim;
Charles can swim;
Therefore Charles is a fish.
6. Henry is a fool because he wears a white necktie.
7. All dogs bark ;
This animal barks ;
Therefore this animal is a dog.

Theme XCIX. —*Write a paragraph proving the truth
of one of the following propositions :* —

1. The government should establish a parcels post.
2. The laws of mind determine the forms of composition.
3. Training for citizenship should be given greater attention in the public schools.
4. The members of the school board should be appointed
by the mayor of the city.
5. In the estimation of future ages —— will be considered the greatest President since Lincoln.

(State your premises. Have you shown that they are
true ?)

181. Evidence. — We may reach belief in the truth of a
specific statement by means of deductive reasoning. Commonly, however, when dealing with an actual state or
occurrence, we present other facts or circumstances that
show its existence. The facts presented may be those of
experience, the testimony of witnesses, the opinion of
those considered as experts in the subject, or a combination of circumstances known to have existed. To be of

any value as arguments, they must be true, and they must be related to the fact that we are trying to prove. These true and pertinent facts we term *evidence*.

Evidence may be direct or indirect. If a man sees a boy steal a bag of apples from the orchard across the way, his evidence is direct. If instead, he only sees him with an empty bag and later with a full one, the evidence will be indirect. If you testify that early in the evening you saw a tramp enter a barn which later in the evening caught fire, your testimony as regards the cause of the fire would be indirect evidence against the tramp. If you can testify that you saw sparks fall from his lighted pipe and ignite a pile of hay in the barn, the evidence which you give will be direct.

Direct evidence has more weight than indirect, but often the latter is nearly equal to the former and is sufficient to convince us. Even the direct testimony of eye-witnesses must be carefully considered. Several persons may see the same thing and yet make very different reports, even though they may all desire to tell the truth. The weight that we shall give to a person's testimony will depend upon his ability to observe and to report accurately what he has experienced, and upon his desire to tell the truth.

Notice in the following selection what facts, specific instances, and circumstances are advanced in support of the proposition. Assuming that they are true, are they pertinent to the proposition?

Certain species of these army ants which inhabit tropical America, Mr. Belt considered to be the most intelligent of all the insects of that part of the world. On one occasion he noticed a wide column of them trying to pass along a nearly perpendicular slope of crumbling earth, on which they found great difficulty in obtaining a foothold. A number succeeded in retaining their positions, and further strengthened them by laying hold of their neighbors. They then remained in this position, and allowed the column to march securely and easily over their bodies. On another occasion a column was crossing a stream of water by a very narrow branch of a tree, which only permitted them to go in single file. The ants widened the bridge by a number clinging to the sides and to each other, and this allowed the column to pass over three or four deep. These ants, having no permanent nests, carry their larvæ and pupæ with them when marching. The prey they capture is cut up and carried to the rear of the army to be distributed as food.

—ROBERT BROWN: *Science for All.*

Theme C. — *Present all the evidence you can either to prove or disprove one of the following propositions :* —

Select some question of local interest as : —

1. The last fire in our town was of incendiary origin.
2. The football team from —— indulged in "slugging" at the last game.
3. Our heating system is inadequate.
4. It rained last night.

If you prefer, choose one of the following subjects : —

1. The Stuart kings were arbitrary rulers.
2. The climate of our country is changing.
3. Gutenberg did not invent the printing press.
4. The American Indians have been unjustly treated by the whites.
5. Nations have their periods of rise and decay.

(Are the facts you use true ? Are they pertinent ? Do you know of facts that would tend to show that your proposition is not true ?)

182. Number and Value of Reasons. — Although a statement may be true and pertinent it is seldom sufficient for proof. We need, as a rule, several such statements. If you are trying to convince a friend that one kind of an automobile is superior to another, and can give only one reason for its superiority, you no doubt will fail in your attempt. If, however, you can give several reasons, you may succeed in convincing him. Suppose you go to your principal and ask to be allowed to take an extra study. . You may give as a reason the fact that your parents wish you to take it. He may not think that is a sufficient reason for your doing so, but when he finds that with your present studies you do not need to study evenings, that one of them is a review, and that you have been standing well in all your studies, he may be led to think that it will be wise for you to take the desired extra study.

While we must guard against insufficiency of reasons, we must not forget that numbers alone do not convince. One good reason is more convincing than several weak ones. Two or three good reasons, clearly and definitely stated, will have much more weight than a large number of less important ones.

EXERCISES

A. Give a reason or two in addition to the reasons already given in each of the following : —

1. It is better to attend a large college than a small one, because the teachers are as a rule greater experts in their lines of work.

2. The school board ought to give us a field for athletics as the school ground is not large enough for practice.

3. Gymnasium work ought to be made compulsory. Otherwise many who need physical training will neglect it.

4. The game of basket ball is an injury to a school, since it detracts from interest in studies.

5. Rudolph Horton will make a good class president because he has had experience.

B. Be able to answer orally any two of the following :

1. Prove to a timid person that there is no more danger in riding in an automobile than there is in riding in a carriage drawn by horses. Use but one argument, but make it as strong as possible.

2. Give two good reasons why the superstition concerning Friday is absurd.

3. What, in your mind, is the strongest reason why you wish to graduate from a high school? For your wishing to go into business after leaving the high school? For your wishing to attend college?

4. What are the two or three strongest arguments in favor of woman's suffrage? Name two or three arguments in opposition to it.

C. Name all the points that you can in favor of the following. Select the one that you consider the most important.

1. Try to convince a friend that he ought to give up the practice of cigarette smoking.

2. Show that athletics in a high school ought to be under the management of the faculty.

3. Show that athletics should be under the management of the pupils themselves.

4. Macbeth's ambition and not his wife was the cause of his ruin.

5. Macbeth's wife was the cause of his ruin.

Theme CI. — *Select one of the subjects in the exercise above, and write out two or three of the strongest arguments in its favor.*

(Consider the premises, especially those which are not expressed. Is your argument deductive or inductive?)

183. The Basis of Belief. — If you ask yourself, Why do I believe this ? the answer will in many cases show that your belief in the particular case under consideration arises because you believe some general principle or theory which applies to it.

One person may believe that political economy should be taught in high schools because he believes that it is the function of the high school to train its pupils for citizenship, and that the study of political economy will furnish this training. Another person may oppose the teaching of political economy because he believes that pupils of high school age are not sufficiently mature in judgment to discuss intelligently the principles of political economy, and that the study of them at that age does not furnish desirable training for citizenship. It is evident that an argument between these two concerning the teaching of political economy in any particular school would consist in a discussion of the conflicting general theories which each believed to be true.

We have shown in Section 179 that one high school principal might believe that boys should be allowed to choose their own studies because he believed that they would not generally select the easy ones ; while another principal would oppose free electives because he believes that boys would choose the less difficult studies. The proposition that "The United States should retain its hold on the Philippines" involves conflicting theories of the function of this government. So it will be found with many of our beliefs that either consciously or unconsciously they are based on general theories. It is important in argument to know what these theories are, and especially to consider what may be the general theories of those whom we wish to convince.

184. Appeals to General Theory, Authority, and Maxims.
— A successful argument in deductive form must be based
upon principles and theories that the audience believes.
A minister in preaching to the members of his church may
with success proceed by deductive methods, because the
members believe the general principles upon which he
bases his arguments. But in addressing a mixed audience,
many of whom are not church members, such an argument
might not be convincing, because his hearers might deny
the validity of the premises from which his conclusions
were drawn. In such a case he must either keep to
general theories which his auditors do believe, or by inductive methods seek to prove the truth of the general
principles themselves.

If in support of our view we quote the opinion of some
one whom we believe competent to speak with weight and
authority upon the question, we must remember that it
will have weight with our audience only if they too look
upon the person as an authority. It proves nothing to a
body of teachers to say that some educational expert believes as you do unless they have confidence in him as a
man of sound judgment. On the other hand, it may count
against a proposition to show that it has not been endorsed
by any one of importance or prominence.

In a similar way a maxim or proverb may be quoted in
support of a proposition. If a boy associates with bad
company, we may offer the maxim, " Birds of a feather flock
together," in proof that he is probably bad too. Such
maxims or proverbs are brief statements of principles
generally believed, and the use of them in an argument
is in effect the presentation of a general theory in a form
which appeals to the mind of the hearer and causes him to
believe our proposition.

185. Argument by Inference. — The statement of a fact may be introduced into an argument, not because the fact itself applies directly to the proposition we wish to prove, but because it by inference suggests a general theory which does so apply. Though the reader may not be conscious of it, the presence of this general theory may influence his decision even more than it would if it had been explicitly stated.

An argument implies that there are two sides to a question. Which you shall take depends on the way you look on it, that is, on what may be called your mental point of view. Therefore any fact, allusion, maxim, comparison, or other statement which may cause you to look at the question in a different light or from a different point of view may be used as an argument. In effect, it calls up a general theory whose presence affects your decision. Notice how brief the argument is in the following selection from Macaulay: —

Many politicians of our time are in the habit of laying it down as a self-evident proposition, that no people ought to be free till they are fit to use their freedom. The maxim is worthy of the fool in the old story, who resolved not to go into the water till he had learned to swim. If men are to wait for liberty till they become wise and good in slavery, they may indeed wait forever.

— MACAULAY : *Milton.*

186. Summary. — To summarize the preceding paragraphs, the authority we quote, the maxims we state, the facts we adduce become valuable because they appeal to general theories already believed by the reader. Success in argument demands, therefore, that we consider carefully what theories may probably be in the mind of our audience, and that we present our argument in such a way as to appeal to those theories.

Theme CII. — *Write a short argument, using one of the following:* —

1. A young boy is urging his father to permit him to attend an entertainment. Give his reasons as he would give them to his father.
2. Suppose the father refuses the request. Write out his reasons.
3. Try to convince a companion just entering high school to take the college preparatory course instead of the commercial course.

(Are your reasons true and pertinent? To what general theories have you appealed? Consider the coherence of each paragraph.)

187. Arrangement of Arguments. — We have learned that in arguing we need to consider how those whom we address arrive at the belief they hold, and that it will assist us to this knowledge of others if we consider our own beliefs and the manner of their establishing. We must present our material in the order that convinces. Each case may differ so from every other that no general rule can be followed, but the consideration of some general principles of arrangement will be of assistance. It is the purpose of the following paragraphs to point out in so far as possible the most effective order of arrangement.

188. Possibility, Probability, and Actuality. — It has been stated, in Section 175, that reasoning leads to probable truth, and that this probability may become so strong as to be accepted as certainty. In common speech this difference is borne in mind, and we distinguish a fact or event that is only possible from one that is probable ; and likewise one that is only probable from one in which the probability approaches so near to certainty as to con-

vince us that it actually did exist or occur. Our arguments may therefore be directed to proving possibility,
probability, or actuality.

If we believe that an event actually occurred, the belief
implies that it was both possible and probable. Therefore, if we wish a person to believe in the actual occurrence
of an event, we must first be sure that he does not question the possibility of its existence, and then we must show
him that it probably did take place. Only as we can
make it extremely probable have we the right to say that
we have shown its actual occurrence.

A mother finding some damage done to one of the
pictures on the wall could not justly accuse her young
son unless by the presence of a chair or stepladder it had
been possible for him to reach the picture. This possibility, reënforced by a knowledge of his tendency to mis-
chief, and by the fact that he was in the house at the time
the damage was done, would lead to the belief that he
probably was guilty. Proof that he was actually responsible for the damage would still be lacking, and it might
later be discovered that the injury had been done
accidentally by one of the servants.

Possibility, probability, and actuality merge into one
another so gradually that no sharply defined distinctions
can be observed. It is impossible to say that a certain
argument establishes possibility, another probability, and
a third the actuality of an event. One statement may do
all three, but any proof of actuality must include arguments
showing both possibility and probability. A person accused of murder attempts to demonstrate his innocence by
proving an *alibi;* that is, he attempts to show that he was
at some other place at the time the murder was committed
and so cannot possibly be guilty. Such an alibi, estab-

lished by reliable witnesses, is positive proof of innocence, no matter how strong the evidence pointing to probable guilt may be.

189. Argument from Cause. — We have learned, in Section 49, that the relation of cause and effect is one which is ingrained in our nature. We accept a proposition as plausible if a cause which we consider adequate has been assigned. Our belief in a proposition often depends upon our belief in some other proposition which may be accepted as a cause.

Thus, in the following, the truth of one proposition leads to the belief that the other is also true : —

a. Henry has studied hard this year, therefore he will pass his college entrance examinations.

b. The man has severed an artery, therefore he will probably bleed to death before the physician arrives.

c. It will soon grow warmer, because the sun has risen.

An argument from cause may be of itself conclusive evidence of the fact. But, for the most part, such arguments merely establish the possibility or probability of the proposition and so render it ready for proof. In our arrangement of material, we therefore place such arguments *first*.

190. Argument from Sign. — Cause and effect are so closely united that when an effect is observed we assume that there has been a cause, and we direct our argument to proving what it is. An effect is so associated with its cause that the existence of an effect is a sign of the existence of a cause, and such an argument is called an *argument from sign*. Reasoning from sign is very common in our daily life. The wild geese flying south indicate the approach of cold weather. The baby's toys show that he has been in the room. A man's hat found beside a rifled safe will convict him of the crime. A dog's track in the garden is positive proof that a dog has been there.

If the effect observed is always associated with the same cause, the argument is conclusive. If I observe as an effect that the river has frozen over during the night, I have no doubt that it has been caused by a lowering of the temperature.

If two or three possible causes exist, our argument becomes conclusive only by considering them all and showing that all but one did not produce the observed effect. If the principal of a school knows that one of three boys broke a window light, he may be able to prove which one did it by finding out the two who did not. If a man is found shot to death, the coroner's jury may prove that he was murdered by showing that he did not commit suicide. If there are many possible causes, the method of elimination becomes too tedious and must be abandoned. If you find that your horse is lame, it would be difficult to prove which of the many possible causes actually operated to produce the lameness, though the attendant circumstances might point to sóme one cause and so lead you to assume that it was the one.

Under *arguments from sign* should be included also those cases when we pass directly from one effect to another that arises from the same cause; as, "I hear the windmill turning, it will be a good day to sail;" or, "These beans are thrifty, therefore if I plant potatoes here I shall get a good crop." In these sentences the wind and the fertile soil are not mentioned, but we pass directly from one effect to another.

As used by rhetoricians, arguments from sign include also arguments from attendant circumstances. If we have observed that two events have happened near together in time, we accept the occurrence of one as a sign that the other will follow. When we hear the factory whistle blow, we conclude that in a few minutes the workmen will pass our window on their way home. Such a conclusion is based upon a belief established by an inductive process. The degree of probability that it gives depends upon the number of times that it has been observed to act without failure. If we have seen two boys frequently together, the presence of one is a sign of the probable presence of the other. A camp fire would point to the recent presence of some one who kindled it.

In using an argument from sign care must be taken not to confuse the relation of cause and effect with that of contiguity in time or place. Do not allege that which happened at the same time or near the same place as a cause. If you do use an attendant circumstance, be sure that it adds something to the probability.

191. Argument from Example. — It has been pointed out in the study of inductive reasoning (Section 176) that a single example may suffice to establish a general notion of a class. In dealing with objects of the physical world, if essential and invariable qualities of the object are considered, they may be asserted to be qualities of each member of the class, and such an argument from an individual to all the members of the class is convincing. They thus rank with arguments from sign as effective in proving the certainty of a proposition.

In dealing with human actions, on the other hand,

examples are seldom proofs of fact. We cannot say that all men will act in a certain way under given circumstances because one man has so acted. Nevertheless, arguments by examples are frequently used and are especially powerful when we wish not only to convince a man, but also to persuade him to action. This persuasion to action must be based on conviction, and in such a case the argument from sign that convinces the man of the truth of a proposition should precede the example that urges him to action. After convincing a friend that there are advantages to be derived from joining a society, he may be persuaded to join by naming those who have joined.

192. Argument from Analogy. — Analogy is very much relied upon in practical life. Reasoning from analogy depends upon the recognition of similarity in regard to some particulars followed by the inference that the similarity extends to other particulars. As soon as it was known that the atmospheric conditions of the planet Mars are similar to those of the earth, it was argued by analogy that Mars must also be inhabited.

An analogy is seldom conclusive and, though it is often effective in argument, it must not be taken as proof of fact. The mind very readily observes likenesses, and when directed toward the establishing of a proposition easily overlooks the differences. In order to determine the strength of an argument from analogy, attention should be given to the differences existing between the two propositions considered. False analogies are very common. We must guard against using them, and especially against allowing ourselves to be convinced by them. Even when the resemblance is so slight as to render analogy impossible, it may serve to produce a metaphor that often has the effect of argument.

It is much easier to captivate the fancy with a pretty or striking figure than to move the judgment with sound reason. . . . His (the speaker's) picture appeals to the mind's visible sense, hence his power over us, though his analogies are more apt to be false than true. . . .

The use of metaphor, comparison, analogy, is twofold — to enliven and to convince; to illustrate and enforce an accepted truth, and to press home and clinch one in dispute. An apt figure may put a new face upon an old and much worn truism, and a vital analogy may reach and move the reason. Thus when Renan, referring to the decay of the old religious beliefs, says that the people are no poorer for being robbed of false bank notes and bogus shares, his comparison has a logical validity. . . .

The accidental analogies or likenesses are limitless, and are the great stock in trade of most writers and speakers. An ingenious mind finds types everywhere, but real analogies are not so common. The likeness of one thing to another may be valid and real, but the likeness of a thought with a thing is often merely fanciful. . . .

I recently have met with the same fallacy in a leading article in one of the magazines. "The fact revealed by the spectroscope," says the writer, "that the physical elements of the earth exist also in the stars, supports the faith that a moral nature like our own inhabits the universe." A tremendous leap — a leap from the physical to the moral. We know that these earth elements are found in the stars by actual observation and experience; but a moral nature like our own —this is assumed, and is not supported by the analogy.

—JOHN BURROUGHS: *Analogy, True and False.*

Notice the use of analogy in the argument below.

There is only one cure for the evils which newly acquired freedom produces; and that cure is freedom. When a prisoner first leaves his cell he cannot bear the light of day: he is unable to discriminate colors, or recognize faces. But the remedy is, not to remand him into his dungeon, but to accustom him to the rays of the sun. The blaze of truth and liberty may at first dazzle and bewilder nations which have become blind in the house of bondage. But, let them gaze on, and they will soon be able to bear it. In a few years men learn to reason. The extreme violence of opinions subsides. Hostile theories correct each other. The scattered elements of truth cease to contend and begin to coalesce, and at length a system of justice and order is educed out of the chaos.

— MACAULAY: *Milton.*

193. Summary of Arrangement. — The necessity of argument arises because some one does not believe the truth of a proposition. In order to establish in his mind a belief, we must present our arguments in an orderly and convincing way. This order will usually be that of showing him first the possibility and then the probability, leading him finally as near to certainty as we can. We may say, therefore, that we should use arguments from cause, arguments from sign, and arguments from example in the order named.

Another principle of arrangement is that inductive argument will usually precede deductive argument. We naturally proceed by induction to establish general truths which, when established, we may apply. If our audience already believe the general theories, the inductive part may be omitted.

Both of these principles of arrangement should be considered with reference to that of a third, namely, climax. Climax means nothing more than the orderly progression of our argument to the point where it convinces our hearer. We call that argument which finally convinces him the strongest, and naturally this should be the end of the argument. Of several proofs of equal grade, one that will attract the attention of the hearer should come first, while the most convincing one should come last.

In arranging arguments attention needs also to be given to coherence. One proof may be so related to another that the presentation of one naturally suggests the other. Sometimes, for the sake of climax, the coherent order must be abandoned. More often the climax is made more effective by following the order which gives the greatest coherence.

Theme CIII. — *Prove one of the following propositions:*
1. The Presidential term should be extended.
2. Bookkeeping is of greater practical value than any other high school study.
3. In cities all buildings should be restricted to three stories in height.
4. Sumptuary laws are never desirable.
5. No pupil should carry more than four studies.
6. This school should have a debating society.

(Have you proved possibility, probability, or actuality? Have you used arguments from cause, sign, or example? Consider the arrangement of your arguments. Consider the analogies you have used, if any. Can you shorten your theme without weakening it?)

194. The Brief. — Arrangement is of very great importance in argument. In fact, it is so important that much more care and attention needs to be given to the outline in argument, and the outline itself may be more definitely known to the hearer than in the other forms of discourse. In description and narration especially, it detracts from the value of the impressions if the reader becomes aware of the plan of composition. In exposition a view of the framework may not hinder clear understanding, but in argument it may be of distinct advantage to have the orderly arrangements of our arguments definitely known to him whom we seek to convince.

The brief not only assists us in making our own thought orderly and exact, but it enables us to exclude that which is trivial or untrue. An explanation may fail to make every point clear and yet retain some valuable elements, but an argument fails of its purpose if it does not establish a belief. A single false argument or even a trivial one may so appeal to a mind prejudiced against the proposition that all the valid proofs fail to convince. This single weakness is at once used by our opponent to show that our other arguments are false because this one is. A committee once endeavored to persuade the governor of a state not to sign a certain bill, but they defeated themselves because their opponents pointed out to the governor that two of the ten reasons which they presented were false and that the committee presenting them knew they were false. This cast a doubt upon the honesty of the committee and the validity of their whole argument, and the governor signed the bill.

The brief differs from the ordinary outline in that it is composed of complete sentences rather than of topics.

Notice the following example.

Term examinations should be abolished.

AFFIRMATIVE

I. There is no necessity for such examinations.

1. The teacher knows the pupil's standing from his daily recitations.

2. Monthly reviews or tests may be substituted if desirable.

II. The evils arising from examinations more than offset any advantages that may be derived from them.

1. The best pupils are liable to work hardest, unduly overtaxing their strength.

2. Pupils often aim to pass rather than to know their subject.

3. A temptation to cheat is placed before them.

III. Examinations are not a fair test of a pupil's ability.

1. A pupil may know his subject as a whole and yet not be able to answer one or two of the questions given him.

2. A pupil who has done poor work during the term may cram for an examination and pass very creditably.

3. Pupils are liable to be tired out at the end of the term and often are not able to do themselves justice.

NEGATIVE

If the writer should choose to defend the negative of the above proposition, the brief might be as follows : —

I. Examinations are indispensable to school work.

1. In no other way can teachers find out so well what their pupils know about their subjects, especially in large classes.

2. They are essential as an incentive to pupils who are inclined to let their work lag.

II. As a rule they are fair tests of a pupil's ability.

1. Pupils who prepare the daily recitations well are almost sure to pass a good examination.

2. Pupils who cram are likely to write a hurried, faulty examination.

3. It seldom happens that many in a class are too worn out to take a term examination.

III. They prepare the pupils for later examinations.

(1) For college entrance examinations.

(2) For examinations at college.

(3) For civil service examinations.

(4) For examinations for teachers' certificates.

EXERCISES

A. Write out subordinate propositions proving the main subdivisions. Also change the arrangement when you think it desirable.

1. Two sessions are preferable to one in a high school.
   - (1) One long session is too fatiguing to both teachers and pupils.
   - (2) Boys and girls as a rule study better at school than they do at home.
   - (3) The time after school is long enough for recreation.
2. The pupils of this high school should be granted a holiday during the street (county or state) fair.
   - (1) They will all go at least one day.
   - (2) It will cause less interruption in the school work if they all go the same day.
3. Women should be allowed to vote.
   - (1) They are now taxed without representation.
   - (2) Whenever they have been allowed to take part in the affairs of the government, it has been an advantage to that government.
   - (3) Many of them are much more intelligent than some men who vote.

B. Write out briefs for the following propositions (affirmative or negative): —

1. High school studies should be made elective in the last two years of the course.
2. The government should own and control the railroads of our country.
3. The old building on the corner of —— Street ought to be removed.
4. Latin should not be made a compulsory study.

5. Reading newspapers is unprofitable.
6. Laws should be made to prohibit all adulteration of foods.
7. We are all selfish.
8. A system of self-government should be introduced into our school.

Theme CIV. — *Write out the argument for one of the preceding propositions.*

(Examine the brief carefully before beginning to write. Can you improve it?)

Theme CV. — *Write a theme proving one of the following propositions:* —

1. Immigration is detrimental to the United States.
2. The descriptions in *Ivanhoe* are better than those in the *House of the Seven Gables*.
3. Argument is of greater practical value than exposition.
4. The Mexican Indians were a civilized race when America was discovered.
5. The standing army of the United States should be increased.
6. All police officers should be controlled by the state and not by the city.

(Have you used arguments from cause, sign, or example? Are they arranged with reference to the principles of arrangement? (Section 192.) Consider each paragraph and the whole theme with reference to unity.)

Theme CVI. — *Write a debate on some question assigned by the teacher.*

(To what points should you give attention in correcting your theme? Read Section 79.)

195. Difference between Persuasion and Argument. — Up to this point we have considered argument as having for its aim the proof of the truth of a proposition. If we consider the things about which we argue most frequently, we shall find that in many of them we aim to do more than merely to convince the hearer. We wish to convince him in order to cause him to act. We argue with him in order to persuade him to do something. Such an argument aims to establish the wisdom of a course of action and is termed *persuasion*. Persuasion differs from argument in its aim. In argument by an appeal principally to the reason, we aim to convince. In persuasion by an appeal mainly to the feelings, we aim to move to action.

196. Importance of Persuasion. — Persuasion deals with the practical affairs of life, and for that reason the part that it performs is a large and important one. All questions of advantage, privilege, and duty are included in the sphere of persuasion. Since such questions are so directly related to our business interests, to our happiness, and to our mode of conduct and action, we are constantly making use of persuasion and quite as constantly are being influenced by it. Our own welfare and happiness depends to so great an extent upon the actions of others that our success in life is often measured by our ability to persuade others to act in accordance with our desires.

197. Necessity of Persuasion. — It is frequently not enough to convince our hearer of the truth of a proposition. Often a person believes a proposition, yet does not act. If we wish action, persuasion must be added to argument. If we always acted at the time we were convinced, and in accordance with our convictions, there would be no need of persuasion. Strange as it seems, we often believe one thing and do just the opposite, or we are indifferent and do nothing at all. We all know that disobedience to the laws of health brings its punishment — yet how many of us act as if we did not believe it at all! The indifferent pupil is positive that he will fail if he does not study. He knows that he ought to apply himself diligently to his work. There is no excuse for doing otherwise, yet he neglects to act and failure is the result.

198. Motive in Persuasion. — The motive of persuasion depends upon the nature of the question. The motives that we have in mind may be selfish, or, on the other hand, they may be supremely unselfish. We may urge others to act in order to bring about our own pleasure or profit ; we may urge them to act for their own self-interest or for the interest of others. We may appeal to private or public interest, to social or religious duty. When a boy urges his father to buy him a bicycle, he has his own pleasure in mind. When we urge people to take care of their health, we have their interest in view ; and when we urge city improvements or reforms in politics, we are thinking of the welfare of people in general.

199. The Material of Persuasion. — Persuasion aims to produce action and may make use of any of the forms of discourse that will fit that purpose. We may describe the beauty of the Adirondacks or narrate our experiences there in order to persuade a friend to accompany us on a camping trip. We may explain the workings of a new invention in order to persuade a capitalist to invest money in its manufacture. Or we may by argument demonstrate that there is a great opportunity for young men in New

Orleans, hoping to persuade an acquaintance to move there. When thus used, description, narration, exposition, and argument may become persuasion; but their effectiveness depends upon their appeal to some fundamental belief or feeling in the person addressed. Our description and narration would not bring to the Adirondacks a man who cared nothing for scenery and who disliked camp life. The explanation of our invention would not interest a capitalist unless he was seeking a profitable investment. Our argument would not induce a man to move to New Orleans if his prejudice against the South was greater than his desire for profit and position. In each case there has been an appeal to some belief or sentiment or desire of the person whom we seek to persuade.

200. Appeal to the Feelings. — Persuasion, therefore, in order to produce action must appeal largely to the feelings. But all persons are not affected in the same way. In order to bring about the same result we may need to make a different appeal to different individuals. One person may be led to act by an appeal made to his sense of justice, another by an appeal made to his patriotism, while still another, unmoved by either of these appeals, may be led to act by an appeal made to his pride or to his love of power. If we would be successful in persuading others, we ought to be able to understand what to appeal to in individual cases. Children may be enticed by candy, and older persons may be quite as readily influenced if we but choose the proper incentive. It is our duty to see that we are persuaded only by the presentation of worthy motives, and that in our own efforts to persuade others we do not appeal to envy, jealousy, religious prejudices, race hatred, or lower motives.

EXERCISES

Show how an appeal to the feelings could be made in the following. To what particular feeling or feelings would you appeal in each case?

1. Try to gain your parents' permission to attend college.
2. Urge a friend to give up card playing.
3. Try to persuade your teachers not to give so long lessons.
4. Persuade others to aid an unfortunate family living in your community.
5. Induce the school board to give you a good gymnasium.
6. Persuade a tramp to give up his mode of life.
7. Try to get some one to buy your old bicycle.
8. Urge your country to act in behalf of some oppressed people.
9. Urge a resident of your town to give something for a public park.

Theme CVII. — *Write out one of the preceding.*

(Consider what you have written with reference to coherence and climax.)

201. Argument with Persuasion. — In some cases we are sure that our hearers are already convinced as to the truth of a proposition. Then there is no need of argument and persuasion is used alone, but more frequently both are used. Argument naturally precedes persuasion, but with few exceptions the two are intermixed and even so blended as to be scarcely distinguishable the one from the other. A good example of the use of both forms is found in the speech of Antony over the dead body of

Cæsar in Shakespeare's *Julius Cæsar*. Read the speech and note the argument and persuasion given in it. What three arguments does Antony advance to prove that Cæsar was not ambitious? Does he draw conclusions or leave that for his listeners to do? Where is there an appeal to their pity? To their curiosity? To their gratitude? What is the result in each case of the various appeals?

In the following examples note the argument and persuasion. Remember that persuasion commences when we begin to urge to action. Notice what feelings are appealed to in the persuasive parts of the speeches.

They tell us, Sir, that we are weak, unable to cope with so formidable an adversary. But, when shall we be stronger? Will it be the next week, or the next year? Will it be when we are totally disarmed and when a British guard shall be stationed in every house? Shall we gather strength by irresolution and inaction? Shall we acquire the means of effectual resistance, by lying supinely on our backs and hugging the delusive phantom of hope, until our enemies shall have bound us hand and foot? Sir, we are not weak, if we make a proper use of the means which the God of nature hath placed in our power. Three millions of people, armed in the holy cause of liberty, and in such a country as that which we possess, are invincible by any force which our enemy can send against us. Besides, Sir, we shall not fight our battles alone. There is a just God who presides over the destinies of nations; and who will raise up friends to fight our battles for us. The battle, Sir, is not to the strong alone; it is to the vigilant, the active, the brave. Besides, Sir, we have no election. If we were base enough to desire it, it is now too late to retire from the contest. There is no retreat, but in submission and slavery. Our chains are forged! Their clanking may be heard on the plains of Boston! The war is inevitable — and let it come! I repeat it, Sir, let it come! — It is vain, sir, to extenuate the matter. Gentlemen may cry peace, peace — but there is no peace. The war is actually begun! The next gale that sweeps from the north will bring to our ears the clash of resounding arms! Our brethren are already in the field. Why stand we here, idle? Is life so dear, is peace so sweet, as

to be purchased at the price of chains and slavery? Forbid it,
Almighty God! I know not what course others may take; but as for
me, give me liberty, or give me death.

— PATRICK HENRY.

The pictures in the American newspapers of the starving reconcentrados are true. They can all be duplicated by the thousands. I
never before saw, and please God, I may never again see, so deplor-
able a sight as the reconcentrados in the suburbs of Matanzas. I can
never forget to my dying day the hopeless anguish in their despairing
eyes. Huddled about their little bark huts, they raised no voice of
appeal to us for alms as we went among them. . . . Men, women, and
children stand silent, famishing with hunger. Their only appeal
comes from their sad eyes, through which one looks as through an
open window into their agonizing souls.

The Government of Spain has not appropriated and will not appropriate one dollar to save these people. They are now being attended
and nursed and administered to by the charity of the United States.
Think of the spectacle! We are feeding the citizens of Spain; we
are nursing their sick; we are saving such as can be saved, and yet
there are those who still say it is right for us to send food, but we
must keep hands off. I say that the time has come when muskets
ought to go with the food. . . .

The time for action has, then, come. No greater reason for it can
exist to-morrow than exists to-day. Every hour's delay only adds
another chapter to the awful story of misery and death. Only one
power can intervene — the United States of America. Ours is the one
great nation of the New World, the mother of American republics.
She holds a position of trust and responsibility toward the peoples
and the affairs of the whole Western Hemisphere. .

Mr. President, there is only one action possible, if any is taken —
that is, intervention for the independence of the island. But we cannot intervene and save Cuba without the exercise of force, and force
means war; war means blood. The lowly Nazarene on the shores of
Galilee preached the divine doctrine of love, "Peace on earth, good
will toward men." Not peace on earth at the expense of liberty and
humanity. Not good will toward men who despoil, enslave, degrade,
and starve to death their fellow-men. I believe in the doctrine of
Christ, I believe in the doctrine of peace; but, Mr. President, men
must have liberty before there can come abiding peace.

Intervention means force. Force means war. War means blood. But it will be God's force. When has a battle for humanity and liberty ever been won except by force? What barricade of wrong, injustice, and oppression has ever been carried except by force? Force compelled the signature of unwilling royalty to the great Magna Charta; force put life into the Declaration of Independence and made effective the Emancipation Proclamation; force beat with naked hands upon the iron gateway of the Bastile and made reprisal in one awful hour for centuries of kingly crime; force waved the flag of revolution over Bunker Hill and marked the snows of Valley Forge with blood-stained feet; force held the broken line at Shiloh, climbed the flame-swept hill at Chattanooga, and stormed the clouds on Lookout heights; force marched with Sherman to the sea, rode with Sheridan in the valley of Shenandoah, and gave Grant victory at Appomattox; force saved the Union, kept the stars in the flag, made " niggers " men.

Others may hesitate, others may procrastinate, others may plead for further diplomatic negotiations, which means delay; but for me, I am ready to act now, and for my action I am ready to answer to my conscience, my country, and my God.

— JOHN MELLEN THURSTON: *Speech in United States Senate*, March, 1898.

EXERCISES

1. A young boy is trying to gain his father's permission to attend an evening entertainment with some other boys. Make a list of his appeals to his father's reason; to his father's feelings. Make a list of his father's objections. Is there any appeal to his son's feelings?

2. Suppose you are about to address the voters of your city on the question of granting saloon licenses. Make a list of appeals to their reason; to their intellect. Remember that appeals to the feelings are made more forcible by descriptive and narrative examples than by direct general appeals.

3. Urge your classmates to vote for some member of your class for president. What qualifications should a good class president have?

Theme CVIII. — *Select one of the subjects concerning which you have written an argument; either add persuasion to the argument or intermix them.*

(What part of your theme is argument and what part persuasion? Does the introduction of persuasion affect the order of arrangement ?)

Theme CIX. — *Select one of the subjects given on page 361 of which you have not yet made use. Write a theme appealing to both feeling and intellect.*

(Are your facts true and pertinent ? Consider the arrangement.)

Theme CX. — *Write a letter to a friend who went to work instead of entering the high school. Urge him to come to the high school.*

(What arguments have you made ? To what feelings have you appealed ?)

Theme CXI. — *Use one of the following as a subject for a persuasive theme :* —

1. Induce your friends not to play ball on Memorial Day.
2. Ask permission to be excused from writing your next essay.
3. Persuade one of your friends to play golf.
4. Induce your friends not to wear birds on their hats.
5. Write an address to young children, trying to persuade them not to be cruel to the lower animals.

202. Questions of Right and Questions of Expediency. — Arguments that aim to convince us of the wisdom of an action are very common. In our home life and in our social and religious life these questions are always arising. They may be classified into two kinds: (1) those which answer the question, Is it right? and (2) those which answer the question, Is it expedient?

The moral element enters into questions of right. It is always wise for us to do that which is morally right, but sometimes we are in doubt as to what course of action is morally right. Opinions differ concerning what is right, and for that reason we spend much time in defending our opinions or in trying to make others believe as we do. In answering such a question honestly, we must lose sight of all advantage or disadvantage to ourselves. When asked to do something we should at once ask ourselves, Is it right? and when once that is determined one line of action should be clear.

An argument which aims to answer the question, Is it expedient? presupposes that there are at least two lines of action each of which is right. It aims to prove that one course of action will bring greater advantages than any other. Taking all classes of people into consideration we shall find that they are arguing more questions of expediency than of any other kind. Every one is looking for advantages either to himself or to those in whom he is interested. A question of expediency should never be separated from the question of right. In determining either our own course of action or that which we attempt to persuade another to follow, we should never forget the presupposition of a question of expediency that either course is right.

EXERCISES

1. Name five questions that you have been called upon to decide as to whether they were right or wrong.
2. Name five similar questions that are liable to arise in every one's experience.

3. Name five questions of right concerning which opinions very often differ.

4. Is an action that is right for one person ever wrong for another?

Theme CXII. — *Write out the reasons for or against one of the following:* —

1. Should two pupils ever study together?
2. Is a lie ever justifiable?
3. Was Shylock's punishment too severe?
4. Woman's suffrage should be established.
5. The regular party nominee should not always be supported.

EXERCISES

Give reasons for or against the following: —

1. We should abolish class-day exercises.
2. The study of science is more beneficial than the study of language.
3. Foreign skilled laborers should be excluded from the United States.
4. Hypnotic entertainments should not be allowed.
5. The study of algebra should not be made compulsory in a high school.
6. *Uncle Tom's Cabin* should be excluded from school libraries.
7. Physical training should be compulsory in public schools.
8. High school secret societies should not be allowed.

Theme CXIII. — *Write an argument of expediency using one of the subjects named in the preceding exercise.*

(What advantages have you made most prominent? To what feelings have you appealed?)

Theme CXIV. — *Write a narration in which the hero is called upon to decide whether some course of action is right or wrong.*

(Consider the theme as a narration. Does it fulfill the requirements of Chapter IX? (See Summary.) Consider just the arguments used. Are the arguments sufficient to bring conviction to the reader that the hero decided rightly?)

203. Refutation. — No question is worth argument unless there are two sides to it — unless there is a chance for some doubt in the mind of the hearer as to which side seems most reasonable. Many questions are of such a nature that in trying to convince our hearers of some truth, we often find it necessary to show them, not only the truth of a proposition or the expediency of a course of action, but also the falsity of some opposing proposition or the inexpediency of the opposite course of action. This tearing to pieces another's argument, is called refutation, or destructive argument. A successful debater shows nearly if not equal skill in tearing down his opponent's arguments as in building up his own.

Even in arguments in which no one takes the opposite side at the given time, we must not forget that there are points on the opposite side which are likely to arise in the minds of our hearers. Just as the skillful teacher must know the difficulties that will arise in the minds of the pupils even though they are not expressed, so must the skillful debater consider the objections that his hearer will mentally set up against his argument. It is well, however, for the debater to avoid overemphasizing objections. Sometimes his discussion gives the objections a weight that they would not otherwise have. It is not wise to set up "a man of straw" for the purpose of knocking him down.

Notice the refutation in the following argument.: —

In no respect is the difference of opinion as to the methods of fishing so pronounced and disturbing among anglers as the diverse ones of fishing "up" and "down" stream.

"Fishing up stream" has many advocates who assert that as trout always lie with their heads up current, they are less likely to see the fisherman or the glint of his rod when the casts are made; that the discomfort and fatigue accompanying wading against strong rapids is amply repaid by the increased scores secured; that the flies deftly thrown a foot or two above the head of a feeding trout float more life-like down the current than those drawn against it by the line, when they are apt to exhibit a muscular power which in the live insect would be exaggerated and unnatural.

On the other hand, the "down stream" fisherman is equally assertive as to the value of his method. He feels the charm of gurgling waters around his limbs, a down current that aids rather than retards or fatigues him in each successive step of enjoyment in his pastime; as he casts his fifty or more feet of line adown the stream, he is assured that he is beyond the ken of the most keen-sighted and wary trout; that his artificial bugs, under the tension of the current seaming it from right to left, reaches every square inch of the "swim," as English rodsters term a likely water, and coming naturally down stream, just the direction from whence a hungry trout is awaiting it, are much more likely to be taken, than those thrown against the current, with, doubtless, a foot or more of the leader drooping and bagging before the nose of a trout, with a dead bug, soaked and bedraggled, following slowly behind.

By wading "down stream" its advocates do not mean splashing and lifting the feet above the surface, sending the water hither and yon on to the banks, into the pools, with the soil of silt or mud or fine gravel from the bottom, polluting the stream many yards ahead, and causing every fish to scurry to the shelter of a hole in the bank or under a shelving rock. They intend that the rodster shall enter the water quietly, and, after a few preliminary casts to get the water gear in good working order to proceed down stream by sliding rather than lifting his feet from the bottom, noiselessly and cautiously approaching the most likely pools or eddies behind the rocks in mid stream, or still stretches close to the banks, where the quiet reaches broaden down stream, where nine chances in ten, on a good trout water, one or more fish will be seen lazily rising and feeding.

Again, the down-stream angler contends that when a fish is fastened on a hook, taking the lure in a current, that he is more likely to be well hooked, hence more certain of capture when the line is tense, than when rising to a floating bug at the end of a looping line and leader. Certainly it is very difficult when casting against the current to keep the line sufficiently taut to strike quickly and effectively a rising trout, which as a rule ejects the artificial lure the instant he feels the gritty impact of the steel.

In fishing down stream, the advocate of the principle that the greater the surface commotion made by the flies used, the surer the rise and catch, has an advantage over his brother who always fishes " fine " and with flies that do not make a ripple. Drawing the artificial bugs across and slightly up stream over the mirrored bosom of a pool is apt to leave a wake behind them which may not inaptly be compared with the one created by a small stern-wheel steamer ; an unnatural condition of things, but of such is a trout's make-up.

— W. C. HARRIS : *Fishing Up or Down Stream.*

Theme CXV. — *Persuade a friend to choose some sport from one of the following pairs :* —

      1. Canoeing or sailing.
      2. Bicycling or automobiling.
      3. Golf or polo.
      4. Basket ball or tennis.
      5. Football or baseball.

Theme CXVI. — *Choose one side of a proposition. Name the probable points on the other side and write out a refutation of them.*

Theme CXVII. — *State a proposition and write the direct argument.*

Theme CXVIII. — *Exchange theme CXVII for one written by a classmate and write the refutation of the arguments in the theme you receive.*

(Theme CXVII and the corresponding Theme CXVIII should be read before the class.)

SUMMARY

1. Argument is that form of discourse which attempts to prove the truth of a proposition.
2. Inductive reasoning is that process by which from many individual cases we establish the probable truth of a general proposition.
3. The establishing of a general truth by induction requires —
     a. That there be a large number of facts, circumstances, or specific instances supporting it.
     b. That these facts be true.
     c. That they be pertinent.
     d. That there be no facts proving the truth of the contrary proposition.
4. Deductive reasoning is that process which attempts to prove the truth of a specific proposition by showing that a general theory applies to it.
5. The establishing of the truth of a specific proposition by deductive reasoning requires —
     a. A major premise that makes an affirmation about *all* the members of a class.
     b. A minor premise that states that the individual under consideration belongs to the class named.
     c. A conclusion that states that the affirmation made about the class applies to the individual. These three statements constitute a syllogism.
6. An enthymeme is a syllogism with but one premise expressed.

7. Errors of deduction arise —
    a. If terms are not used throughout with the same meaning.
    b. If the major premise does not make a statement about every member of the class denoted by the middle term.
    c. If either premise is false.

8. Belief in a specific proposition may arise —
    a. Because of the presentation of evidence which is true and pertinent.
    b. Because of a belief in some general principle or theory which applies to it.

  In arguing therefore we —
    a. Present true and pertinent facts, or evidence; or
    b. Appeal directly to general theories, or by means of facts, maxims, allusions, inferences, or the quoting of authorities, seek to call up such theories.

9. Classes of arguments : —
    a. Arguments from cause.
    b. Arguments from sign and attendant circumstances.
    c. Arguments from example and analogy.

10. Arrangement.
    a. Arguments from cause should precede arguments from sign, and arguments from sign should precede arguments from example.
    b. Inductive arguments usually precede deductive arguments.
    c. Arguments should be arranged with reference to climax.
    d. Arguments should be arranged, when possible, in a coherent order.

11. In making a brief the above principles of arrange-
    ment should be observed. Attention should be
    given to unity so that the trivial and false may be
    excluded.

12. Persuasion is argument that aims to establish the
    wisdom of a course of action.

13. Persuasion appeals largely to the feelings.

    a. Those feelings of satisfaction resulting from
        approval, commendation, or praise, or the
        desire to avoid blame, disaster, or loss of
        self-esteem.

    b. Those feelings resulting from the proper and
        legitimate use of one's powers.

    c. Those feelings which arise from possession,
        either actual or anticipated.

14. Persuasion is concerned with —

    a. Questions of right.

    b. Questions of expediency.

APPENDIX

I. ELEMENTS OF FORM

1. Importance of Form. — The suggestions which have been made for the correction of the Themes have laid emphasis upon the thought. Though the thought side is the more important, yet careful attention must also be given to the form in which it is stated. If we wish to express our thoughts so that they will be understood by others, we shall be surer to succeed if we use the forms to which they are accustomed. The great purpose of composition is the clear expression of thought, and this is aided by the use of the forms which are conventional and customary.

Wrong habits of speech indicate looseness and carelessness of thought, and if not corrected show a lack of training. In speaking, our language goes directly to the listener without revision. It is, therefore, essential that we pay much attention to the form of the expression so that it may be correct when we use it. Our aim should be to avoid an error rather than to correct it.

Similarly in writing, your effort should be given to avoiding errors rather than to correcting those already made. A misspelled word or an incorrect grammatical form in the letter that you send to a business man may show you to be so careless and inaccurate that he will not wish to have you in his employ. In such a case it is only the avoidance of the error that is of value. You must determine for yourself that the letter is correct before you send it. This same condition should prevail with reference to your school themes. The teacher may return these for correction, but you must not forget that the purpose of this correction is merely to emphasize the correct form so that you will use it in your next theme. It will be helpful to have some one point out your individual mistakes, but it is only by attention to them on your own part and by a definite and long-continued effort to avoid them that you will really accomplish much toward the establishing of correct language habits. In this, as in other things, the most rapid progress will be made by doing but one thing at a time.

Many matters of form are already familiar to you. A brief statement of these is made to serve as a review and in order to secure uniformity in class work.

1. *Neatness.* — All papers should be free from blots and finger marks. Corrections should be neatly done. Care in correcting or interlining will often render copying unnecessary.

2. *Legibility.* — Excellence of thought is not dependent upon penmanship, and the best composition may be the most difficult to read. A poorly written composition is, however, more likely to be considered bad than one that is well written. A plain, legible, and rapid handwriting is so valuable an accomplishment that it is well worth acquiring.

3. *Paper.* — White, unruled paper, about 8½ by 11 inches, is best for composition purposes. The ability to write straight across the page without the aid of lines can be acquired by practice. It is customary to write on only one side of the paper.

4. *Margins.* — Leave a margin of about one inch at the left of the sheet. Except in formal notes and special forms there will be no margin at the right. Care should be taken to begin the lines at the left exactly under each other, but the varying length of words makes it impossible to end the lines at the right at exactly the same place. A word should not be crowded into a space too small for it, nor should part of it be put on the next line, as is customary in printing, unless it is a compound one, such as steam-boat. Spaces of too great length at the end of a line may be avoided by slightly lengthening the preceding words or the spaces between them.

5. *Spacing.* — Each theme should have a title. It should be placed in the center of the line above the composition, and should have all important words capitalized. Titles too long for a single line may be written as follows : —

MY TRIP TO CHICAGO
ON A BICYCLE

With unruled paper some care must be taken to keep the lines the same distance apart. The spaces between sentences should be somewhat greater than those between words. Paragraphs are indicated by indentations.

6. *Corrections.* — These are best made by using a sharp knife or an ink eraser. Sometimes, if neatly done, a line may be drawn through an incorrect word and the correct one written above it. Omitted words may be written between the lines and the place where they belong indicated by a caret. If a page contains many corrections, it should be copied.

7. *Inscription and Folding.* — The teacher will give directions as to inscription and folding. He will indicate what information he wishes, such as name, class, date, etc., and where it is to be written. Each page should be numbered. If the paper is folded, it should be done with neatness and precision.

2. Capitals. — The use of capitals will serve to illustrate the value of using conventional forms. We are so accustomed to seeing a proper name, such as Mr. Brown, written with capitals that we should be puzzled for a moment if we should find it written without. The sentence, Ben Hur was written by Lew Wallace, would look unfamiliar if written without capitals. We are so used to our present forms that beginning sentences with small letters would hinder the ready comprehension of the thought. Everybody agrees that capitals should be used to begin direct questions and quotations, names of deity, days of the week, the months, each line of poetry, the pronoun I, the interjection O, etc., and no good writer will fail to use them. Usage varies somewhat in regard to capitals in some other places. Such expressions as Ohio river, Lincoln school, Jackson county, state of Illinois, once had both names capitalized. The present tendency is to write them as above. Even titles of honor are not capitalized unless they are used with a proper name; for example, He introduced General Grant. The general then spoke.

3. Rules of Capitalization. — 1. Every sentence and every line of poetry begin with capitals.

2. Every direct quotation, except brief phrases and subordinate parts of sentences, begins with a capital.

3. Proper nouns and adjectives derived from proper nouns begin with capitals. Some adjectives, though derived from proper nouns, are no longer capitalized; *e.g.* voltaic.

4. Titles of honor when used with the name of a person begin with capitals.

5. The first word and every important word in the titles of books, etc., begin with capitals.

6. The pronoun I and the interjection O are always capitalized.

7. Names applied to the Deity are capitalized and pronouns referring thereto, especially if personal, are usually capitalized.

8. Important words are often capitalized for emphasis, especially words in text-books indicating topics.

4. Punctuation. — The meaning of a sentence depends largely on the grouping of words that are related in sense to each other. When reading aloud we make the sense clear by bringing out to the hearer this grouping. This is accomplished by the use of pauses and by emphasis and inflection. In writing we must do for the eye what the inflection and pauses do for the ear; and so we use punctuation marks to indicate inflection and emphasis, and especially to show word grouping. They are important because their purpose is to assist in making the sense clear. There are many special rules more or less familiar to you, but they may all be included under the one general statement: Use such marks and only such marks as will assist the reader in getting the sense.

What marks we shall use and how we shall use them will be determined by custom. In order to benefit a reader, marks must be used in ways with which he is familiar. Punctuation changes from time to time. The present tendency is to omit all marks not absolutely necessary to the clear understanding of the sentence.

There are some very definite rules, but there are others that cannot be made so definite, and the application of them requires care and judgment on the part of the writer. Improvement will come only by practice. Sentences should not be written for the purpose of illustrating punctuation. The meaning of what you are writing ought to be clear to you, and the punctuation marks should be put in *as you write,* not inserted afterward.

5. Rules for the Use of the Comma. — 1. The comma is used to separate words or phrases having the same construction, used in a series.

Judges, senators, and representatives were imprisoned.
The country is a good place to be born in, a good place to die in, a good place to live in at least part of the year.

If any conjunctions are used to connect the last two members, the comma may or may not be used in connection with the conjunction.

The cabbage palmetto affords shade, kindling, bed, and food.

2. Words or expressions in apposition should be separated by a comma.

The native Indian dress is an evolution, a survival from long years of wild life.

3. Commas are used to separate words in direct address from the rest of the sentence.

Bow down, dear Land, for thou hast found release.
O, Sohrab, an unquiet heart is thine !

4. Introductory and parenthetical words or expressions are set off by commas.

However, the current is narrow and very shallow here.
This, in a general way, describes the scope of the small parks or playgrounds.

If the parenthetical expression is quite long and not very closely related to the rest of the sentence, the dash or marks of parenthesis are frequently used. Some writers use them even when the connection is somewhat close.

5. The comma is frequently used to separate the parts of a long compound predicate.

Pine torches have no glass to break, and are within the reach of any man who can wield an ax.

6. A comma is often used to separate a subject with several modifiers, or with a long modifier, from the predicate verb.

One of the mistakes often made in beginning the study of birds with small children, is in placing stress upon learning by sight and name as many species of birds as possible.

7. Participial and adjective phrases and adverb phrases out of their natural order should be separated from the rest of the sentence by commas.

A knight, clad in armor, was the most conspicuous figure of all.
To the mind of the writer, this explanation has much to commend it.

8. When negative expressions are used in order to show a contrast, they are set off by commas.

They believed in men, not in mere workers in the great human workshop.

9. Commas are used in complex sentences to separate the dependent clause from the rest of the sentence.

The great majority of people would be better off, if they had more money and spent it.
While the flour is being made, samples are sent every hour to the testing department.

If the connection is close, the comma is usually omitted, especially when the dependent clause comes last.

I will be there when the train arrives.

10. When a relative clause furnishes an additional thought, it should be separated from the rest of the sentence by a comma.

Hiram Watts, who has been living in New York for six years, has just returned to England.

If the relative clause is restrictive, that is, if it restricts or limits the meaning of the antecedent, the comma is unnecessary.

This is the best article that he ever wrote.

11. Commas are used to separate the members of a compound sentence when they are short or closely connected.

Ireland is rich in minerals, yet there is but little mining done there.

> Breathe it, exult in it,
> All the day long,
> Glide in it, leap in it,
> Thrill it with song.

12. Short quotations should be separated from the rest of the sentence by a comma.

"There must be a beaver dam here," he called.

13. The omissions of important words in a sentence should be indicated by commas.

If you can, come to-morrow ; if not, come next week.

6. Rules for the Use of the Semicolon. —1. When the members of a compound sentence are long or are not closely connected, semicolons should be used to separate them.

> Webster could address a bench of judges ; Everett could charm a college ; Choate could delude a jury ; Clay could magnetize a senate, and Tom Corwin could hold the mob in his right hand ; but no one of these men could do more than this one thing.
> — WENDELL PHILLIPS.

> We might as well decide the question now ; for we shall surely be obliged to soon.

2. When the members of a compound sentence themselves contain commas, they should be separated from one another by semicolons.

> As Cæsar loved me, I weep for him ; as he was fortunate, I rejoice at it ; as he was valiant, I honor him ; but, as he was ambitious, I slew him.
> — SHAKESPEARE.

3. The semicolon should be used to precede *as, namely, i.e., e.g., viz.*

> Some adjectives are compared irregularly ; as, good, bad, and little.

4. When a series of distinct statements all have a common

dependence on what precedes or follows them, they may be separated from each other by semicolons.

> When subject to the influence of cold we eat more ; we choose more heat-producing foods, as fatty foodstuffs ; we take more vigorous exercise ; we put on more clothing, especially of the non-conducting kinds — woolens.

7. Rules for the Use of the Colon. — 1. The colon is used before long or formal quotations, before enumerations, and before the conclusion of a previous statement.

> Old Sir Thomas Browne shrewdly observes : " Every man is not only himself. There have been many Diogeneses and many Timons though but few of the name. Men are lived over again. The world is now as it was in ages past. There were none then, but there has been one since, that parallels him, and is, as it were, revived self."
>
> — GEORGE DANA BOARDMAN.

> Adjectives are divided into two general classes : descriptive and definitive adjectives.

> The following members sent in their resignations : Mrs. William M. Murphy, Mrs. Ralph E. Wiltsie, and Mrs. John C. Clark.

2. The colon is used to separate the different members of a compound sentence, when they themselves are divided by semicolons.

> It is too warm to-day ; the sunshine is too bright ; the shade, too pleasant : we will wait until to-morrow or we will have some one else do it when the busy time is over.

8. Rules for the Use of the Period. — 1. The period is used at the close of imperative and declarative sentences.

2. All abbreviations should be followed by a period.

9. Rule for the Use of the Interrogation Mark. — The interrogation mark should be used after all direct questions.

10. Rule for the Use of the Exclamation Mark. — Interjections and exclamatory words and expressions should be followed by the exclamation mark. Sometimes the exclamatory word is only a part of the whole exclamation. In this case, the exclamatory word should be followed by a comma, and the entire exclamation by an exclamation mark.

> See, how the lightning flashes !

11. Rules for the Use of the Dash. — 1. The dash is used to show sudden changes in thought or breaks in speech.

> I can speak of this better when temptation comes my way — if it ever does.

2. The dash is often used in the place of commas or marks of parenthesis to set off parenthetical expressions.

> In the mountains of New York State this most valuable tree — the spruce — abounds.

3. The dash, either alone or in connection with the comma, is used to point out that part of a sentence on which special stress is to be placed.

> I saw unpruned fruit trees, broken fences, and farm implements, rusting in the rain — all evidences of wasted time.

4. The dash is sometimes used with the colon before long quotations, before an enumeration of things, or before a formally introduced statement.

12. Rules for the Use of Quotation Marks. — 1. Quotation marks are used to inclose direct quotations.

> " In all the great affairs of life one must run some risk," she remarked.

2. A quotation within a quotation is usually indicated by single quotation marks.

> " Can you tell me where I can find ' Rienzi's Address ' ? " asked a young lady of a clerk in Brooklyn.

3. When a quotation is interrupted by parenthetical expressions, the different parts of the quotation should be inclosed in quotation marks.

> " Bring forth," cried the monarch, " the vessels of gold."

4. When the quotation consists of several paragraphs, the quotation marks are placed at the beginning of each paragraph and at the close of the last one.

13. Rule for the Use of the Apostrophe. — The apostrophe is used to denote the possessive case, to indicate the omission of letters, and to form the plural of signs, figures, and letters.

In the teacher's copy book you will find several fancy A's and 3's which can't be distinguished from engravings.

II. REVIEW OF GRAMMAR

THE SENTENCE

14. English grammar is the study of the forms of English words and their relationship to one another as they appear in sentences. A *sentence* is a group of words that expresses a complete thought.

15. Elements of a Sentence. — The elements of a sentence, as regards the office that they perform, are the *subject* and the *predicate*. The *subject* is that about which something is asserted, and the *predicate* is that which asserts something about the subject.

Some predicates may consist of a single word or word-group, able in itself to complete a sentence: [The thrush *sings*. The thrush *has been singing*]. Some require a following word or words: [William struck *John* (object complement, or object). Edward became *king* (attribute complement). The people made Edward *king* (objective complement)].

The necessary parts of a sentence are: some name for the object of thought (to which the general term *substantive* may be given); some word or group of words to make assertion concerning the substantive (general term, *assertive*); and, in case of an incomplete assertive, one of the above given completions of its meaning (object complement, attribute complement, objective complement).

In addition to these necessary elements of the sentence, words or groups of words may be added to make the meaning of any one of the elements more exact. Such additions are known as *modifiers*. The word-groups which are used as modifiers are the *phrase* and the *clause*.

[The thrush sings *in the pine woods* (phrase). The wayfarer *who hears the thrush* is indeed fortunate (clause).]

Both the subject and the predicate may be unmodified: [Bees buzz]; both may be modified: [The honey bees buzz in the clover]; one may be modified and the other unmodified: [Bees buzz in the clover].

The unmodified subject may be called the *simple subject*, or, merely, the *subject*. If modified, it becomes the *complete subject*.

The assertive element, together with the attribute complement, if one is present, may be called the *simple predicate*. If modified, it becomes the *complete predicate*.

Some grammarians call the assertive element, alone, the *simple predicate;* modified or completed, the *complete predicate*.

16. Classification of Sentences as to Purpose. — Sentences are classified according to purpose into three classes: *declarative*, *interrogative*, and *imperative* sentences.

A *declarative* sentence is one that makes a statement or declares something: [Columbus crossed the Atlantic].

An *interrogative* sentence is one that asks a question: [Who wrote *Mother Goose ?*].

An *imperative* sentence is one that is used to express a command or entreaty: [" Fling away ambition "].

Each kind of sentence may be of an exclamatory nature, and then the sentence is said to be an *exclamatory* sentence: [How happy all the children are! (exclamatory declarative). " Who so base as be a slave ? " (exclamatory interrogative). " Heap high the farmer's wintry hoard!" (exclamatory imperative)].

Notice that the exclamation point follows the declarative and imperative forms, but the interrogative form is followed by the question mark.

WORDS AND THEIR OFFICES

17. The Individual Elements of which every sentence is composed are *words*. Every word is the sign of some idea. Each of the words *horse, he, blue, speaks, merrily, at,* and *because,* has a certain naming value, more or less definite, for the mind of the reader. Of these, *horse, blue, he, merrily,* have a fairly vivid descriptive power. In the case of *at* and *because,* the main office is, evidently, to express a relation between other ideas: ["I am *at* my post"], ["I go *because* I must"]. The word *speaks* is less clearly a relational word; at first thought it would seem to have only the office of picturing an activity. That it also fills the office of a connective will be evident if we compare the following sentences: He *speaks* in public. He *is* a public *speaker.* It is evident that *speaks* contains in itself the *naming* value represented in the word *speaker,* but also has the *connecting* office fulfilled in the second sentence by *is.*

All words have, therefore, a naming office, and some have in addition a connecting or relational office.

PARTS OF SPEECH

18. Parts of Speech. — When we examine the different words in sentences we find that, in spite of these fundamentally similar qualities, they are serving different purposes. This difference in purpose or use serves as the basis for dividing words into eight classes, called Parts of Speech. Use alone determines to which class a word in any given sentence shall belong. Not only are single words so classified, but any part of speech may be represented by a group of words. Such a group is either a *phrase* or a *clause.*

A *phrase* is a group of words, containing neither subject nor predicate, that is used as a single part of speech.

A *clause* is a group of words, containing both subject and predicate, that is used as part of a sentence. If used as a single part of speech, it is called a *subordinate,* or *dependent,* clause. Some grammarians use the word *clause* for a subordinate statement only.

19. Classification. — The eight parts of speech may be classified as follows : —

    I. Substantives : nouns, pronouns.

    II. Assertives : verbs.

    III. Modifiers : adjectives, adverbs.

    IV. Connectives : prepositions, conjunctions.

    V. Interjections.

20. Definitions. — The parts of speech may be defined as follows : —

(1) A *noun* is a word used as a name.

(2) A *pronoun* is a word used in place of a noun, designating a person, place, or thing without naming it.

(3) An *adjective* is a word that modifies a substantive.

(4) A *verb* is a word that asserts something — action, state, or being — concerning a substantive.

(5) An *adverb* is a word that modifies a verb, adjective, or another adverb.

(6) A *preposition* is a word that shows the relation of the substantive that follows it to some other word or words in the sentence.

(7) A *conjunction* is a word that connects words or groups of words used in the same way.

(8) An *interjection* is a cry expressing emotion, but not forming part of the sentence.

NOUNS

21. Classes of Nouns. — Nouns are divided into two general classes : *proper* nouns [Esther] and *common* nouns [girl].

Common nouns include *abstract* nouns [happiness] and *collective* nouns [army].

Any word mentioned merely *as a word* is a noun : [*And* is a conjunction].

22. Inflection. — A change in the form of a word to denote a change in its meaning is termed *inflection.*

23. Number. — The most common inflection of the noun is that which shows us whether the name denotes one or more than one. The power of the noun to denote one or more than one is termed *number*. A noun that denotes but one object is *singular* in number. A noun that denotes more than one object is *plural* in number.

The plural number of nouns is regularly formed by adding *s* and *es* to the singular [bank, banks; box, boxes].

Other points to be noted concerning the plural of nouns are as follows : —

1. The irregular plural in *en* [child, children].

2. Formation of the plural by internal change [goose, geese].

3. Fourteen nouns ending in *f* or *fe* change the *f* or *fe* into *ves* [leaf, leaves].

4. Nouns ending in *y*, preceded by a consonant, change the *y* to *i* and add *es* [enemy, enemies].

5. Letters, figures, signs, etc., form their plural by adding *'s*: [You have used too many *i*'s].

6. Nouns taken from other languages usually form their plurals according to the laws of those languages [phenomenon, phenomena].

7. A few nouns in our language do not change their form to denote number.

(*a*) Some nouns have the same form for both the singular and the plural [sheep, deer].

(*b*) Some nouns are used only in the plural [scissors, thanks].

(*c*) Some nouns have no plurals [pride, flesh].

(*d*) Some nouns, plural in form, have a singular meaning [measles, news, politics].

8. Compound nouns usually form their plural by pluralizing the noun part of the compound [sister-in-law, sisters-in-law]. If the words of the compound are both nouns, and are of equal importance, both are given a plural ending [manservant,

menservants]. When the compound is thought of as a whole, the last part only is made plural [spoonful, spoonfuls].

9. Proper names usually form their plurals regularly. If they are preceded by titles, they form their plurals either by pluralizing the title or by pluralizing the name [The Misses Hunter or the Miss Hunters. The Messrs. Keene or the two Mr. Keenes. The Masters Burke. The Mrs. Harrisons.]

10. A few nouns have two plurals differing in meaning or use [cloth, cloths, clothes; penny, pennies, pence].

24. Case. — Case is the relation that a noun or pronoun bears to some other word in the sentence.

Inflection of nouns or pronouns for the purpose of denoting case is termed *declension.* There are three cases in the English language: the *nominative,* the *possessive,* and the *objective;* but nouns show only two forms for each number, as the nominative and objective cases have the same form.

25. Formation of the Possessive. — Nouns in the singular, and those in the plural not already ending in *s,* form the possessive regularly by adding *'s* to the nominative [finger, finger's; geese, geese's].

In case the plural already ends in *s,* the possessive case adds only the apostrophe [girls'].

A few singular nouns add only the apostrophe, when the addition of the *'s* would make an unpleasant sound [Moses'].

Compound nouns form the possessive case by adding *'s* to the last word. This is also the rule when two names denoting joint ownership are used: [Bradbury and Emery's Algebra].

Notice that in the following expression the *'s* is affixed to the second noun only: [My sister Martha's book].

Names of inanimate objects usually substitute prepositional phrases to denote possession: [The hardness *of the rock,* not The rock's hardness].

26. Gender. — Gender is the power of nouns and pronouns to denote sex. Nouns or pronouns denoting males are of the *masculine* gender; those denoting females are of the *feminine* gender; and those denoting things without animal life are *neuter* gender.

27. Person. — Person is the power of one class of pronouns to show whether the speaker, the person spoken to, or the person or thing spoken of is designated. According to the person denoted, the pronoun is said to be in the *first*, *second*, or *third* person. Nouns and many pronouns are not inflected for person, but most grammarians attribute person to them because the context of the sentence in which they are used shows what persons they represent.

28. Constructions of Nouns. — The following are the usual constructions of nouns: —

(*a*) The *possessive* case of the noun denotes possession.

(*b*) Nouns in the *nominative* case are used as follows: —

1. As the subject of a verb: [The western *sky* is all aflame].

2. As an attribute complement: [Autumn is the most gorgeous *season* of the year].

3. In an exclamation: [Alas, poor *soul*, it could not be!].

4. In direct address: [O hush thee, my *baby!*].

5. Absolutely: [The *rain* being over, the grass twinkled in the sunshine].

6. As a noun in apposition with a nominative: [Columbus, a *native* of Genoa, discovered America].

(*c*) Nouns in the *objective* case are used as follows: —

1. As the direct object of a verb, termed either the direct object or the object complement: [I saw a *host* of golden daffodils].

2. As the objective complement: [They crowned him *king*].

3. As the indirect object of a verb: [We gave *Ethel* a ring].

4. As the object of a preposition: [John Smith explored the coast of *New England*].

5. As the subject of an infinitive: [He commanded *the man* (*him*) to go without delay].

A Few Special Features

(1) The unusual number of carefully graded subjects suggested for
theme work:

(2) The introduction into each
theme of a single new principle just
developed in the text (See pp. 66, 73,
102, etc.):

(3) Suggestions for theme correction
(See pp. 66, 80, 95, 109, etc.):

(4) Correlation with other school
studies (See pp. 67, 70, 76, 99, 143, 166,
etc.):

(5) Suggestions as to preparation of
lessons and methods of recitation (See pp.
67, 74, 105, 107, etc.):

(6) Modern and interesting illustra-

tive material (See pp.18, 79, 88, 125, 239, 241, 261, etc.). In so many books the illustrative extracts are unattractiv and even difficult to understand.

(7) The concise summaries (See pp. 44, 109, 151, 325, etc.):

(8) The very full treatment of argument (See pp. 138 to 152, and 326 to 378:

(9) The comprehensive summary of grammar (See pp. 328 to 426) sufficient for the four years' course.

6. As the attribute of an expressed subject of the infinitive *to be:* [I thought it to be *John (him)*].

7. As an adverbial noun: [He came last *week*].

8. As a noun in apposition with an object: [Stanley found Livingstone, the great *explorer*].

29. Equivalents for Nouns.

1. Pronoun: [John gave *his* father a book for Christmas].

2. Adjective: [The *good* alone are truly great].

3. Adverb: [I do not understand the *whys* and *wherefores* of the process].

4. A gerund, or infinitive in *ing:* [*Seeing* is *believing*].

5. An infinitive or infinitive phrase: [With him, *to think* is *to act*].

6. Clause: [It is hard for me to believe *that she took the money*]. Noun clauses may be used as subject, object, attribute complement, and appositive.

7. A prepositional phrase: [*Over the fence* is out].

PRONOUNS

30. Antecedent. — The most common equivalent for a noun is the pronoun. The substantive for which the pronoun is an equivalent is called the *antecedent*, and with this antecedent the pronoun must agree in *person, number,* and *gender,* but not necessarily in *case.*

31. Classes of Pronouns. — Pronouns are commonly divided into five classes, and sometimes a sixth class is added: (1) personal pronouns, (2) relative pronouns, (3) interrogative pronouns, (4) demonstrative pronouns, (5) adjective pronouns, (6) indefinite pronouns (not always added).

32. Personal Pronouns. — Personal pronouns are so called because they show by their form whether they refer to the first, the second, or the third person. There are five personal pronouns in common use: *I, you, he, she,* and *it.*

33. Constructions of Personal Pronouns. — The personal pronouns are used in the same ways in which nouns are used. Besides the regular uses that the personal pronoun has, there are some special uses that should be understood.

1. The word *it* is often used in an indefinite way at the beginning of a sentence: [It snows]. When so used, it has no antecedent, and we say it is used *impersonally*.

2. The pronoun *it* is often used as the *grammatical* subject of a sentence in which the *logical* subject is found after the predicate verb: [*It* is impossible for us to go]. When so used the pronoun *it* is called an *expletive*. *There* is used in the same way.

34. Cautions and Suggestions.

1. Be careful not to use the apostrophe in the possessive forms *its, yours, ours,* and *theirs.*

2. Be careful to use the nominative form of a pronoun used as an attribute complement: [It is *I;* it is *they*].

3. Be sure that the pronoun agrees in number with its antecedent. One of the most common violations of this rule is in using *their* in such sentences as the following: — Every boy and girl must arrange *his* desk. Who has lost *his* book ? The use of *every* and the form *has* obliges us to make the possessive pronouns singular.

His may be regarded as applying to females as well as males, where it is convenient not to use the expression *his or her.*

4. The so-called subject of an infinitive is always in the objective case: [I asked *him* to go].

5. The attribute complement will agree in case with the subject of the verb. Hence the attribute complement of an infinitive is in the objective case: [I knew it (obj.) to be *him*]; but the attribute complement of the subject of a finite verb is in the nominative case: [I knew it (nom.) was *he*].

6. Words should be so arranged in a sentence that there will be no doubt in the mind concerning the antecedent of the pronoun.

7. Do not use the personal pronoun form *them* for the adjective *those*: [*Those* books are mine].

35. Compound Personal Pronouns. — To the personal pronouns *my, our, your, him, her, it,* and *them,* the syllables *self* (singular) and *selves* (plural) may be added, thus forming what are termed *compound personal* pronouns. These pronouns have only two uses: —

1. They are used for emphasis: [He *himself* is an authority on the subject].

2. They are also used reflexively: [The boy injured *himself*].

36. The Relative or Conjunctive Pronouns. — The pronouns *who, which, what* (= that which), *that,* and *as* (after *such*) are more than equivalents for nouns, inasmuch as they serve as connectives. They are often named *relative pronouns* because they relate to some antecedent either expressed or implied; they are equally well named *conjunctive pronouns* because they are used as connectives. They introduce subordinate clauses only; these clauses are called *relative clauses,* and since they modify substantives, are also called *adjective clauses.*

37. Uses of Relative Pronouns. — *Who* is used to represent persons, and objects or ideas personified; *which* is used to represent things; *that* and *as* are used to represent both persons and things.

When a clause is used *for the purpose* of pointing out some particular person, object, or idea, it is usually introduced by *that;* but when the clause supplies an additional thought, *who* or *which* is more frequently used. The former is called a *restrictive clause,* and the latter, a *non-restrictive clause.*

[The boy that broke his leg has fully recovered (restrictive).] Note the omission of the comma before *that.* [My eldest brother, who is now in England, will return by June (non-restrictive).] Note the inclosure of the clause in commas. See Appendix 5, rule 10.

In the first sentence it is evident that the intent of the

writer is to separate, in thought, *the boy that broke his leg* from all other boys. Although the clause does indeed describe the boy's condition, it does so *for the purpose* of *limiting* or *restricting* thought to one especial boy among many. In the second sentence the especial person meant is indicated by the word *eldest.* The clause, *who is now in England,* is put in for the sake of giving an additional bit of information.

38. Constructions of Relative Pronouns. — Relative pronouns may be used as subject, object, object of a preposition, subject of an infinitive, and possessive modifier.

The relative pronoun is regarded as agreeing in person with its antecedent. Its verb, therefore, takes the person of the antecedent: [*I,* who *am* your friend, will assist you].

The case of the relative is determined by its construction in the clause in which it is found: [He *whom* the president appointed was fitted for the position].

39. Compound Relative Pronouns. — The compound relative pronouns are formed by adding *ever* and *soever* to the relative pronouns *who, which,* and *what.* These have the constructions of the simple relatives, and the same rules hold about person and case: [Give it to *whoever* wishes it. Give it to *whomever* you see].

40. Interrogative Pronouns. — The pronouns *who, which,* and *what* are used to ask questions, and when so used, are called *interrogative* pronouns. *Who* refers to persons; *what* to things; and *which* to persons or things. Like the relatives *who* has three case forms; *which* and *what* are uninflected.

The implied question in the sentence, I know whom you saw, is, Whom did you see? The introductory *whom* is an interrogative pronoun, and the clause itself is called an *indirect question.*

The words *which, what,* and *whose* may also be used as modifiers of substantives, and when so used they are called *interrogative adjectives:* ["*What* manner of man is this?" *Whose* child is this? *Which* book did you choose?].

41. Demonstrative Pronouns. — *This* and *that*, with their plurals *these* and *those*, are called *demonstrative pronouns*, because they point out individual persons or things.

42. Indefinite Pronouns. — Some pronouns, as *each*, *either*, *some*, *any*, *many*, *such*, etc., are indefinite in character. Many indefinites may be used either as pronouns or adjectives.

Of the indefinites only two, *one* and *other*, are inflected.

	SINGULAR	PLURAL	SINGULAR	PLURAL
NOM. and OBJ.	one	ones	other	others
POSS.	one's	ones'	other's	others'

43. Adjective Pronouns or Pronominal Adjectives. — Many words, as has been noted already, are either pronouns or adjectives according to the office that they perform. If the noun is expressed, the word in question is called a *pronominal adjective;* but if the noun is omitted so that the word in question takes its place, it is called an *adjective pronoun.* [*That* house is white (adjective). *That* is the same house (pronoun).]

ADJECTIVES

44. Classes of Adjectives. — There are two general classes of adjectives: the *descriptive* [blue, high, etc.], so called because they describe, and the *limiting* or *definitive* adjectives [yonder, three, that, etc.], so called because they limit or define. It is, of course, true that any adjective which describes a noun limits its meaning; but it is named from its descriptive power, not from its limiting power.

A very large per cent of all adjectives belong to the first class, — *descriptive* adjectives. *Proper* adjectives and *participial* adjectives form a small part of this large class: [*European* countries. A *running* brook].

45. Limiting or Definitive Adjectives. — The *limiting* adjectives include the various classes of *pronominal adjectives* (all of which have been mentioned under pronouns), the *articles* (*a, an,* and *the*), and adjectives denoting *place* and *number*.

46. Comparison of Adjectives. — With the exception of the words *this* and *that*, adjectives are not inflected for number, and none are inflected for case. Many of them, however, change their form to express a difference in degree. This change of form is called *comparison*. There are three degrees of comparison: the *positive*, the *comparative*, and the *superlative*. Adjectives are regularly compared by adding the syllables *er* and *est* to the positive to form the comparative and superlative degrees. In some cases, especially in the case of adjectives of more than one syllable, the adverbs *more* and *most* are placed before the positive degree in order to form the other two degrees [long, longer, longest; beautiful, more beautiful, most beautiful].

47. Irregular Comparison of Adjectives. — A few adjectives are compared irregularly. As a rule, they are in common use and we should be familiar with the correct forms.

POSITIVE	COMPARATIVE	SUPERLATIVE
bad evil ill	worse	worst
far	farther	farthest
good well	better	best
fore	former	foremost first
late	later latter	latest last
little	less	least
many much	more	most
near	nearer	nearest next
old	older elder	oldest eldest

The following words are used as adverbs or prepositions in the positive degree, and as *adjectives* in the other two degrees: —

(forth)	further	furthest
(in)	inner	{ innermost inmost
(out)	{ outer utter	{ outmost outermost utmost uttermost
(up)	upper	{ upmost uppermost

48. Cautions concerning the Use of Adjectives.

1. When two or more adjectives modify the same noun, the article is placed only before the first, unless emphasis is desired: [He is an industrious, faithful pupil].

2. If the adjectives refer to different things, the article should be repeated before each adjective: [She has a white and a blue dress].

3. When two or more nouns are in apposition, the article is placed only before the first: [I received a telegram from Mr. Richards, *the* broker and real estate agent].

4. *This, these, that,* and *those* must agree in number with the noun they modify: [*This kind* of flowers; *those sorts* of seeds].

5. When but two things are compared, the comparative degree is used: [This is the more complete of the two].

6. When *than* is used after a comparative, whatever is compared should be excluded from the class with which it is compared: [I like this house better than any other house; not, I like this house better than any house].

7. Do not use *a* after *kind of, sort of,* etc.: [What kind of man is he? (not, What kind of *a* man)]. *One* man does not constitute a class consisting of many kinds.

49. Constructions of Adjectives. — Adjectives that merely describe or limit are said to be *attributive* in construction.

When the adjective limits or describes, and, at the same time, adds to the predicate, it is called a *predicate adjective.* Predicate adjectives may be used either as attribute or objective complements: [The sea is *rough* to-day (attribute complement), He painted the boat *green* (objective complement)].

50. Equivalents for Adjectives. — The following are used as equivalents for the typical adjective: —

1. A noun used in apposition: [Barrie's story of his mother, "*Margaret Ogilvy*," is very beautiful].

2. A noun used as an adjective: [A *campaign* song].

3. A prepositional phrase: [His little, nameless, unremember'd acts *of kindness* and *of love*].

4. Participles or participial phrases: [We saw a brook *running* between the alders. Soldiers *hired to serve a foreign country* are called mercenaries].

5. Relative clauses: [This is the house *that Jack built*].

6. An adverb (sometimes called the *locative* adjective): [The book *here* is the one I want].

VERBS

51. Uses of Verbs. — A *verb* is the word or word-group that makes an assertion or statement, and it is therefore the most important part of the whole sentence. It has been already shown that such a verb as *speaks* serves the double purpose of suggesting an activity and showing relation. The most purely *relational* verb is the verb *to be*, which is called the *copula* or *linking verb*, for the very reason that it joins predicate words to the subject: [The lake *is* beautiful]. *To be*, however, is not always a pure *copula*. In such a sentence as, "He that cometh to God must believe that He *is*," the word means *exists*. Verbs that are like the copula, such as, *appear, become, seem*, etc., are called *copulative* verbs. Verbs that are not only relational but have descriptive power, as *sings, plays, runs*, etc., are called *attributive* verbs. They attribute some quality or characteristic to the subject.

52. Classes of Verbs. — According to their uses in a sentence verbs are divided into two classes: *transitive* and *intransitive*.

A *transitive* verb is one that takes a following substantive, expressed or implied, called the *object*, to designate the receiver or the product of the action : [They seized the *city*. They built a *city*]. The transitive verb may sometimes be used *absolutely :* [The horse eats]. Here the object is implied.

An *intransitive* verb is one that does not take an object to complete its meaning ; or, in other words, an intransitive verb is one that denotes an action, state, or feeling that involves the subject only : [He ran away. They were standing at the water's edge].

A few verbs in our language are always transitive, and a few others are always intransitive. The verbs *lie* and *lay, rise* and *raise, sit* and *set*, are so frequently misused that attention is here called to them. The verbs *lie, rise,* and *sit* (usually) are intransitive in meaning, while the verbs *lay, raise,* and *set* are transitive. The word *sit* may sometimes take a reflexive object : [They sat *themselves* down to rest].

The majority of verbs in our language are either transitive or intransitive, according to the sense in which they are used.

> [The fire *burns* merrily (intransitive).
>
> The fire *burned* the building (transitive).
>
> The bird *flew* swiftly (intransitive).
>
> The boy *flew* his kite (transitive).]

Some intransitive verbs take what is known as a *cognate object :* [He died a noble *death.*] Here the object repeats the meaning of the verb.

53. Complete and Incomplete Verbs. — Some intransitive verbs make a complete assertion or statement without the aid of any other words. Such verbs are said to be of *complete predication :* [The snow melts].

All transitive verbs and some intransitive verbs require one or more words to complete the meaning of the predicate. Such verbs are said to be incomplete. Whatever is added to complete the meaning of the predicate is termed a *complement.* The complement of a transitive verb is called the *object complement,*

or simply the *object:* [She found the *book*]. Some transitive
verbs, from the nature of their meaning, take also an *indirect*
object: [I gave *her* the book]. When a word belonging to the
subject is added to an intransitive verb in order to complete
the predicate, it is termed an *attribute complement*. This complement may be either a noun or an adjective : [He is our
treasurer (noun). This rose is *fragrant* (adjective)]. Among
the incomplete intransitive verbs the most conspicuous are the
copula and the copulative verbs.

54. Auxiliary Verbs. — English verbs have so few changes of
form to express differences in meaning that it is often necessary to use the so-called *auxiliary* verbs. The most common
are : *do, be, have, may, must, might, can, shall, will, should, would,
could,* and *ought*. Some of these may be used as principal
verbs. A few notes and cautions are added.

Can is used to denote the ability of the subject.

May is used to denote permission, possibility, purpose, or
desire. Thus the request for permission should be, "May I ? "
not " Can I ? "

Must indicates necessity.

Ought expresses obligation.

Had should never be used with *ought*. To express a moral
obligation in past time, combine *ought* with the perfect infinitive : [I ought *to have done* it].

Should sometimes expresses duty : [You should not go].

Would sometimes denotes a custom : [He would sit there for
hours]. Sometimes it expresses a wish : [Would he were
here !]. For other uses of *should* and *would*, see Appendix 60.

55. Principal Parts. — The main forms of the verb — so important as to be called the *principal parts* because the other
parts are formed from them — are the *root infinitive*, the *preterite (past) indicative*, and the *past participle* [move, moved,
moved ; sing, sang, sung ; be, was, been]. The *present* participle is sometimes given with the principal parts.

56. Inflection. — As is evident from the preceding paragraph, verbs have certain changes of form to indicate change of meaning. Such a change or *inflection*, in the case of the noun, is called *declension;* in the case of the verb it is called *conjugation*. Nouns are *declined;* verbs are *conjugated*.

57. Person and Number. — In Latin, or any other highly inflected language, there are many terminations to indicate differences in person and number, but in English there is but one in common use, *s* in the third person singular: [*He runs*]. *St* or *est* is used after *thou* in the second person singular: [*Thou lovest*].

58. Agreement. — Verbs must agree with their subjects in person and number. The following suggestions concerning agreement may be helpful: —

1. A compound subject that expresses a single idea takes a singular verb: [Bread and milk *is* wholesome food].

2. When the members of a compound subject, connected by *neither . . . nor,* differ as regards person and number, the verb should agree with the nearer of the two: [Neither they nor I *am* to blame].

3. When the subject consists of singular nouns or pronouns connected by *or, either . . . or, neither . . . nor,* the verb is singular: [Either this book or that *is* mine].

4. Words joined to the subject by *with, together with, as well as,* etc., do not affect the number of the verb. The same is true of any modifier of the subject: [John, as well as the girls, *is* playing house. One of my books *is* lying on the table. Neither of us *is* to blame].

5. When the article *the* precedes the word *number,* used as a subject, the verb should be in the singular; otherwise the verb is plural: [*The* number of pupils in our schools *is* on the increase. *A* number of children *have* been playing in the sand pile].

6. The pronoun *you* always takes a plural verb, even if its meaning is singular: [You *were* here yesterday].

7. A collective noun takes a singular or plural verb, according as the collection is thought of as a whole or as composed of individuals.

59. Tense. — The power of the verb to show differences of time is called *tense*. Tense shows also the completeness or incompleteness of an act or condition at the time of speaking. There are three *primary* tenses: *present, preterite (past)*, and *future;* and three *secondary* tenses for completed action: *present perfect, past perfect (pluperfect)*, and *future perfect*.

English has only two simple tenses, the present and the preterite: *I love, I loved*. All other tenses are formed by the use of the auxiliary verbs. By combining the present and past tenses of *will, shall, have, be*, or *do* with those parts of the verb known as infinitives and participles, the various tenses of the complete conjugation of the verb are built up. The formation of the *preterite* tense, and the consequent division of verbs into *strong* and *weak*, will be discussed later.

60. The Future Tense. — The future tense is formed by combining *shall* or *will* with the root infinitive, without *to*.

The correct form of the *future tense* in assertions is here given: —

SINGULAR	PLURAL
1. I shall fall	1. We shall fall
2. Thou wilt fall	2. You will fall
3. He will fall	3. They will fall

Will, in the *first* person, denotes not simple futurity, but determination: [I will (= am determined to) go].

Shall, in the *second* and *third* persons, is not simply the sign of the future tense in declarative sentences. It is used to denote the determination of the speaker with reference to others.

Notice: —

1. In clauses introduced by *that*, expressed or understood, if the noun clause and the principal clause have *different* subjects, the same auxiliary is used that would be used were the subor-

dinate clause used independently: [I fear we *shall* be late. My friend is determined that her son *shall* not be left alone].

2. In all other subordinate clauses, *shall*, for all persons, denotes simple futurity; *will*, an expression of willingness or determination: [He thinks that he *shall* be there. He promises that he *will* be there].

3. In questions, *shall* is always used in the first person; in the second and third persons the same auxiliary is used which is expected in the answer.

(NOTE. — *Should* and *would* follow the rules for *shall* and *will*.)

61. Tenses for the Completed Action.

1. To represent an action as completed at the *present* time, the past participle is used with *have* (*hast*, *has*). This forms the *present perfect* tense: [I *have finished*].

2. To represent an action as completed in *past* time, the past participle is combined with *had* (*hadst*). This forms the *past perfect*, or *pluperfect*, tense: [I *had finished*].

3. To represent action that will be completed in *future* time, *shall have* or *will have* is combined with the past participle. This forms the *future perfect* tense: [I *shall have finished*].

62. Sequence of Tenses. — It is, in general, true that the tense of a subordinate clause changes when the tense of the main verb changes. This is known as the Law of the Sequence (or *following*) of Tenses: [I know he means well. I knew he meant well].

The verb in the main clause and the verb in the subordinate clause are not necessarily in the same tense.

[I think he *is* there.	I thought he was there.
I think he *was* there.	I thought he had been there.
I think he *will be* there.	I thought he would be there.]

In general, the principle may be laid down that in a complex sentence the tense for both principal and subordinate clauses is that which the sense requires.

General truths and present facts should be expressed in the

present tense, whatever the tense of the principal verb: [He believed that truth *is* unchangeable. Who did you say *is* president of your society?].

The *perfect infinitive* is used to denote action completed at the time of the main verb: [I am sorry *to have wounded* you].

63. Mode. — A statement may be regarded as the expression of a fact, of a doubt or supposition, or of a command The power of the verb to show how an action should be regarded is called *mode (mood)*. In our language there is but a slight change of form for this purpose. The distinction of mode which we must make is a distinction that has regard to the thought or attitude of mind of the speaker rather than to the form of the verb.

The *indicative* mode is used to state a fact or to ask questions of fact: [I shall write a letter. Shall I write a letter?].

The *subjunctive* mode indicates uncertainty, unreality, and some forms of condition: [If she were here, I should be glad].

The *imperative* mode expresses a command or entreaty: [Come here].

64. The Subjunctive Mode. — The subjunctive is disappearing from colloquial speech, and the indicative form is used almost entirely.

The verb *to be* has the following indicative and subjunctive forms in the present and preterite: —

	IND.	SUBJ.		IND.	SUBJ.
	I am	I be		I was	I were
	Thou art	Thou be		Thou wast	Thou were
PRESENT	He is	He be	PRETERITE	He was	He were
	We are	We be		We were	We were
	You are	You be		You were	You were
	They are	They be		They were	They were

In other verbs the indicative and subjunctive forms are the same, except that the second and third persons singular subjunctive have no personal endings.

INDICATIVE	Thou learnest	He learns
SUBJUNCTIVE	Thou learn	He learn

The subjunctive idea is sometimes expressed by verb phrases, containing the auxiliary verbs *may* (*might*), *would*, or *should*. *May*, *would*, and *should* are not, however, always subjunctive. In " I *may* go" (may = am allowed to), *may* is indicative. In "you *should* go" (= ought to), *should* is indicative.

The subjunctive mode is used most frequently to express:—

1. A wish: [The Lord be with you].

2. A condition regarded as doubtful: [If it be true, what shall we think?], or a condition regarded as untrue: [If I were you, I should go]. When condition is expressed by the subjunctive without *if*, the verb precedes the subject: [Were my brother here, he could go with me].

3. A purpose: [He studies that he may learn].

4. Exhortations: [Sing we the song of freedom].

5. A concession,—supposed, not given as a fact: [Though he be my enemy, I shall pity him].

6. A possibility: [We fear lest he be too late].

The tenses of the subjunctive require especial notice. In conditional clauses, the *present* refers either to present or future time: [Though the earth be removed, we shall not fear].

The *preterite* refers to present time. It implies that the supposed case is not a fact: [If he were here, I should be much pleased].

The *pluperfect* subjunctive expresses a false supposition in past time: [If you had been here, this would not have happened].

The phrases with *may, might, can, must, could, would*, and *should* are sometimes called the *potential mode*, but the constructions all fall within either the indicative or the subjunctive uses, and a fourth mode is only an incumbrance.

65. The Imperative Mode.—The imperative is the mode of command and entreaty. It has but one form for both singular and plural, and but one tense,—the present. It has but one person,

— the second. The subject is usually omitted. The case of direct address, frequently used with the imperative, should not be confused with the subject. In, "John, hold my books," the subject is *you,* understood. Were *John* the subject, the verb must be *holds.* *John* is, here, a compellative, or vocative.

66. Voice. — Verbs are said to be in the *active* voice when they represent the subject as acting, and in the *passive* voice when they represent the subject as being acted upon. Intransitive verbs, from their very nature, have no passive voice. Transitive verbs may have both voices, for they may represent the subject either as acting or as being acted upon.

The direct object in the active voice generally becomes the subject in the passive; if the subject of the active appears in the passive, it is the object of the preposition *by :* [My dog loves me (active). I am loved by my dog (passive)].

Verbs of calling, naming, making, and thinking may take two objects referring to the same person or thing. The first of these is the direct object and the second is called the objective complement: [John called him *a coward*]. The objective complement becomes an attribute complement when the verb is changed from the active to the passive voice: [He was called *a coward* by John].

Certain verbs take both a direct and an indirect object in the active : [John paid him nine *dollars*]. If the indirect object becomes the subject in the passive voice, the direct object is known as the *retained object :* [He was paid nine *dollars* by John].

67. Infinitives. — The infinitive form of the verb is often called a verbal noun, because it partakes of the nature both of the verb and of the noun. It is distinguished from the *finite,* or true, verb because it does not make an assertion, and yet it assumes one. While it has the modifiers and complements of a verb, it at the same time has the uses of a noun.

There are two infinitives : the *root infinitive* (commonly preceded by *to*, the so-called *sign* of the infinitive), and the *gerund*, or *infinitive in -ing*.

1. Root infinitive: [*To write* a theme requires practice].

2. Gerund: [*Riding* rapidly is dangerous]. In each of these sentences the infinitive, in its capacity as noun, stands as the subject of the sentence. In 1, *to write* shows its verb nature by governing the object *theme ;* in 2, *riding* shows its verb nature by taking as a modifier the adverb *rapidly.*

Each form of the infinitive is found as the subject of a verb, as its object, as an attribute complement, and as the object of a preposition. The root infinitive, together with its subject in the objective case, is used as the object of verbs of knowing, telling, etc.: [I know *him to be a good boy*]. See also Appendix 85 for adjective and adverbial uses.

The infinitive has two tenses: the *present* and the *perfect.* The *present* tense denotes action which is not completed at the time of the principal verb: [He tries *to write.* He tried *to write.* He will try *to write*]. The *perfect* infinitive denotes action complete with reference to the time of the principal verb: [I am glad *to have known* her].

68. Participles. — Participles are verbal adjectives: [The girl *playing* the piano is my cousin]. *Playing,* as an *adjective,* modifies the noun *girl ;* it shows its *verbal* nature by taking the object *piano.*

The *present participle* ends in *-ing.* When the *past participle* has an ending, it is either *-d, -ed, -t,* or *-en.* The *perfect participle* is formed by combining *having* with a past participle; as, *having gone.*

There is danger of confusing the present participle with the gerund, or infinitive in *-ing,* unless the adjective character of the one and the noun character of the other are clearly distinguished: [The boy, *driving* the cows to pasture, was performing his daily task (participle). *Driving* the cows to pasture was his daily task (gerund)].

Participles are used to form verb-phrases. The present participle is used for the formation of the progressive conjugation; the past participle, for the formation of the compound or perfect tenses. Participles are also used in all the adjective constructions.

One especial construction requires notice, — the *absolute* construction, or the *nominative absolute*, as it is called: [*The ceremony having been finished*, the people dispersed]. The construction here is equivalent to a clause denoting *time* or *cause* or some *circumstance* attendant on the main action of the sentence. The participle is sometimes omitted, but the substantive must not be, lest the participle be left apparently belonging to the nearest substantive; as, Walking home, the rain began to fall. As the sentence stands, *walking* modifies *rain*.

69. Conjugation. — The complete and orderly arrangement of the various forms of a verb is termed its conjugation. Complete conjugations will be found in any text-book on English grammar.

The passive voice must not be confused with such a form as the progressive conjugation of the verb. The passive consists of a form of *to be* and a *past participle:* [I am instructed]. The progressive tenses combine some form of *to be* with a *present* participle: [I am instructing].

It may be well to distinguish here between the passive voice and a past participle used as an attribute complement of the verb *be*. Both have the same form, but there is a difference of meaning. The passive voice always shows action received by the subject, while the participle is used only as an adjective denoting condition: [James *was tired* by his day's work (passive voice). James was *tired* (attribute complement)].

70. Weak and Strong Conjugations. — Verbs are divided into two classes as regards their conjugations. It has been the custom to call all verbs which form the preterite and past participle by adding *-d* or *-ed* to the present, *regular* verbs [love, loved, loved], and to call all others *irregular*. A better classification, based on more careful study of the history of the English verb, divides verbs into those of the *weak* and those of the *strong* conjugations.

The *weak verbs* are those which form the preterite by adding -*ed*, -*d*, or -*t* to the present: *love, loved.* There is also infrequently a change of vowel: *sell, sold ; teach, taught.*

All verbs which form the preterite without the addition of an ending are *strong verbs.* There is usually a change of vowel. The termination of the past participle in -*n* or -*en* is a sure indication that a verb is *strong.* Some verbs show forms of both conjugations.

A complete list of *strong* verbs cannot be given here, but a few of the most common will be given, together with a few *weak* verbs, in the use of which mistakes occur.

Present	Preterite	Past Participle
am	was	been
arise	arose	arisen
bear	bore	borne, born [1]
begin	began	begun
bid (command)	bade	bidden
bite	bit	bitten
blow	blew	blown
break	broke	broken
bring	brought	brought
burst	burst	burst
catch	caught	caught
choose	chose	chosen
climb	climbed	climbed
come	came	come
do	did	done
drink	drank	drunk [2]
drive	drove	driven
drown	drowned	drowned
eat	ate	eaten
fall	fell	fallen
fly	flew	flown
freeze	froze	frozen

[1] Used only in the passive sense of " born into the world."

[2] *Drunken* is an adjective.

get	got	got
give	gave	given
go	went	gone
grow	grew	grown
have	had	had
hide	hid	hidden
hurt	hurt	hurt
know	knew	known
lay	laid	laid
lie (recline)	lay	lain
lead	led	led
read	rĕad	rĕad
ride	rode	ridden
ring	rang	rung
run	ran	run
see	saw	seen
shake	shook	shaken
show	showed	shown
sing	sang	sung
sink	sank	sunk
sit	sat	sat
slay	slew	slain
speak	spoke	spoken
spring	sprang	sprung
steal	stole	stolen
swell	swelled	{ swelled / swollen }
swim	swam	swum
take	took	taken
tear	tore	torn
throw	threw	thrown
wear	wore	worn
wish	wished	wished
write	wrote	written

CAUTION. — Do not confuse the preterite with the past participle. Always use the past participle form in the compound tenses.

ADVERBS

71. Classes of Adverbs. — Adverbs vary much as to their use and meaning. It is therefore impossible to make a very accurate classification, but we may divide them, according to use, into *limiting, interrogative,* and *conjunctive* adverbs.

Limiting adverbs modify the meaning of verbs, etc.: [He rows *well*].

Interrogative adverbs are used to ask questions: [*When* shall you come? He asked *where* we were going (indirect question)].

Conjunctive adverbs introduce clauses: [We went to the seashore, *where* we stayed a month]. Here *where* is used as a connective and also as a modifier of *stayed*.

Conjunctive adverbs introduce the following kinds of clauses:

1. Adverbial clauses: [Go *where* duty calls].

2. Adjective clauses: [This is the very spot *where* I put them].

3. Noun clause: [I do not know *how* he will succced].

Adverbs may also be classified, according to meaning, into adverbs of *manner, time, place,* and *degree.* The classification is not, however, a rigid one.

Adverbs of *manner* answer the question How? Most of these terminate in *-ly.* Some few, however, are identical in form with adjectives of like meaning: [She sang very loud].

Adverbs of *time* answer the question When?

Adverbs of *place* answer the question Where? This class, together with the preceding two classes, usually modify verbs.

Adverbs of degree answer the question To what extent? These adverbs modify verbs, adjectives, and other adverbs.

72. Phrasal Adverbs. — Certain phrases, adverbial in character, cannot easily be separated into parts. They have been called *phrasal adverbs;* as, arm-in-arm, now-a-days, etc.

73. Inflection. — Some adverbs, like adjectives, are compared for the purpose of showing different degrees of quality or quantity.

The comparative and superlative degrees may be formed by adding the syllables *er* and *est* to the positive degree. The great majority of adverbs, however, make use of the words *more* and *most* or *less* and *least* to show a difference in degree : [Fast, faster, fastest; skillfully, more skillfully, most skillfully; carefully, less carefully, least carefully].

Some adverbs are compared irregularly : —

badly	worse	worst
ill (evil)		
far	farther	farthest
forth	further	furthest
late	later	latest
		last
little	less	least
much	more	most
nigh	nigher	nighest
		next
well	better	best

74. Suggestions and Cautions concerning the Use of Adverbs.

1. Some words, as *fast*, *little*, *much*, *more*, and others, have the same form for both adjective and adverb, and use alone can determine what part of speech each is.

(Adjective) He is a fast driver. She looks well (in good health).

(Adverb) How fast he walks! I learned my lesson well.

2. Corresponding adjectives and adverbs usually have different forms which should not be confused.

(Adjective) She is a good student.

(Adverb)   He works well.

3. The adjective, and not the adverbial, form should be used after a copulative verb, since adverbs cannot modify substantives : [I feel bad; not, I feel badly].

4. Two negatives imply an affirmative. Hence only one should be used to denote negation : [I have nothing to say. I have no patience with him].

75. Equivalents for Adverbs.

1. A phrase : [The child ran away *with great glee*].

2. A clause : [I will go canoeing *when the lake is calm*].

3. A noun : [Please come *home*. I will stay five *minutes*].

PREPOSITIONS

76. Classes of Prepositions. — The *simple* prepositions are: *at, after, against, but, by, down, for, from, in, of, off, over, on, since, through, till, to, under, up,* and *with.*

Other prepositions are either derived or compound: such as, *underneath, across, between, concerning,* and *notwithstanding.*

77. Suggestions concerning the Use of Prepositions. — Mistakes are frequently made in the use of the preposition. This use cannot be fully discussed here, but a partial list of words with the required preposition will be given.

afraid *of.*

agree *with* a person.

agree *to* a proposal.

bestow *upon.*

compare *to* (to show similarity).

compare *with* (to show similarity or difference).

comply *with.*

conform *to.*

convenient *for* or *to.*

correspond *to* or *with* (a thing).

correspond *with* (a person).

dependent *on.*

differ *from* (a person or thing).

differ *from* or *with* (an opinion).

different *from.*

disappointed *in.*

frightened *at* or *by.*

glad *of.*

need *of.*

profit *by.*

scared *by.*

taste *of* (food).

taste *for* (art).

thirst *for* or *after.*

Like, originally an adjective or adverb, is often, in some of its uses, called a preposition. It governs the objective case, and should not be used as a conjunction: [She looks like *me;* not, She looks like I do]. The appropriate *conjunction* here would be *as:* [She speaks *as* I do].

The prepositions *in* and *at* denote rest or motion *in* a place; *into* denotes motion *toward* a place: [He is *in* the garden. He went *into* the garden].

78. Prepositional Phrases. — The preposition, with its object, forms what is termed a prepositional phrase. This phrase is *adjective* in force when it modifies a substantive;

and *adverbial*, when it modifies a verb, adjective, or other adverb: [In the cottage *by the sea* (adjective). He sat *on the bench* (adverb)].

Some prepositions were originally adverbs; such as, *in, on, off, up*, and *to*. Many of them are still used adverbially or as adverbial suffixes: [The ship lay to. A storm came on].

CONJUNCTIONS

79. Classes of Conjunctions. — Conjunctions are divided according to their use into two general classes: the *coördinate* and the *subordinate* conjunctions.

Coördinate conjunctions are used to connect words, phrases, and clauses of equal rank; *subordinate* conjunctions connect clauses of unequal rank.

The principal coördinate conjunctions are *and, but, or, nor,* and *for. And* is said to be *copulative* because it merely adds something to what has just been said. Other conjunctions having a copulative use are *also, besides, likewise, moreover,* and *too;* and the correlative conjunctions, *both . . . and, not only . . . but also,* etc. These are termed *correlative* because they occur together. *But* is termed the *adversative* coördinate conjunction because it usually introduces something adverse to what has already been said. Other words of an adversative nature are *yet, however, nevertheless, only, notwithstanding,* and *still. Or* is alternative in its force. This conjunction implies that there is a choice to be made.

Other similar conjunctions are *either . . . or, neither . . . nor, or, else. Either . . . or* and *neither . . . nor* are termed *correlative* conjunctions, and they introduce alternatives. *For, because, such,* and *as* are *coördinate* conjunctions only in such a case as the following: [She has been running, for she is out of breath].

Some of the most common conjunctions of the *subordinate* type are those of place and time, cause, condition, purpose, comparison, concession, and result. *That* introducing a subordinate clause may be called a *substantive* conjunction: [I knew *that* I ought to go].

There are a number of subordinate conjunctions used in pairs which are called *correlatives*. The principal pairs are *as . . . so, as . . . as, so . . . as, if . . . then, though . . . yet*.

80. Simple and Compound Sentences. — In the first section of this review the parts of a sentence were named as the *subject* and *predicate*.

The *subject* may itself consist of two parts joined by one of the coördinating conjunctions: [Alice *and* her cousin are here]. The predicate may be formed in a similar fashion: [John played *and* made merry all day long]. Both subject and predicate may be so compounded: [John *and* Richard climbed the ladder *and* jumped on the hay].

In all these cases the sentence, consisting as it does of but one subject and one predicate, is said to be *simple*.

When two clauses — that is, two groups of words containing each a subject and predicate — are united by a coördinate conjunction, the sentence is said to be *compound:* [John wished to play Indian, *but* Richard preferred to play railroad].

The coördinating conjunction need not actually appear in the sentence. Its omission is then indicated by the punctuation: [John wished to play Indian; Richard preferred another game].

81. Subordinate Conjunctions and Complex Sentences. — A *subordinate* conjunction is used to join a subordinate clause to a principal clause, thus forming a *complex* sentence. The test to be applied to a clause in order to ascertain whether it is a subordinate clause, is this: if any group of words in a sentence, containing a subject and predicate, fulfills the office of some single part of speech, it is a *subordinate* clause. In the sentence, "I went because I knew that I must," the clause, "because I knew that I must" states the reason for the action named in the main clause. It, therefore, stands in *adverbial* relation to the verb "went." "That I must" is the object of

" knew." It, therefore, stands in a *substantive* relation to the verb.

Subordinate clauses are often introduced by subordinate conjunctions (sometimes by relative pronouns or adverbs); but, whenever such a clause appears in a sentence, otherwise simple, the sentence is *complex.* If it appears in a sentence otherwise compound, the sentence is *compound-complex.*

The different types of subordinate clauses will be discussed later.

SENTENCE STRUCTURE

82. Phrases. — Phrases are classified both as to structure and use.

From the standpoint of structure, a phrase is classified from its introductory word or words, as : —

1. *Prepositional :* [They were *in the temple*].
2. *Infinitive :* [He tried *to make us hear*].
3. *Participial :* [*Having finished my letter*].

Classified as to use, a phrase may be —

1. A *noun :* [*To be good* is *to be truly great*].
2. An *adjective :* [The horse is an animal *of much intelligence*].
3. An *adverb :* [He lives *in the city*].

83. Clauses. — It has been already shown that clauses may be either principal or subordinate. A principal clause is sometimes defined as " one that can stand alone," and so is independent of the rest of the sentence. This is misleading, for, although true in most cases, it does not hold in cases like the following : —

1. As the tree falls, so it must lie.
2. That sunshine is cheering, cannot be denied.

The genuine test for the subordinate clause is the one already given in connection with the study of the subordinate conjunction. It must serve the purpose of some single part of speech. All other clauses are principal clauses.

84. **Classification of Subordinate Clauses.** — *A.* Subordinate clauses may be classified into *substantive* and *modifying* clauses.

Substantive clauses show the various substantive constructions. Thus: —

1. Subject: [*" Thou shalt not covet,"* is the tenth commandment].

2. Object: [I know *what you wish*].

3. Appositive: [The truth *that the earth is spherical* is generally believed].

4. Attribute complement: [The truth is *that she is not well*].

Modifying clauses show adjective and adverbial constructions. Thus: —

1. Adjective: [The house *which you see* is mine].

2. Adverb: [I will go *when* it is possible].

B. Subordinate clauses may also be classified according to the introductory word.

(*a*) Clauses introduced by *relative* or *interrogative pronouns: who, which, what, that* (= who or which), *as* (after such), and the compound relatives, *whoever, whichever, whatever* (the first three are both relative and interrogative): [The school *that stands on the hillside* is painted white. I know *whom you mean*].

(*b*) Clauses introduced by a relative or interrogative adjective: [The man *whose library is well furnished* is rich. I see *which way I ought to take*].

(*c*) Clauses introduced by a relative or interrogative adverb, such as *when, whenever, since* (referring to time), *until, before, after, where, whence, whither, wherever, why, as, how:* [I know the house *where he lives*].

(*d*) Clauses introduced by a subordinate conjunction, such as *because, since* (= because), *though, although, if, unless, that* (= in order that), *as, as if, as though, then:* [I will go *since you wish it*].

C. Subordinate clauses may also be classified according to the nature of the thought expressed.

(*a*) General description: [The house, *which stands on the hill,* has a fine view].

(*b*) Place: [The house *where he was born* is torn down].

(*c*) Time: [He works *whenever he can*].

(*d*) Cause: [*Since you wish it,* I will go].

(*e*) Concession: [*Although he is my friend,* I can see his faults].

(*f*) Purpose: [Run, *that you may obtain the prize*].

(*g*) Result: [She was so tired *that she stumbled*].

(*h*) Condition: [*If it rains,* we shall not go].

(*i*) Comparison: [You look *as if you were tired*].

Note that the subordinate clauses in the above examples are modifying clauses.

(*j*) Direct quotation: [She said, "*I will go*"].

(*k*) Indirect statement: [She said *that she would go*].

(*l*) Indirect question: [I knew *where his house was*].

Note that the subordinate clauses in the above examples are substantive clauses.

85. The Framework of a Sentence has been already described as consisting of the *subject*, the *verb*, and, if the verb be incomplete, of some completing element, *object* or *attribute complement*. Occasionally an *objective complement* must be added. Besides these elementary parts, both subject and predicate may have modifiers.

The usual modifiers of the subject are: —

1. Adjective: [The *golden* bowl is broken].

2. Adjective phrase: [The house *on the hill* is beautiful].

3. Adjective clause: [The house *which stands on the hill* is beautiful].

4. Noun or pronoun in possessive case: [*Helen's* paint box is lost].

5. Noun in apposition: [Mr. Merrill, the *president* of the club, will open the debate].

6. Adverb used as an adjective: [My *sometime* friend].

7. Infinitive used adjectively: [Work *to do* is a blessing].

8. Participle: [The child, *lagging* behind, lost her way].

The modifiers of the predicate are: —

1. Adverb: [The snow melted very *quickly*].

2. Noun used adverbially: [I walked *a mile*].

3. Infinitive used adverbially: [We were called together *to decide* an important question].

4. Adverbial phrase: [She ran *along the road*].

5. Adverbial clause: [Go *when you can*].

6. Nominative absolute: [The *speeches being over*, the audience dispersed].

Occasionally, adverbs and phrases of adverbial character modify the entire thought in a sentence, rather than some single word: [*To speak plainly*, I cannot go. *Perhaps* I may help you].

LIST OF SPECIAL WORDS

86. **Special Words.** — A list is here given of words which appear as various parts of speech: —

a   (1) Adjective: *A* book. (2) Preposition: I go *a*-fishing.

about   (1) Preposition: Walk *about* the house. (2) Adverb: We walked *about* for an hour. *By, over, up*, etc., are used in the same way.

above   (1) Preposition: The sun is *above* the horizon. (2) Adverb: Go *above*. (3) Noun: Every good gift is from *above*. (4) Adjective: The *above* remarks are discredited. *Below* has the same uses.

after   (1) Preposition: *After* our sail. (2) Conjunctive adverb: He came *after* she went away.

all   (1) Pronoun: *All* went merry as a marriage bell. (2) Noun: I gave my *all*. (3) Adjective: *All* hands to the rescue. (4) Adverb: The work is *all* right.

as

(1) Conjunctive pronoun: I give such *as* I have. (2) Conjunctive adverb: I am not so old *as* she. (3) Adverb: What other grief is *as* hard to bear? (4) Conjunction: *As* it was hot, we did not go. (5) Preposition: I warned her *as* a friend. (6) Compound Conjunction: He looks *as* if he were not well.

before

(1) Preposition: He stood *before* the door. (2) Conjunctive Adverb: I will do it *before* I go. (3) Adverb: She has never been here *before*.

both

(1) Adjective: *Both* white and red pines are beautiful. (2) Pronoun: *Both* are yours. (3) Conjunction: She is *both* good and beautiful.

but

(1) Conjunction: John reads *but* Richard plays. (2) Preposition: All *but* him are at home. (3) Adverb: We can *but* fail.

either

(1) Adjective: *Either* dress is becoming. (2) Conjunction: *Either* this dress or the other is becoming. (3) Pronoun: *Either* is right.

fast

(1) Noun: A long *fast*. (2) Verb: They *fast* often. (3) Adverb: The rain fell *fast*. (4) Adjective: He is a *fast* walker.

for

(1) Subordinate Conjunction: I must go, *for* I promised. (2) Coördinate Conjunction: She stayed at home, *for* I saw her. (3) Preposition: I have nothing *for* you.

hard

(1) Adjective: *Hard* labor. (2) Adverb: He works *hard*.

like

(1) Noun: We may never see her *like* again. (2) Adjective: This process gives *like*

results. (3) Adverb: *Like* as a father pitieth his children. (4) Preposition: She looks *like* me. (By some grammarians *like* in this case is considered an *adjective* with the preposition *to* omitted.) (5) Verb: You *like* your work.

little   (1) Adjective: A *little* bread. (2) Noun: I wish a *little*. (3) Adverb: He laughs *little*. *Much* has the same uses.

many a   (1) Adjective: *Many a* tree.

notwithstanding (1) Preposition: *Notwithstanding* the rain, we were content. (2) Conjunction or Preposition: She is happy, *notwithstanding* (the fact that) she is an invalid.

only   (1) Adjective: This is the *only* way. (2) Adverb: *Only* experienced persons need apply. (3) Conjunction: I should go, *only* it is stormy.

since   (1) Preposition: *Since* that day I have not seen her. (2) Conjunction: *Since* you lost it, you must replace it. (3) Adverb: I have not seen her *since*. (4) Conjunctive Adverb: You have been here *since* I have.

still   (1) Adjective: The lake is *still*. (2) Adverb: The tree is *still* lying where it fell. (3) Conjunction: He is entertaining; *still* he talks too much. (4) Verb: Oil is said to *still* the waves. (5) Noun: In the *still* of noonday the song of the locust was loud.

than   (1) Conjunction: I am older *than* she. (2) Preposition: *Than* whom there is none wiser.

that   (1) Demonstrative Pronoun: *That* is right.

(2) Conjunctive Pronoun: He *that* lives nobly is happy. (3) Adjective: *That* book is mine. (4) Conjunction: I say this *that* you may understand my position. (5) Substantive Conjunction: *That* this is true is evident.

the   (1) Adjective (article): *The* lake. (2) Adverb: *The* more . . . *the* merrier.

then   (1) Adverb: I shall know *then*. (2) Conjunction: If you so decide, *then* we may go.

there   (1) Adverb: The stream runs *there*. (2) Expletive: *There* are many points to be considered. (3) Interjection: *There! there!* it makes no difference!

what   (1) Conjunctive Interrogative Pronoun: I heard *what* you said. (2) Interrogative Pronoun: *What* shall I do? (3) Interrogative Adjective: *What* game do you prefer? (4) Conjunctive Adjective: I know *what* books he enjoys. (5) Adverb: *What* with this and *what* with that, he finally got his wish. (6) Interjection: *What! what!*

while   (1) Noun: A long *while*. (2) Verb: To *while* away the time. (3) Conjunctive Adverb: I stay in *while* it snows.

III. FIGURES OF SPEECH

87. Figures of Speech. — A figure of speech is a change from the usual form of expression for the purpose of producing a greater effect. These changes may be effective either because they are more pleasing to us or because they are more forcible, for or both reasons.

While figurative language is a change from the usual mode of expression, we are not to think of it as being unnatural. It is, in fact, as natural as plain language, and nearly every one, from the illiterate to the most learned, makes use of it, more or less, in his ordinary conversation. This arises from the fact that we all enjoy comparisons and substitutions. When we say that we have been pegging away all day at our work, or that the wind howls, or that the man has a heart of steel, we are making use of figures of speech. Figurative language ranges from these very simple expressions to the beautiful figures of speech found in so much of our poetry. Written prose contains many beautiful and forcible examples, but it is in poetry that we find most of them.

88. Simile. — A simile is an expressed comparison between objects belonging to different classes. We must remember, however, that all resemblances do not constitute similes. If we compare two trees, or two beehives, or two rivers, our comparison is not a simile. If we compare a tree to a person, a beehive to a schoolroom, or time to a river, we may form a good simile, since the things compared do not belong to the same class. The best similes are those in which the ideas compared have one strong point of resemblance, and are unlike in all other respects.

1. How far that little candle throws its beams !
   So shines a good deed in a naughty world.

   — SHAKESPEARE.

2. For very young he seemed, tenderly reared ;
   Like some young cypress, tall, and dark, and straight.

   — MATTHEW ARNOLD.

3. In the primrose-tinted sky
   The wan little moon
   Hangs like a jewel dainty and rare.

   — FRANCIS C. RANKIN.

89. Metaphor. — A metaphor differs from a simile in that the comparison is implied rather than expressed. They are essentially the same as far as the comparison is concerned, and usually the one kind may be easily changed to the other. In a simile we say that one object *is like* another, in a metaphor we say that one object *is* another.

EXERCISES

Select the metaphors in the following and change them to similes : —

> 1. In arms the Austrian phalanx stood,
>   A living wall, a human wood.
>
> — JAMES MONTGOMERY.

> 2.   The familiar lines
>   Are footpaths for the thoughts of Italy.
>
> — LONGFELLOW.

> 3. Life is a leaf of paper white,
>   Whereon each one of us may write
>   His word or two, and then comes night.
>
> — LOWELL.

90. Personification. — Personification is a special form of the metaphor in which life is attributed to inanimate objects or the characteristics of persons are attributed to objects, animals, or even to abstract ideas.

EXERCISES

Explain why the following quotations are examples of personifications : —

> 1. The day is done ; and slowly from the scene
>   The stooping sun upgathers his spent shafts
>   And puts them back into his golden quiver.
>
> — LONGFELLOW.

> 2. Time is a cunning workman and no man can detect his joints.
>
> — CHARLES PIERCE BURTON.

> 3. The sun is couched, the seafowl gone to rest,
>   And the wild storm hath somewhere found a nest.
>
> — WORDSWORTH.

> 4. See the mountains kiss high heaven,
>   And the waves clasp one another ;

> No sister flower would be forgiven
> If it disdained its brother.
>
> — SHELLEY.

91. Apostrophe. — Apostrophe is like personification, but has an additional characteristic. When we directly address inanimate objects or the absent as if they were present, we call the figure of speech thus formed apostrophe.

The following are examples of apostrophe : —

> 1. Break, break, break,
>   At the foot of thy crags, O Sea !
>
> — TENNYSON.

> 2. Backward, turn backward, O Time, in your flight,
>   Make me a child again just for to-night !
>   Mother, come back from the echoless shore,
>   Take me again to your heart as of yore.
>
> — ELIZABETH AKERS ALLEN.

92. Metonymy. — Metonymy consists in substituting one object for another, the two being so closely associated that the mention of one suggests the other.

> 1. The pupils are reading George Eliot.
> 2. Each hamlet heard the call.
> 3. Strike for your altars and your fires.
> 4. Gray hairs should be respected.

93. Synecdoche. — Synecdoche consists in substituting a part of anything for the whole or a whole for the part.

> 1. A babe, two summers old.
> 2. Give us this day our daily bread.
> 3. Ring out the thousand years of woe,
>   Ring in the thousand years of peace.
> 4. Fifty mast are on the ocean.

94. Other Figures of Speech. — Sometimes, especially in older rhetorics, the following so-called figures of speech are added to the list already given : irony, hyperbole, antithesis, climax, and interrogation. The two former pertain rather to style, in fact, are qualities of style, while the last two might properly be placed along with kinds of sentences or paragraph development. Since these so-called figures are not all mentioned elsewhere in this text, a brief explanation and example of each will be given here.

1. *Irony* consists in saying just the opposite of the intended meaning, but in such a way that it emphasizes that meaning.

> What has the gray-haired prisoner done ?
> Has murder stained his hands with gore ?
> Not so ; his crime is a fouler one —
> God made the old man poor.
>
> — WHITTIER.

2. *Hyperbole* is an exaggerated expression used to increase the effectiveness of a statement.

> He was a man of boundless knowledge.

3. *Antithesis* consists merely of contrasted statements. This may be found in a single sentence or it may be extended through an entire paragraph.

> Look like the innocent flower,
> But be the serpent under it.
>
> — SHAKESPEARE.

4. *Climax* consists of an ascendant arrangement of words or ideas.

> I came, I saw, I conquered.

5. When a question is asked, not for the purpose of obtaining information but in order to make speech more effective, it is called the figure of *interrogation*. An affirmative question denies and a negative question affirms.

> 1. Am I my brother's keeper ?
> 2. Am I not free ?

IV. LIST OF SYNONYMS

Abandon, cast off, desert, forswear, quit, renounce, withdraw from.
Abate, decrease, diminish, mitigate, moderate.
Abhor, abominate, detest, dislike, loathe.
Abiding, enduring, lasting, permanent, perpetual.
Ability, capability, capacity, competency, efficacy, power.

Abolish, annul, eradicate, exterminate, obliterate, root out, wipe out.

Abomination, curse, evil, iniquity, nuisance, shame.

Absent, absent-minded, absorbed, abstracted, oblivious, preoccupied.

Absolve, acquit, clear.

Abstemiousness, abstinence, frugality, moderation, sobriety, temperance.

Absurd, ill-advised, ill-considered, ludicrous, monstrous, paradoxical, preposterous, unreasonable, wild.

Abundant, adequate, ample, enough, generous, lavish, plentiful.

Accomplice, ally, colleague, helper, partner.

Active, agile, alert, brisk, bustling, energetic, lively, supple.

Actual, authentic, genuine, real.

Address, adroitness, courtesy, readiness, tact.

Adept, adroit, deft, dexterous, handy, skillful.

Adequate, adjoining, bordering, near, neighboring.

Admire, adore, respect, revere, venerate.

Admit, allow, concede, grant, suffer, tolerate.

Admixture, alloy.

Adverse, disinclined, indisposed, loath, reluctant, slow, unwilling.

Aerial, airy, animated, ethereal, frolicsome.

Affectation, cant, hypocrisy, pretense, sham.

Affirm, assert, avow, declare, maintain, state.

Aged, ancient, antiquated, antique, immemorial, old, venerable.

Air, bearing, carriage, demeanor.

Akin, alike, identical.

Alert, on the alert, sleepless, wary, watchful.

Allay, appease, calm, pacify.

Alliance, coalition, compact, federation, union, fusion.

Allude, hint, imply, insinuate, intimate, suggest.

Allure, attract, cajole, coax, inveigle, lure.

Amateur, connoisseur, novice, tyro.

Amend, better, mend, reform, repair.

Amplify, develop, expand, extend, unfold, widen.

Amusement, diversion, entertainment, pastime.

Anger, exasperation, petulance, rage, resentment.

Animal, beast, brute, living creature, living organism.

Answer, rejoinder, repartee, reply, response, retort.

Anticipate, forestall, preclude, prevent.

Apiece, individually, severally, separately.

Apparent, clear, evident, obvious, tangible, unmistakable.

Apprehend, comprehend, conceive, perceive, understand.

Arraign, charge, cite, impeach, indict, prosecute, summon.

Arrogance, haughtiness, presumption, pride, self-complacency, supercili-
ousness, vanity.

Artist, artificer, artisan, mechanic, operative, workman.

Artless, boorish, clownish, hoidenish, rude, uncouth, unsophisticated.

Assent, agree, comply.

Assurance, effrontery, hardihood, impertinence, impudence, incivility,
insolence, officiousness, rudeness.

Atom, grain, scrap, particle, shred, whit.

Atrociousness, barbaric, barbarous, brutal, merciless.

Attack, assault, infringement, intrusion, onslaught.

Attain, accomplish, achieve, arrive at, compass, reach, secure.

Attempt, endeavor, essay, strive, try, undertake.

Attitude, pose, position, posture.

Attribute, ascribe, assign, charge, impute.

Axiom, truism.

Baffle, balk, bar, check, embarrass, foil, frustrate, hamper, hinder, impede,
retard, thwart.

Banter, burlesque, drollery, humor, jest, raillery, wit, witticism.

Beg, plead, press, urge.

Beguile, divert, enliven, entertain, occupy.

Bewilderment, confusion, distraction, embarrassment, perplexity.

Bind, fetter, oblige, restrain, restrict.

Blaze, flame, flare, flash, flicker, glare, gleam, gleaming, glimmer, glitter,
light, luster, shimmer, sparkle.

Blessed, hallowed, holy, sacred, saintly.

Boasting, display, ostentation, pomp, pompousness, show.

Brave, adventurous, bold, courageous, daring, dauntless, fearless, gallant,
heroic, undismayed.

Bravery, coolness, courage, gallantry, heroism.

Brief, concise, pithy, sententious, terse.

Bring over, convince, induce, influence, persuade, prevail upon, win over.

Calamity, disaster, misadventure, mischance, misfortune, mishap.

Candid, impartial, open, straightforward, transparent, unbiased, unpreju-
diced, unreserved.

Candor, frankness, truth, veracity.

Caprice, humor, vagary, whim.

Caricature, burlesque, parody, travesty.

Catch, capture, clasp, clutch, grip, secure.

Cause, consideration, design, end, ground, motive, object, reason, purpose.

Caution, discretion, prudence.

Censure, criticism, rebuke, reproof, reprimand, reproach.

Character, constitution, disposition, reputation, temper, temperament.

Characteristic, peculiarity, property, singularity, trait.

Chattering, garrulous, loquacious, talkative.

Cheer, comfort, delight, ecstasy, gayety, gladness, gratification, happiness, jollity, satisfaction.

Churlish, crusty, gloomy, gruff, ill-natured, morose, sour, sullen, surly.

Class, circle, clique, coterie.

Cloak, cover, gloss over, mitigate, palliate, screen.

Cloy, sate, satiate, satisfy, surfeit.

Commit, confide, consign, intrust, relegate.

Compassion, forbearance, lenience, mercy.

Compassionate, gracious, humane.

Complete, consummate, faultless, flawless, perfect.

Confirm, corroborate.

Conflicting, discordant, discrepant, incongruous, mismated.

Confused, discordant, miscellaneous, various.

Conjecture, guess, suppose, surmise.

Conscious, aware, certain.

Consequence, issue, outcome, outgrowth, result, sequel, upshot.

Continual, continuous, incessant, unbroken, uninterrupted.

Credible, conceivable, likely, presumable, probable, reasonable.

Customary, habitual, normal, prevailing, usual, wonted.

Damage, detriment, disadvantage, harm, hurt, injury, prejudice.

Dangerous, formidable, terrible.

Defame, deprecate, disparage, slander, vilify.

Defile, infect, soil, stain, sully, taint, tarnish.

Deleterious, detrimental, hurtful, harmful, mischievous, pernicious, ruinous.

Delicate, fine, minute, refined, slender.

Delightful, grateful, gratifying, refreshing, satisfying.

Difficult, hard, laborious, toilsome, trying.

Digress, diverge, stray, swerve, wander.

Disown, disclaim, disavow, recall, renounce, repudiate, retract.

Dispose, draw, incline, induce, influence, move, prompt, stir.

Earlier, foregoing, previous, preliminary.

Effeminate, feminine, womanish, womanly.

Emergency, extremity, necessity.

Empty, fruitless, futile, idle, trifling, unavailing, useless, vain, visionary.

Erudition, knowledge, profundity, sagacity, sense, wisdom.

Eternal, imperishable, interminable, perennial, perpetual, unfailing.
Excuse, pretense, pretext, subterfuge.
Exemption, immunity, liberty, license, privilege.
Explicit, express.

Faint, faint-hearted, faltering, half-hearted, irresolute, languid, listless, purposeless.
Faithful, loyal, stanch, trustworthy, trusty.
Fanciful, fantastic, grotesque, imaginative, visionary.
Fling, gibe, jeer, mock, scoff, sneer, taunt.
Flock, bevy, brood, covey, drove, herd, litter, pack.
Fluctuate, hesitate, oscillate, vacillate, waver.
Folly, imbecility, senselessness, stupidity.

Grief, melancholy, regret, sadness, sorrow.

Hale, healthful, healthy, salutary, sound, vigorous.

Ignorant, illiterate, uninformed, uninstructed, unlettered, untaught.
Impulsive, involuntary, spontaneous, unbidden, voluntary, willing.
Indispensable, inevitable, necessary, requisite, unavoidable.
Inquisitive, inquiring, intrusive, meddlesome, peeping, prying.
Intractable, perverse, petulant, ungovernable, wayward, willful.
Irritation, offense, pique, resentment.

Probably, presumably.

Reliable, trustworthy, trusty.
Remnant, trace, token, vestige.
Requite, repay, retaliate, satisfy.

V. LIST OF WORDS FOR EXERCISES IN WORD USAGE

Ability, capacity.
Accept, except.
Acceptance, acceptation.
Access, accession.
Accredit, credit.
Act, action.
Admire, like.
Admittance, admission.
Advance, advancement, progress, progression.
Affect, effect.
After, afterward.
Aggravating, irritating, provoking, exasperating.
Allege, maintain.
Allow, guess, think.
Allusion, illusion, delusion.
Almost, most, mostly.
Alone, only.
Alternate, choice.

Among, between.
Amount, number, quantity.
Angry, mad.
Apparently, evidently.
Apt, likely, liable.
Arise, rise.
At, in.
Avocation, vocation.
Awfully, very.

Balance, rest, remainder.
Begin, commence.
Beside, besides.
Both, each, every.
Bring, fetch.
By, with.

Calculate, intend.
Carry, bring, fetch.
Casuality, casualty.
Character, reputation.
Claim, assert.
Clever, pleasant.
College, university, school.
Completeness, completion.
Compliment, complement.
Confess, admit.
Construe, construct.
Contemptible, contemptuous.
Continual, continuous.
Convince, convict.
Council, counsel.
Couple, pair.
Credible, creditable, credulous.
Custom, habit.

Deadly, deathly.
Decided, decisive.
Decimate, destroy.
Declare, assert.
Degrade, demean.
Depot, station, R. R.

Discover, invent.
Drive, ride.

Each other, any other, one another.
Emigration, immigration, migration.
Enormity, enormousness.
Estimate, esteem.
Exceptional, exceptionable.
Expect, suppose.

Falseness, falsity.
Fly, flee.
Funny, odd.

Grant, give.

Habit, practice.
Haply, happily.
Healthy, healthful, wholesome.
Human, humane.

Lady, woman.
Last, latest, preceding.
Learn, teach.
Lease, hire.
Less, fewer.
Lie, lay.
Loan, lend.
Love, like.

Mad, angry.
Majority, plurality.
Manly, mannish.
May, can.
Mutual, common.

Necessities, necessaries.
Nice, pleasant, attractive.
Noted, notorious.

Observation, observance.
Official, officious.

Oral, verbal.

Part, portion.
Partly, partially.
Persecute, prosecute.
Person, party.
Practicable, practical.
Prescribe, proscribe.
Prominent, predominant.
Purpose, propose.

Quite, very, rather.

Relation, relative.
Repair, mend.
Requirement, requisite.
Rise, raise.

Scholar, pupil, student.

Sensible of, sensitive to.
Series, succession.
Settle, locate.
Sewage, sewerage.
Shall, will.
Should, would.
Sit, set.
Splendid, elegant.
Statement, assertion.
Statue, statute, stature.
Stay, stop.

Team, carriages.
Transpire, happen.

Verdict, testimony.

Without, unless.
Womanly, womanish.

INDEX

Gateway Series of English Texts

General Editor, HENRY VAN DYKE, Princeton University

The English Texts which are required for entrance to college, edited by eminent authorities, and presented in a clear, helpful, and interesting form. A list of the volumes and of their editors follows. More detailed information will be gladly supplied on request.

Shakespeare's Merchant of Venice. Professor Felix E. Schelling, University of Pennsylvania. **35 cents.**

Shakespeare's Julius Cæsar. Dr. Hamilton W. Mabie, "The Outlook." **35 cents.**

Shakespeare's Macbeth. Professor T. M. Parrot, Princeton University. **40 cents.**

Milton's Minor Poems. Professor Mary A. Jordan, Smith College. **35 cents.**

Addison's Sir Roger de Coverley Papers. Professor C. T. Winchester, Wesleyan University. **40 cents.**

Goldsmith's Vicar of Wakefield. Professor James A. Tufts, Phillips Exeter Academy. **45 cents.**

Burke's Speech on Conciliation. Professor William MacDonald, Brown University. **35 cents.**

Coleridge's The Ancient Mariner. Professor Geo. E. Woodberry, Columbia University. **30 cents.**

Scott's Ivanhoe. Professor Francis H. Stoddard, New York University. **50 cents.**

Scott's Lady of the Lake. Professor R. M. Alden, Leland Stanford Jr. University. **40 cents.**

Macaulay's Milton. Rev. E. L. Gulick, Lawrenceville School. **35 cents.**

Macaulay's Addison. Professor Charles F. McClumpha, University of Minnesota. **35 cents.**

Carlyle's Essay on Burns. Professor Edwin Mims, Trinity College, North Carolina. **35 cents.**

George Eliot's Silas Marner. Professor W. L. Cross, Yale University. **40 cents.**

Tennyson's Princess. Professor Katharine Lee Bates, Wellesley College. **40 cents.**

Tennyson's Gareth and Lynette, Lancelot and Elaine, and **The Passing of Arthur.** Dr. Henry van Dyke, Princeton University. **35 cents.**

Macaulay's Life of Johnson. Professor J. Scott Clark, Northwestern University. **35 cents.**

AMERICAN BOOK COMPANY

A History of English Literature

By REUBEN POST HALLECK, M.A. (Yale)

Cloth, 12mo, 499 pages.   With numerous illustrations.   Price $1.25.

Halleck's History of English Literature is a concise and interesting text-book of the history and development of English literature from the earliest times to the present.   While this work is sufficiently simple to be readily comprehended by high school students, the treatment is not only philosophic, but also stimulating and suggestive, and will naturally lead to original thinking.

The book is a history of literature and not a mere collection of biographical sketches.   Only enough of the facts of an author's life are given to make students interested in him as a personality, and to show how his environment affected his work.   The author's productions, their relation to the age, and the reasons why they hold a position in literature, receive treatment commensurate with their importance.

One of the most striking features of the work consists in the way in which literary movements are clearly outlined at the beginning of each of the chapters.   Special attention is given to the essential qualities which differentiate one period from another, and to the animating spirit of each age.   The author shows that each period has contributed something definite to the literature of England, either in laying characteristic foundations, in presenting new ideals, in improving literary form, or in widening the circle of human thought.

At the end of each chapter a carefully prepared list of books is given to direct the student in studying the original works of the authors treated.   He is told not only what to read, but also where to find it at the least cost.

The book contains as a frontispiece a Literary Map of England in colors, showing the counties, the birthplaces, the homes, and the haunts of the chief authors, specially prepared for this work.

Copies of Halleck's History of English Literature will be sent, prepaid, to any address on receipt of price.

American Book Company

New York   •   Cincinnati   •   Chicago

(90)

An Introduction to the

Study of American Literature

BY

BRANDER MATTHEWS
Professor of Literature in Columbia University

Cloth, 12mo, 256 pages   -   -   -   Price, $1.00

A text-book of literature on an original plan, and conforming with the best methods of teaching.

Admirably designed to guide, to supplement, and to stimulate the student's reading of American authors.

Illustrated with a fine collection of facsimile manuscripts, portraits of authors, and views of their homes and birthplaces.

Bright, clear, and fascinating, it is itself a literary work of high rank.

The book consists mostly of delightfully readable and yet comprehensive little biographies of the fifteen greatest and most representative American writers. Each of the sketches contains a critical estimate of the author and his works, which is the more valuable coming, as it does, from one who is himself a master. The work is rounded out by four general chapters which take up other prominent authors and discuss the history and conditions of our literature as a whole ; and there is at the end of the book a complete chronology of the best American literature from the beginning down to 1896.

Each of the fifteen biographical sketches is illustrated by a fine portrait of its subject and views of his birthplace or residence and in some cases of both. They are also accompanied by each author's facsimile manuscript covering one or two pages. The book contains excellent portraits of many other authors famous in American literature.

Copies of Brander Matthews' Introduction to the Study of American Literature will be sent prepaid to any address, on receipt of the price, by the Publishers :

American Book Company

New York   •   Cincinnati   •   Chicago

THE MODERN MATHEMATICAL SERIES

FOR COLLEGES AND SECONDARY SCHOOLS

LUCIEN AUGUSTUS WAIT
General Editor
Senior Professor of Mathematics in Cornell University

ANALYTIC GEOMETRY
> By J. H. Tanner, Ph.D., Assistant Professor of Mathematics, Cornell University, and Joseph Allen, A.M., Instructor in Mathematics in the College of the City of New York. Cloth, 8vo, 410 pages $2.00

DIFFERENTIAL CALCULUS
> By James McMahon, A.M., Assistant Professor of Mathematics, Cornell University, and Virgil Snyder, Ph.D., Instructor in Mathematics, Cornell University. Cloth, 8vo, 351 pages $2.00

INTEGRAL CALCULUS
> By D. A. Murray, Ph.D., Professor of Mathematics, Dalhousie College. Cloth, 8vo, 302 pages $2.00

DIFFERENTIAL AND INTEGRAL CALCULUS
> By Virgil Snyder, Ph.D., Instructor in Mathematics, Cornell University, and John Irwin Hutchinson, Ph.D., Instructor in Mathematics, Cornell University. Cloth, 8vo, 320 pages $2.00

ELEMENTARY GEOMETRY—PLANE
> By James McMahon, Assistant Professor of Mathematics in Cornell University. Half leather, 12mo, 358 pages, $0.90

ELEMENTARY ALGEBRA
> By J. H. Tanner, Ph.D., Assistant Professor of Mathematics, Cornell University. Half leather, 8vo, 374 pages . . $1.00

ELEMENTARY GEOMETRY—SOLID
> By James McMahon. (In preparation.)

ALGEBRA FOR COLLEGES
> By J. H. Tanner. (In preparation.)

The advanced books of this series treat their subjects in a way that is simple and practical, yet thoroughly rigorous and atttactive to both teacher and student. They meet the needs of students pursuing courses in engineering and architecture in any college or university. The elementary books are designed to implant the spirit of the other books into secondary schools, and will make the work in mathematics, from the very start, continuous and harmonious.

AMERICAN BOOK COMPANY